Congress and the Common Good

CONGRESS AND THE COMMON GOOD

ARTHUR MAASS

Basic Books, Inc., Publishers

NEW YORK

Library of Congress Cataloging in Publication Data

Maass, Arthur.
  Congress and the common good.

Includes bibliographical references and index.
  1. United States. Congress. 2. Presidents—
United States. 3. United States—Executive depart-
ments. I. Title.
JK1061.M3 1983   328.73'07456   83–71019
ISBN 0–465–01385–6

Contents

Contents

Preface

THE SEED of this book is the lectures that I have given at Harvard on executive–legislative relations and on Congress over the last twenty-three years, in Gov. 130, the basic undergraduate course on U.S. national government, and in courses and research seminars for graduate students.

The book is on political institutions and procedures. I am interested in how legislative institutions at different levels—the whole House, legislative leadership groups, committees, congressmen's offices—receive advice from those to whom they are accountable; how they exercise the discretion that is available to them, especially how they deliberate; and how they instruct those who will carry out their decisions. Since congressional decision making is almost always dominated by the nature of relations between the Executive and Congress, attention is also given to the several levels of executive institutions and to connections between them and Congress—between bureaus and committees, for example, or the White House and congressional leadership groups. I am interested also in the reciprocal relations between political institutions, on the one hand, and elections, public opinion, and the conduct of individual political actors, on the other. But the focus throughout is institutions, not political behavior.

The book is on Congress, yet it is directed principally to the House of Representatives rather than the Senate. There are a number of reasons for this. The House is easier to study. The sample of actors is more than four times as large and the chamber has more structure. Political scientists have studied the House more than the Senate and it is a great advantage to be able to use their data and findings. Nonetheless, the general mode of executive–legislative relations developed in chapter 1 applies equally to both Houses, and special attention is given to the Senate in three types of situations: first, where the Senate acts for Congress as a whole because it alone has constitutional authority, as in the case of confirmation of executive officials; second, where the Senate's actions, more than those of the House, have determined the Executive's conduct in executive–legislative relations, as in the case of making secret documents available to Congress; and third, where the Senate has differentiated its role from that of the House, as in the case of appropriation procedures.

The manuscript was completed on July 1, 1982, and, with rare exceptions, does not include developments in executive–legislative relations since the end of 1981.

This book is dedicated to the bright and stimulating young scholars who have assisted me and taught sections in Gov. 130 and to those who, by writing their doctoral dissertations with my advice on topics treated in this book, have been responsible for some of its findings and conclusions. Their names are recorded at the end of this Preface, and it will be observed that most of them have gone on to distinguished careers as teachers, scholars, or practitioners of American politics.

Professor Don K. Price consented for nineteen years to lecture on the presidency in this course, and I should like to take this opportunity to salute the "winner of the Price-Laski debates," as the *Harvard Crimson*, with a straight face, described him when Price initially accepted an appointment at Harvard in 1958. They were referring, of course, to a debate between Price and Harold J. Laski in the *Public Administration Review*, 1943–1944, on whether the parliamentary or presidential system was more suited to the United States, Price defending the latter. Harvard students were familiar with the debate in part because it had been required reading in Government 1.

In addition to those to whom this book is dedicated, I am glad to be able to express my gratitude here to two bright young scholars, Mary R. Musca and Elaine K. Swift, who lent their talents to collecting data and evaluating critically—oh so critically!—my first draft. Because of their heightened sense of relevance, many of my favorite examples are excised. When occasionally I protested their judgment, they responded with devastating effect that my focus should be institutions, not personalities. As a result, Abner J. Mikva, Charles H. Percy, Charles E. Schumer, Patsy T. Mink, and others will never know how relevant was their conduct on certain occasions to the analysis of this book. Susan H. Robinson's creative expertise is in literary fiction, but she has excelled in converting this big social science manuscript into publisher's copy. After all, it's intelligence and reading that count. The Institute for Educational Affairs, Inc., offered a small grant to help pay for these assistants and for other incidental expenses in preparing the manuscript. It is difficult to get such small grants, and the Institute and its directors, Leslie Lenkowsky and Philip N. Marcus, are to be congratulated for providing them with no foundation fuss. I hope the book justifies their confidence.

This book is dedicated to:

	Years	Current Position
Archie D. Barrett	T*(1971)	Professional staff member, subcommittee on Investigations, House Armed Services Committee
Frans R. Bax	C†(1973–75); T(1976)	Intelligence analyst, CIA
Thomas G. Berggren	C(1977–78)	Attorney in charge, London office, Morrison & Foerster
Richard K. Betts	C(1971–73)	Senior fellow, Brookings Institution
Gary E. Bombardier	C(1968–71)	Associate staff, House Committee on Appropriations, for Matthew F. McHugh, (D. NY)
Lawrence D. Brown	C(1970–72)‡	Senior fellow, Brookings Institution
Joseph Cooper	T(1961)§	Professor of political science, Rice University
Robert J. Doris	C(1975–76)	Consultant, Boston Consulting Group, Menlo Park, CA
E. Duane Draper	C(1982–83)	Attorney; teaching fellow in government, Harvard University
Yaron Ezrahi	C(1968–69)	Senior lecturer in political science, Hebrew University of Jerusalem
Booth Fowler	C(1964–67)	Professor of political science, University of Wisconsin, Madison

*   "T" indicates Ph.D. thesis (a) written under Maass, *and* (b) on a subject discussed in this book (year completed).
†   "C" indicates section leader or course assistant in Gov. 130 (years of service).
‡   Brown has also lectured on the Executive in Gov. 130, 1976 to date; and he kindly read the manuscript of this book.
§   Cooper also joined Maass in a research seminar on congressional supervision of the Executive, 1961–66.

Barney Frank	C(1962–64, 66–67)	Member of Congress (D. MA)
James M. Gerhardt	C(1964–66)	Professor of political science, Southern Methodist University
Adela Gondek	C(1974–76)	Assistant professor of political science, Rider College
Charles T. Goodsell	T(1960)	Professor of public policy, Virginia Polytechnic Institute
Doris Kearns Goodwin	C(1968–70)	Scholar and author, Lincoln, MA
George D. Greenberg	C(1967–68)	Program analyst, U.S. Department of Health and Human Services
Thane Gustafson	C(1973–74)	Political science department, RAND Corporation
Douglas S. Hobbs	C(1962–64)	Professor of political science, University of California, Los Angeles
John R. Johannes	T(1970)	Professor of political science, Marquette University
Ralph T. Jones	C(1967–68)	Analyst, Abt Associates
Robert A. Katzmann	C(1975–77)	Research associate, Brookings Institution
Michael W. Kirst	C(1963–64); T(1964)	Professor of education and business administration, Stanford University
Ronald J. Kurth	C(1969–70)	Rear Admiral, Director, Politico-Military Policy Division, U.S. Navy
William Lasser	C(1980–81)	Teaching fellow in government, Harvard University
Arthur B. Levy	T(1970)	Professor of political science, University of South Florida
Gordon Calvin MacKenzie	T(1975)	Professor of government, Colby College
David Mayhew	C(1960–61)	Professor of political science, Yale University
R. Shep Melnick	C(1976–78); T(1979)*	Assistant professor of government, Harvard University
Andrew W. Parkin	C(1976–77)	Lecturer in politics, Flinders University of South Australia
Charles Pruitt	C(1978–81)	Assistant professor of government, St. Olaf College

* Melnick also lectured on the federal courts and administrative law in Gov. 130, 1979-1982; and he kindly read the manuscript of this book.

Martin M. Shapiro	C(1958–62)	Professor of law, University of California, Berkeley
Ernest Spaeth	C(1958–59)	President, Johns-Manville Europe, Paris
John Tierney	C(1977–79)	Assistant professor of political science, Boston College
Mark Tipermas	C(1972–74)	Project manager, ICF, Inc., Washington, D.C.
Cheryl L. Wires	C(1978–80)	Teaching fellow in government, Harvard University

PART I

Framework for Analysis

1

What Does Congress Do?
A Model of Executive-
Legislative Relations

IN ORDER to describe and explain Congress, in order, even, to collect and organize the data that are most important in regard to Congress, one needs a framework for analysis, a model. My purpose in chapters 1 through 4 is to present one such model, which will then be used as the basis for inquiry in the remainder of this book. The model is fundamentally different from those that dominate contemporary studies of Congress and the presidency.

Most of the dominant models are based on interest group theory, holding that the duty of governmental institutions in the United States is to facilitate the articulation by particular groups of their partisan interests; to organize a political process for the purpose of aggregating and mutually adjusting these group interests; and to design and implement governmental programs in accordance with the results of this bargaining process. The public interest is then defined as the outcome of a process called partisan mutual adjustment *(pma)*—the aggregation and reconciliation of those particular interests that assert themselves. Practitioners of interest group theory believe that this formulation describes realistically how our institutions function. They also believe that it satisfies the requirements of government in a democratic, constitutional state, such as the United States. This is so, they say, because ours is a pluralist society, with a large number of groups promoting many interests, and citizens are free to associate with any number of these. Furthermore, the process of *pma* is conducted in accordance with certain minimal rules of fair play.[1]

Some analysts have adopted an extreme version of this model that is based on individuals rather than groups. The purpose of the political process in this case is to reconcile the private, largely economic interests of all citizens in a manner similar to utility maximization as it occurs in economic markets.

I have rejected *pma* and utility maximization models because they are so far from being realistic and because it is questionable that they satisfy the requirements of a democratic system of government. Much of what Congress and the President do cannot be described adequately by using these models. Take the Ninety-fifty Congress, 1977–1978, as an example. Interest group theories do not throw much light on the major issue, which was ratification and implementation of the Panama Canal treaties. After lengthy hearings, the Senate debated the treaties for thirty-eight days before approving them by a margin of one vote more than the two-thirds needed, and both House and Senate spent additional time on issues related to their implementation once the treaties were ratified. Although various conservative organizations opposed the treaties vigorously, while the Carter Administration and a number of liberal groups lobbied vigorously for them, the deliberative process leading to their ratification did not involve in any important way the aggregation and reconciliation of particular interests. Nor do such theories help explain many other important issues considered by that Congress, such as the use of governmental funds to finance abortions, on which there were eleven roll-call votes in the House within a period of five months, with additional votes in the House and many in the Senate; or the ethics and standards of conduct of the civil service, senior executive officers, and members of Congress, which at times appeared to preoccupy both President Jimmy Carter and the Congress.

Furthermore, *pma* and utility maximization models, when they are used as the dominant framework for study, lead to incomplete and in some cases incorrect analyses of the relations between Congress and the Executive, most especially of the process by which the Executive builds support in Congress for the President's programs. These models also lead, as we shall see, to faulty analyses of (1) the relations between congressional committees and the whole House; (2) voting in Congress, more specifically the relative importance of the several factors that influence the votes of members; (3) the relation of constituency service as an activity of members of Congress to the legislative process and to congressional oversight of administration; and (4) the extent to which Congress is concerned with broad program policies or with narrow individual projects, including the role of "pork barrel" in executive–legislative relations. On these and other important characteristics of our national government, models based on interest group theory are likely to be insufficient or misleading. More generally, they fail to give sufficient emphasis, as I see it, to either leadership or accountability in government.

The alternative model used in this book holds that the duty of governmental institutions is to promote the articulation by groups and individuals of their preferences for the political community, and that these preferences are likely to be different from the parochial preferences of interest groups and the preferences of individuals for their own narrow economic well-being. Instead of conducting a political process that simply aggregates and reconciles narrow group or individual interests, government conducts a process of deliberation and discussion that results in decisions that are based on broader community interests, and it designs and implements programs in accordance with these decisions. It is within the framework of this process that the narrower interests of groups and individuals are reconciled. And it is within this framework that studies of Congress that are based on *pma* should be evaluated and used.

Both Congress and the Executive will be judged, then, by how well they represent, promote, and protect the public interest of the political community at large and how well they resist control by special and particular interests. To impart meaning to this criterion for evaluating Congress and the Executive, I shall describe a political process that is conceived in terms of public or community interest. This process is more complex, to be sure, than one based on partisan mutual adjustment, but the results represent the real world, not a vast oversimplification of it, and at the same time they offer a view of how we govern ourselves that is more honorable than that suggested by the trading of advantages by special interests.

The Discussion Model: Basics

Virtually all theoretical discussions of the constitutional democratic state discriminate between the community or society on the one hand and the government or state on the other, each possessing unique functions. This dualism between community and government should be explained briefly, for we can derive from it a meaning for the public interest and an understanding of the relation of legislative and executive institutions to it.

FUNCTIONS OF THE COMMUNITY

The community's unique political function is to reach agreement on the standards of the common life. A constitutional democratic system is based on the capacity of its citizens to debate and determine the standards by which they wish to live in political community. There can be no higher respect for the integrity of each person in a political community than that he be free to, and encouraged to, participate in determining these standards which are, of course, not fixed, but continually being resolved.

The community in which discussion and resolution of standards takes place is basically one of voluntary association. The religious, the social, the economic —in short, the common life of society—is lived by individuals in all manner of social relationships—churches, trade unions, fraternal organizations, business corporations, service clubs, single-issue advocacy groups. And the community's political function is to foster a process of discussion that results in agreement on standards for the community as a whole and in a propensity to reexamine them.

FUNCTIONS OF THE STATE

The state serves the community in order to make more effective the community's function relating to common standards. In doing so the state must understand the principles that govern the common life and in some ways interpret them, but the state does not and should not seek to prescribe these standards. More specifically, the state has three unique functions according to the model presented here.

First it guarantees those political and economic conditions that are essential in order to enable all to participate in citizenship. Thus the state maintains for its members minimum standards of political rights and legal rights— freedom of speech, press, association, voting, and fair trial. Equally, the state maintains economic rights for all its members by guaranteeing minimum economic conditions—minimum wages, unemployment compensation, public support for education. This theory of the democratic state recognizes, as did Aristotle, that citizens possessed of political and legal rights may nonetheless be unable to participate in any real sense in the community because of their poverty; and it justifies the government's responsibility for preventing this.

To provide the opportunity for effective participation in citizenship, the state also acquires and puts at the disposal of all citizens accurate information about the community—for example, data on population, inflation, unemployment, cost of living—so that the community can decide intelligently on its objectives. Finally, included in its first function, the state defends the community from external attack and from internal violence.

The second unique function of the state is to provide institutions for focusing on issues and on areas of community agreement, and for translating such agreements into rules and criteria that are sufficiently specific to serve as guides to governmental action, where such action is desired by the community. The state's third function is to carry out activities in accordance with these criteria. The focus of this book is, for the most part, on how these last two functions are served by the institutions of American government.

A CONTINUOUS PROCESS OF DISCUSSION

One can view the operation of a democratic community and democratic government as being composed of four stages. The first stage is discussion in the community where the broad standards are agreed on. Here the state plays no part other than that which I have described as its first unique function. But the next stages—the electoral process, the legislative process, and the administrative process—are organized by the state. They are the means through which discussion and interpretation of standards are carried to greater and greater specificity, from general issue to concrete decision. Each stage is part of a continuous process of discussion and debate; each takes over from a previous stage, discharging a selective function, and hands on to a next stage, performing an instructive function. At the same time, each stage or process has a duty and a set of institutions of its own. That is, while each receives instructions from the previous stage, it has a specific deliberative discretion. Let me state briefly how the three processes that are organized by government operate.

The *electoral process* takes over from the community discussion stage. The process involves additional discussion. At the moment of choice, individuals are selected as representatives and instructed to carry discussion to a further and more precise point in the legislative process. It is not essential that the programs of electoral candidates be detailed and specific; the later stages of discussion will accomplish this. Instead, the essence of the selective function of the electorate consists in the choice of citizens who, in their personal capacities, are fitted to discharge the task of deliberation and discussion at the legislative stage.

The *legislative process* takes over from the electoral stage and translates into rules of law the general ideas endorsed by the electorate. The legislators—both the President and Congress—by means of special techniques for discussion and decision, including the capacity to use effectively more information than the electorate can use, accomplish something which their constituents are incapable of accomplishing. In the legislative process the basic objectives and standards that are to govern the government's activities in any area are laid down, usually by statute.

Finally, through the *administrative process* the legislative standards are translated into rules and regulations that are immediately useful for governmental action, and the actions of government are conducted in accordance with these rules and regulations. The translation of statutory standards into rules and regulations is in effect the last stage of discussion and a part of the

7

state's second function of providing institutional means for focusing on issues and translating them into action guides. The government's subsequent actions based on these rules and regulations constitute the state's third function, to carry out activities in accordance with standards set in the process of discussion.

Thus the administrative process includes part of the second function of the state—translating broad objectives into specific rules—and all of the third function—conducting programs. It is difficult to draw a rigid line separating these two activities of the administrative process. The logic of the legislative process leads to administrative discretion in policymaking. The exercise of this discretion is most apparent in the issuance of rules and regulations by administrative agencies. No statute, no matter how detailed, is likely to answer all questions that come before administrators who are inevitably and properly concerned with refining the governing criteria.

Institutionalization of the Processes of Discussion

To this point the analysis has been in terms of governmental processes, but what about the institutions that conduct these processes? Most of the duties of both Congress and the Executive are related to the legislative and administrative processes. But more specifically, what are the reasons for a governing body chosen as is our Congress? One reason is to divide power at the center of government, in this case among Congress, the Executive, and the courts. Keeping government weak by keeping it divided is not the principal rationale for Congress, however. There are other reasons which can be grouped under several headings.

POPULAR CONTROL OVER THE ADMINISTRATIVE PROCESS

First is the need for popular control over the administrative process. It has always been a premise of constitutional democratic government that bureaucracies suffer from inherent tendencies to be parochial, to aggregate power— tendencies that can destroy the responsibility of government. Thus bureaucracy needs to be subjected continuously to informed criticism. There are several means for doing this: the chief executive, the courts, professional standards of the bureaucracy, direct relations between the public and the bureaus of government; but all of these, while necessary, are not sufficient. Congressional control is also required.

The chief executive, as an elected representative of the people, subjects the bureaucracy to popular control. The supervision that he can provide has limitations, however. It can be exercised only by the President's top political aides in the executive branch, and they are continually in danger of becoming captives of their departments—by their own lack of expertise, by the departments' quiet persistence, quiet obstruction, and command of facts. The large number of political executives in government who are appointed by the President or by cabinet officers and agency heads for the purpose of giving the departments and agencies the President's political direction—these "strangers" in Washington, as Professor Hugh Heclo has called them—have on the whole failed to take control of the bureaucracy.

Example. President Richard M. Nixon at the beginning of his second term in 1973 felt that he could not rely on the departments and agencies to promote his domestic programs, involving, among other things, a "new federalism," revenue sharing, and block grants; that his cabinet officers and other political appointees had become captives of their own departments. Thus Nixon undertook to implant in each department and agency, at the assistant secretary level and below, men and women who were personally loyal to him and his programs, many of them from the White House. This experiment failed for reasons too lengthy to go into here, but it illustrates the problems and limitations of presidential control over the bureaucracy and over the corps of political executives.[2]

Control of the bureaucracy by the courts was in the past largely negative —prohibiting certain actions—and after the fact. In recent years judges have been much more active in overseeing administrative action. There is a new administrative law. But it is concerned more with protecting minorities from abuse and protecting private property from public taking than with subjecting the bureaucracy to broad popular influence and control.

Professional standards of the public service, the restraints represented by a career civil service and by professional elites within the service, are important in insuring responsible conduct of public affairs, but these, too, are no substitute for popular oversight, as we shall see in later chapters.

As for direct relations between governmental bureaus and the public, what is sometimes called "people power," these develop almost inevitably into direct relations between a bureau and a special public, namely, the bureau's clientele. The direct relations of the Interstate Commerce Commission with the public are mostly direct relations between the agency and representatives of the railroads and truckers. Similarly, the direct public relations of the several poverty agencies are mostly with those who represent the poor. As such, these direct public relations cannot be very effective in insuring broad popular control over the agencies' programs.

In short, congressional oversight, as a supplement to these other forms, is needed to guarantee the capacity of the people to call the bureaucracy to account.

A second reason for Congress is the need for popular control over the legislative process. In the administrative process the Executive leads; the Congress controls. In the legislative process the normal situation is no different. The legislature is not the dominant influence in the legislative process. The President is more influential. He leads and Congress controls. Leadership in this context means two things: to initiate the legislative process, that is, to perform its early stages, and to impel it, or to continuously drive the process forward.

There are good reasons for executive leadership of the legislative process. The first stage of the process usually involves identifying a problem and raising an issue to determine whether or not legislation is desirable. In this, the President's personal leadership is likely to be very effective, based on his election, his press coverage, and the issues and programs that he highlights in his formal messages to Congress at the beginning of each session—the State of the Union, the Budget, and the Economic report—and in subsequent messages on special topics.

An issue having been raised, the early stages of the legislative process are mainly a matter of evaluating alternative solutions to particular problems and of concentrating on the more promising possibilities. This requires, among other things, access to great stores of information and expertise. Again, the Executive, with its massive professional establishment, is better able to provide these than is the legislature.

The early stages of the legislative process also involve insuring that policy proposals are coordinated and consistent, that the proposals, for example, of the Department of Agriculture for food for the poor are consistent with those of the Department of Health and Human Services for welfare payments and the Department of Housing and Urban Development for housing subsidies for the poor. This type of coordination requires central direction of the policy-initiating process; and the Executive, with its hierarchical organization, is better able to provide this than the legislature with its decentralized, committee-based organization, where collegiality dominates hierarchy.

Having initiated a legislative proposal, the Executive then normally impels it by clearing it with interested parties who may not have been involved in choosing the preferred solution, recommending it, and working for its adoption. For this last task the Executive uses, among others, the technique and resources of legislative liaison, about which more later in this chapter.

Having said, then, that executive leadership is the normal requirement, we can delineate the legislature's role in the legislative process, which is to criticize and control. Control in this context means to exercise a check upon executive leadership, to oversee it, to criticize and influence it, and to approve, reject, or amend specific executive proposals.

There is probably no better index of the degree to which executive proposals are actively or passively acceptable to the community than the voice of the legislature. When Hubert Humphrey was vice president in 1965 he said in a speech:

> The members of Congress provide a direct link between the national government and the almost 195 million persons who comprise this republic. Surely this connection is vital in keeping our national government responsive to the needs and opinions of the American people. . . . Through reasonable discussion, through taking into account the views of many, Congress amends and refines legislative proposals so that once a law is passed it reflects the collective judgment of a diverse people.[3]

This results from the composition of the Congress and the manner in which its members are elected, but also from the fact that the American legislature can serve effectively as a focal point for the expression and organization of opinion.

Example. In 1968 President Lyndon B. Johnson proposed the development of an antiballistic missile (ABM) system which both houses of Congress then approved by large majorities, although a number of members were strongly opposed. The next year President Richard M. Nixon proposed further development and deployment of the ABM, and this time opponents used the institutions and procedures of Congress to focus national attention on the issue. As a result, the pros and cons of the ABM became a great national debate, and two close roll-call votes in which the Senate opponents were defeated (51–49 and 50–50) assumed the character of an exciting national drama.

On February 4, 1969, a bipartisan group of senators, including Mike Mansfield (D. MT and majority leader), J. William Fulbright (D. AR and chairman of the Foreign Relations Committee), John Sherman Cooper (R. KY), Edward M. Kennedy (D. MA), Jacob K. Javits (R. NY), Edward W. Brooke (R. MA), and George S. McGovern (D. SD), made concerted speeches on the floor opposing the ABM, which attracted great attention in the mass media. These opponents then helped to organize an impressive group of anti-ABM scientists whose testimony before the Foreign Relations and Armed Services Committees was widely reported and used for additional floor speeches. Finally, they debated the issue on the floor for approximately one month before the hairbreadth votes of August 8. The congressional opponents were unable to convince a majority of their colleagues, but they were able to use Congress's means for controlling the legislative process to elevate a fairly technical question to an issue of broad national concern. Subsequently the ABM was scaled down, in part due to the thorough debate on the subject in 1969.

Example. The Food and Drug Administration proposed in March 1977 to ban saccharin because evidence from animal experiments linked it to an increased risk of bladder cancer. Committees in the House and Senate held hearings on the new rule. These hearings helped to induce an avalanche of constituency complaints to which Congress responded by passing a bill, which the President signed, delaying the ban for eighteen months while new studies were made. Congress had been the focal point for the expression and organization of opinion. The moratorium was extended for two years in 1979 and again in 1981.

UNIQUE CONTRIBUTIONS OF CONGRESS

A third reason or group of reasons for a popularly elected legislature relates to the unique contributions that such a body can make to the success of democratic government—qualitative contributions that apply to Congress's duties in both the administrative process and the legislative process.

The legislature can bring to both the administrative and legislative processes certain qualities of the *nonexpert*. The collective, nontechnical mind of the legislature contains insights and sensitivities that are likely to go beyond the perception and ken of any group of experts. Thus it was the lay Congress that helped to discredit the tyranny of the military experts during the Vietnam War. New techniques of decision making that have been developed in the last ten to fifteen years—multiple-objective planning, benefit-cost analysis, planning-programming-budgeting, evaluation, and others—-have increased the capacity of nonexperts in both Congress and the Executive to make decisions on issues that involve a great deal of technical data. We shall return to this subject in chapter 13.

The legislature can also bring to both the administrative and legislative processes an open mind—the *capacity for change*. It can make the Executive see the obvious and do something about it. It was Congress that drove home the obvious fact that some of the intelligence operations of the CIA in the 1950s and 1960s were inconsistent with the basic moral standards of our democratic system of government, compelling the Executive to consider, propose, and adopt changes in the CIA's methods and procedures.

Finally, and perhaps obviously, the legislature's *constituency is different* from the President's. The constituency of the House of Representatives is the sum of popular majorities in 435 single-member districts; whereas that of the President is roughly the sum of popular majorities in the fifty states. This fact enables the Congress to provide a complement to the views of the President so that their interaction in both administration and legislation results in a more valid refinement of community consensus than would otherwise be the case.

The Model of Executive–Legislative Relations

There is, then, no correspondence between the legislative process and the duties and responsibilities of the legislature; nor between the executive or administrative process and the duties and responsibilities of the Executive. The legislature plays a role in both policy and administration, in both the legislative process and in the administrative process. The same is true of the Executive. This is illustrated in table 1.1, which shows that there is no basis for distinguishing the President from the Congress if one considers the processes of government in which they participate, but a solid basis for distinction can be found in the roles that they play in these processes. The Executive's role is leadership—to initiate and impel; the Congress's, control—to oversee and to approve, reject, or amend.

TABLE 1.1
Roles of the Executive and Congress

Institution	Processes	Roles
Executive	Legislative and administrative	Initiation and leadership
Congress	Legislative and administrative	Oversight and control Secondary role: initiation in legislative process

This model contradicts several stereotypes of the relations between Congress and the Executive, one of which is derived from a literal reading of the Constitution. Article I, Section 1, provides that all legislative powers shall be vested in a Congress of the United States; Article II, Section 1, that the Executive power shall be vested in a President of the United States. We find in fact that both Congress and the President share in legislative and executive powers. A related stereotype results from efforts of the federal courts, especially the U.S. Supreme Court, to determine legislative intent in ambiguous statutes. This they do by reference to legislative histories, which the courts construct from congressional documents—bills, committee reports, floor debates—and frequently from certain selected documents only. Yet it is likely that the provisions they seek to interpret were initially drafted by the executive branch, where alternatives were also considered, and that somewhere in the executive establishment there are papers that document this.

The courts in these cases base their opinions of legislative intent on incomplete legislative histories, and this practice lends support to the stereotype that Congress alone legislates, or that Congress is necessarily the principal actor in

13

the legislative process. It may be asking too much of the courts to do complete and proper legislative histories; the executive documents may be difficult to find. Indeed Justice Robert Jackson, in a frequently quoted opinion, recommended that courts not go beyond committee reports, not even to committee hearings and floor debates.[4] This being the case, perhaps the courts should be more modest and restrained in their efforts to interpret legislative intent, and more aggressive in demanding that the legislators themselves—the Executive and Congress—clarify ambiguous statutory provisions. But this question is more complex than these comments suggest and beyond the scope of this book.

Table 1.1 represents the only form of legislative–executive relations in the administrative process. Congress simply cannot initiate or conduct administration. And it represents the principal or dominant form of legislative–executive relations in the legislative process. In the legislative process, however, there is a secondary mode in which Congress may lead and initiate.

CONGRESSIONAL LEADERSHIP OF THE LEGISLATIVE PROCESS:
A SECONDARY MODE OF EXECUTIVE–LEGISLATIVE RELATIONS

The President selects his program, picks his priorities, and for the President's program the President is the leader. For subjects that the President elects not to initiate, for subjects that are not on the President's program, Congress can and sometimes does take the lead. On these occasions there is a leadership reserve in the Congress, and it is one of the main strengths of the American system of government, one that is not to be found in any other major parliamentary government in the world.

This leadership reserve, however, can be used with success only episodically, not regularly. As we have seen, the early stages of the legislative process involve the collection of large quantities of data, the availability of large numbers of experts, and the capacity to coordinate. Congress is limited by the lack of resources and organization typically needed for these tasks.

Furthermore, the President is free at any time to include any subject in his program and thereby to be the leader. The Executive always has the resources for this. As a general rule, whenever the President is disposed toward leadership, it is his to be had. As Speaker Carl B. Albert (D. OK) said to Gerald R. Ford soon after Ford was sworn in as President in 1974: "It is obvious that under our system, 535 members of Congress cannot fashion and pass a legislative program without the President."

Example. In 1975 the Democrats, with an overwhelming majority in both the House and the Senate, announced with maximum exposure in the media that they would initiate a comprehensive energy program for the nation, discarding President

Ford's proposed program. But jurisdiction over energy matters lay with several committees in both Houses, so there was no institutional means for initiating a comprehensive program. In an effort to overcome this, the House and Senate Democratic caucuses set up Democratic task forces on energy, but their proposals, which were scarcely comprehensive programs to start with, were rejected by the legislative committees to which they were subsequently referred. This effort by Congress to disregard the President's role as initiator of a highly complex and comprehensive program and to assume this role themselves was a crashing failure.

In fact, there is much evidence to show that Congress prefers that the President take the lead. During Congress's unsuccessful effort to fashion energy legislation in 1975, Representative Alan W. Steelman (R. TX) said:

> The legislative body can never be depended on to be the initiator. . . . There are just too many of us in the House. . . . Our role is to properly air options and to come up with some response. We are reduced to a reaction role to presidential policy initiatives, which can be a good working of checks and balances.

Representative Bob Eckhardt (D. TX) agreed with this analysis, describing Congress as "a machine with a V-8 engine into which different forces come from different directions. The President is the ignition system."

> *Example.* President Lyndon B. Johnson in 1964 proposed to Congress that the minimum wage be raised. He said in his message to Congress: "It is not a question of whether to raise the Federal minimum wage but when and by how much." He then made no recommendations on these matters, but left them up to Congress, counseling the members to weigh carefully the effects of any increase on the economy. Members of the House Committee on Education and Labor chided the President for passing the buck to Congress. The subcommittee chairman said: "We feel we need some guidelines."

Furthermore, there are few cases of pure congressional leadership in which Congress on its own (or relatively on its own, since the executive branch is necessarily involved to some degree) performs all steps in initiating and impelling the legislative process. The Taft-Hartley Labor Management Act of 1947, passed over President Harry S Truman's veto, is one example, and there are others. But for the most part, Congress shares leadership with the Executive in a variety of ways. Based on the analysis of John R. Johannes, these can be reduced to four other categories in addition to the first and infrequent category of pure congressional leadership.[5]

A second category comprises instances in which an executive department or agency performs the first steps but finds the road blocked when the White House decides against following through. The program usually dies unless Congress can be implicated—unless Congress will provide the political initiative that the President usually supplies. If Congress does take the leadership at this point, this combines executive expertise with the political motivation of the legislature. On lesser matters, this pattern is not uncommon; on major matters, it is infrequent.

Example. Civil Rights Act, 1957. Attorney General Herbert Brownell, Jr., and a number of Justice Department lawyers, as well as congressional liberals led by House Judiciary Committee chairman Emmanuel Celler (D. NY), favored major new civil rights legislation. In the absence of President Dwight D. Eisenhower, who was recovering from a heart attack, Brownell requested and received approval at a cabinet meeting to prepare such legislation in late autumn 1955. After the bill had been drafted, however, Eisenhower, in April 1956, decided against any major civil rights proposal. Brownell was asked not to proceed with the legislation, to which he agreed reluctantly. However, in a letter to Congress supporting a minor civil rights bill to which the White House had no objection, Brownell spoke of a need for stronger legislation, which was "a not so thinly veiled invitation for would-be congressional initiators to request Justice Department assistance." Whereupon a member of the Judiciary Committee asked Brownell for specific legislative recommendations, to which he responded with the Department's draft bill, which then became the basis of the 1957 Act.

A third category is the reverse of the second. Here it is Congress that begins consideration of a particular problem and carries its work through several stages. Before the members can finish, however, the President, with all of the advantages inherent in his office, steps in to take over. His purpose in doing so may be to assure results that are more akin to executive interpretations of what is needed, in which case he is likely to submit his own bill. Or his purpose may be to claim credit, in which case he may give such a wholehearted endorsement of the congressional proposal that it becomes associated with his leadership.

Example. National Traffic and Motor Vehicle Safety Act, 1966. In 1965 Ralph Nader published a devastating critique of the safety of American automobiles, *Unsafe at Any Speed*. Nader, crusading for national attention to his cause, convinced his home-state senator, Abraham Ribicoff (D. CT), chairman of the Subcommittee on Executive Reorganization of the Committee on Government Operations, to conduct hearings. Although the subcommittee had no clear jurisdiction over the matter, its hearings became the means for arousing public opinion and developing the outline of legislation. President Lyndon B. Johnson thereupon added the subject to his legislative program and presented a draft bill which was subsequently heavily amended by Congress.

The *Washington Post* (30 August 1966) said in an editorial: "The auto safety bill that the Congress sent to the President is a remarkable achievement. In an era when the Executive branch ordinarily has assumed the initiative in suggesting and formulating legislation, the auto safety bill can be counted as a prime example of legislative initiative. Congressional hearings on auto safety last year prodded the Administration into submitting a bill early this session. The finished legislation is a substantial improvement."

In the fourth category Congress demands that the Executive lead. Congress may take several steps in the initiation of legislation and then decide that the technical expertise or the political power of the administration is required, and it may try to compel the President to provide these. Or Congress may decide at the outset that the President should initiate legislation and then try to compel him to do so. In either case, Congress, or its committees, demands executive leadership.

Example. National Aeronautics and Space Administration (NASA) Act, 1958 —the statute which established NASA and the program that sent an American to the moon. The Soviets orbited their first Sputnik in October and November 1957, when the United States had no capacity to send satellites into outer space. There were contrasting responses to this event from the White House and Congress. President Dwight D. Eisenhower remained serene, assuring the nation that there were scientists in the Defense Department's Advanced Research Projects Agency (ARPA) working on the problem. Congress became excited, and several committees opened hearings on why the United States was so far behind the Soviets. The most important of these was chaired by the Senate majority leader, Lyndon B. Johnson (D. TX), who was also chairman of the Preparedness Investigating Subcommittee of the Senate Armed Services Committee. Johnson devoted a great deal of time and attention to the hearings, with the aid of a specially recruited staff. The hearings were conducted in a bipartisan manner. Witnesses included famous scientists and representatives of the armed services, the Defense Department, and defense and related industries.

In a January 1958 informal report to the Senate, Johnson called for a number of policy changes, including creation of a civilian space agency. While making it clear that there was sufficient support in Congress to pass such legislation, he said that he would wait for an Administration proposal. House Speaker Sam Rayburn agreed with his Texas colleague, telling reporters that there "should be leadership in the executive branch. But if the Administration does not come forward with a bold program, a reasonable program, then Congress will come forward with a bold, workable program."

To strengthen this threat Congress took steps to equip itself for the job of policymaking in a new field. During February and March both chambers established special committees for space matters, and the Senate committee was directed to report to the Senate by June its recommendations on legislation to deal with the problem.

To the Administration it had now become clear that a proposal for a space program would have to be made to preclude any further congressional initiatives in policymaking. By early April a bill was presented to Congress which, with amendments, was enacted in July.

The fifth category covers cases in which the President seeks to shift the duty of leadership and initiation to Congress. He may decide that it is better to let Congress carry the ball, or fumble it, as the case may be. The example cited earlier in which President Johnson left it to Congress to decide when and by how much the minimum wage should be increased exemplifies this category.

Clearly there is substantial overlap among these categories. Congress, by picking up an executive proposal that was spurned by the President (category two), might force him into reconsidering (category four). Furthermore, although these categories have been designed to deal with congressional leadership in legislation, which I have called the secondary mode, several of them relate also to executive leadership, for there are few examples of pure presidential initiation, just as there are few of pure congressional leadership.

The Public Interest

This model of executive–legislative relations and the analysis of governmental functions from which it derives enables us to say more about the public interest of the political community. Remember that each successive stage in the political process involves a refinement of standards reached in the previous stage, so that the criterion for evaluating the performance of political institutions at any stage involves reference to the previous stage to see if the selective function has been performed in accordance with instructions; and that the ultimate criterion, the first stage, is no less than the community's agreements on the standards of the common life, which are of necessity general and broad. *Thus the public interest is related to breadth of view.*

When the legislators (the President and Congress) exercise their discretion and seek agreement among themselves on policy, their standard of conduct is determined by the earlier stages of electoral process and community discussion. Periodically the electorate, using this standard, will pass formal judgment on the legislators; between elections the electorate and the community will provide intelligence to the legislators which the legislators will evaluate and use as they see fit in the exercise of their discretion. Where the legislators are unable to reach agreement on an issue, they will often refer it back to the community, or periodically to the electorate, for further discussion and agreement.

Similarly, the standard of public interest followed by administrators in the exercise of their discretion will relate to the legislative and electoral processes and ultimately to community discussion. To illustrate, let us consider the responsibility of bureau chiefs in carrying out programs.[6] We can make a distinction between what they do in administering laws on the one hand, and on the other hand, how they report on what they have done and how they recommend what should be done. In carrying out the law, the administrators' discretion may not be very broad. Of the determinants of their actions, three-fifths may be ministerial, in the sense that the policies are stated clearly and specifically by the legislation, and two-fifths may be left to their discretion. In their ministerial duties they follow the specific provisions of the law with fairness, impartiality, and energy. With respect to their discretion, however, the standard of conduct is breadth of view according to the discussion model. They seek to refine the law's intent by the broadest possible view of the consequences resulting from the exercise of the discretion that is available to them. In applying this standard, administrators look beyond the specific provisions of the statute, which may be quite specialized in nature, to the broader consensus attained in the electoral process and in the community. In reporting on what their bureaus have done and in recommending what they should do in the future, especially the latter, the administrators' discretion is almost complete. It is here, therefore, that the standard of breadth of view is most effective.

The public interest, then, is identified with a political process that emphasizes breadth of view. This does not mean that the provision of public services by the federal government is necessarily more in the public interest than having them provided by local governments or the economic market, for reliance on local governments and on the market may be broad national objectives. The point is rather that decisions on whether to favor nationalism or localism in this context are made in a political process that focuses on the broad interests of the nation.

To specify the public interest in any particular case, political decision makers will set a value on nationalism or localism as well as on other variables that are closely related to the public interest—for example, the rate of discount to be used in determining the present value of future benefits of governmental programs, due process, and equal protection. But my purpose is not to define the substance of the public interest, that is, the values that may be assigned to these several variables.[7] It is, rather, to understand the process by which institutions determine these values, especially the institutions and procedures of executive–legislative relations. For this purpose a model that relates the public interest to breadth of view, as it is achieved in a continuous process of community and political discussion, is both realistic and useful.

This view of the public interest, based on discussion and deliberation as a means for determining what citizens want for the political community, is not in vogue with many political scientists who, although they are concerned as am I with process rather than substance of the public interest, emphasize interest group theories. For them the *public* interest is, as we have said, the result of a conflict and adjustment of *particular* interests operating under certain so-called rules of the game—a process frequently called partisan mutual adjustment.

Assumptions of the Discussion Model

Before comparing the consequences of using one or the other of these models for analysis of governmental institutions, I should say more about the basic assumptions of the discussion model, for they are substantially different from those of the alternative *pma* model.

POLITICAL PARTICIPATION

The first assumption of the discussion model is that citizens are in some degree politically active and that they are not greatly subject to manipulation by politicians. This assumption contradicts many studies of political behavior published since 1950 and relied upon by supporters of *pma*. Robert A. Dahl once contradicted Aristotle, holding that "obviously man is not instinctively a political animal." He based his conclusion on public opinion surveys which showed that most citizens were indifferent to and poorly informed about political life, and voting studies that revealed low levels of participation in elections.[8] These data do not necessarily undermine the discussion model, however, for several reasons.

Students of political behavior have begun to express doubts about the questions and metrics that have been used to measure political involvement.[9] A frequently cited index relates to the relatively high percentage of citizens who could not name their congressman when asked to do so. But recent studies have shown that citizens are often able to recognize and evaluate candidates without being able to recall their names from memory. (How frequently have you searched in vain for a name in introducing a good friend at a party?) According to Thomas E. Mann and Raymond E. Wolfinger, "Scholars have underestimated the level of public awareness of congressional candidates primarily because of faulty measures." There are other examples.

In finding that voters were intellectually disorganized and uninformed about governmental policies, the opinion surveyors used as their standard of evaluation a definition of rational voting that demanded too much of citizens and ignored the roles of representative institutions in policymaking and of retrospective voting in choosing representatives. The authors of *The American Voter*, for example, set five necessary conditions that citizens must meet to qualify as issue-oriented (that is, rational, responsible) voters: (1) the citizen must express an opinion on an issue; (2) the citizen must have knowledge of current government policy on the issue; (3) the citizen must have knowledge of the policy alternatives offered by the competing parties; (4) the citizen must feel sufficiently strongly about the issue to make use of the aforementioned knowledge in casting his vote. Not surprisingly, fewer than one-third of the potential electorate met the conditions.[10] But how relevant are they? Such conditions for voters might possibly be pertinent in a plebiscitary democracy, but they are neither possible nor necessary in a democracy with representative institutions that carry on discussion in a legislative process subsequent to elections. As Morris P. Fiorina has said: "Perhaps we find the electorate wanting because our tests are wanting. If so, we are the irresponsible ones for pronouncing others irresponsible on the basis of such tests."[11]

The opinion surveyors assumed that voters' choices were based principally on their evaluations of the alternative programs proposed by different candidates, and for this reason, presumably, citizens needed to be well informed and highly rational concerning a large number of issue domains. As early as 1966 V. O. Key, in his last book, pointed out, with reference to presidential elections, that there was a large element of retrospective judgment in voters' decisions, which did not require the types of information presumed to be necessary to choose between alternative candidates' programs.[12] Voters respond most clearly, he said, to those events they have experienced and observed; proposals for the future, being hazy and uncertain, neither engage the voter nor govern his actions in the same degree. Key was quick to point out that a combination of the electorate's retrospective judgment and the custom of party accountability enabled the electorate in fact to exercise a strong prospective influence, for parties and candidates "must worry, not about the meaning of past elections, but about their fate in future elections," and they conduct themselves accordingly.

Key's analysis was not pursued systematically for about fifteen years, until Fiorina completed a major study on retrospective voting. He found it to be applicable to congressional as well as presidential elections, although his formulation is somewhat more complex than Key's.

> Retrospective judgments have direct impacts on the formation of future expectations and on party identification, and through these factors, indirect influences on the vote. Simple retrospective evaluations—the most primitive kind of political issue— stand at the base of the pyramid. They feed indirectly into performance judgments, directly and indirectly into party identification and future expectations, and indirectly into the vote. These simplest of all issues have a pervasive influence on the citizen's voting decision.[13]

Finally, several recent studies report a significant rise in issue consistency among voters and in issue voting, which the authors attribute to changes in the issues and among the voters.[14] These may be due also, at least in part, to shortcomings in the earlier studies. Regardless, there is now ample evidence that citizens have the capacity to govern under a political system that is based on a process of continuous discussion.

Turning next to the overall level of political participation in the United States, it is relatively high and increasing. Citizens participate in all manner of political activities. Using the categories of a 1972 study of political participation in the United States by Sidney Verba and Norman H. Nie, 22 percent are political inactives, while 71 percent are active (7 percent are unclassifiable). The actives include "communalists" who are active in community politics but not in political campaigns (20 percent); "campaigners" who are active in political campaigns but not in community politics (15 percent); "complete activists" (11 percent); "parochial participants" who are active with respect to particular issues but are not involved in broader community politics or political campaigns (4 percent); "voting specialists" who, although they vote in both national and local elections, are not active in community politics and political campaigns (21 percent).[15] Voting is, therefore, one dimension of a rich and complex system of democratic discussion in the United States.

At the same time, nonvoting has been a persistent phenomenon. In the past, nonvoters were explained away as the consequence of legal restrictions and malfunctions in socialization. However, with legal barriers largely gone, with political information and communication high, and with a raised political consciousness in the electorate, nonvoting persists, and the question is what threshold of voting participation is needed to sustain a democratic state based on the concept of continuous discussion. Totalitarian regimes appear to require over 95 percent participation, but what is the figure for a deliberative state? Is 55 percent of the voting-age population, the current level, enough?

The literature of political science, surprisingly, contains few answers to this question. According to one recent study of voting in presidential elections:

> The least-educated, the very poor, Puerto Ricans, Chicanos, and people who move shortly before an election vote less than others. The voting strength of Southerners, the young, elderly, unemployed, unmarried, and blacks, is also reduced. . . . These findings would suggest that low turnout tilts the political system towards the right. . . . The flaw in this argument is an excess of economic determinism. What is important in politics is not the census pigeonholes that people fall into but rather their partisan affiliations and political opinions. In these respects, people who vote are not very different from the entire population.[16]

The authors conclude that the political consequences of low turnout are "surprisingly small." In fact, we just don't know what these consequences are, since, if the politically inactive portions of the population were suddenly mobilized, there is no guarantee that their political attitudes would not change in the process. Nonetheless, with political participation on the whole high and increasing, the current levels of voting are, it seems to me, more than sufficient to support a deliberative state based on the discussion model.

As for manipulation of voters, it was once popular among political commentators to say that citizens were beguiled by campaign tricks, demagogic rhetoric, and television debates, but there is little evidence to support these claims. As Key said in his study of presidential elections: "The perverse and unorthodox argument of this little book is that voters are not fools." The American voter and electorate are neither "straight-jacketed by social determinants" nor "moved by subconscious urges triggered by devilishly skillful propagandists."[17]

POLITICAL BEHAVIOR

The second assumption of the discussion model relates to political behavior, apart from the question of retrospective voting. Each individual plays a number of roles in his life and each role can lead him to a unique response to a given choice situation. Thus individuals have the capacity to respond to issues —to formulate their preferences concerning them—in several ways, including what they believe to be good for themselves, largely their economic self-interests; what they believe to be good for particular sectional, occupational, social, or religious groups; and what they believe to be good for the political community. The difference among these can be defined in terms of breadth of view. Responses are community, rather than privately, oriented to the extent that individuals have given greater emphasis to their estimates of the consequences of their choices for the larger community. Furthermore, the responses that individuals give in any choice situation will depend in significant part on how questions are asked of them. This means not simply the way questions are worded, but the total environment in which they are put and discussed.

Social science literature is filled with studies of role differentiation.[18] A classic experiment relates to the attitudes of college students on birth control. Questions with relevance to the church (for example, should birth control information be provided to married individuals who desire it?) were asked of Catholic students randomly divided into two groups. One group met in a small room where they were made aware of their common religious membership. The other group met in a large auditorium, along with hundreds of other students of many religions, where no effort was made to establish awareness of common religious beliefs. Although all of the students were instructed to respond with their "own personal opinions," there was a significant difference between the replies of the Catholic group that were aware of their common religious membership and the unaware group. The former approximated more closely the traditional Catholic position against birth control. The question

23

was the same for both groups, but individual responses depended on the institutional environment in which the question was asked.

Individuals, then, have multiple preference functions. Their responses to choice situations depend on which of these they call forth or use, and this depends in part on the institutional environment.

MEASUREMENT OF COMMUNITY-ORIENTED RESPONSES

The third assumption is that for individuals' participation in the political community the broader responses are the relevant ones and these can be measured. This assumption, too, contradicts many of the studies of political behavior published since the 1950s. These studies, based on public opinion and voting surveys, have shown, among other things, that citizens vote according to their narrow economic or demographic interests, and that there is so great a diversity of these individual values in society that meaningful and measurable community responses cannot be found. In the year 1960, for example, the authors of *The American Voter* reported that citizens' policy preferences often reflected little more than "primitive self-interest," and James Prothro and Charles Grigg reported, in an influential article, that they could find no community consensus on policy issues.[19]

Typically those who have found in their studies of political behavior that citizens pursue only their narrow economic interests and that there is little or no community consensus have been either not aware of the hypothesis, or they have been unsympathetic with the hypothesis, that citizens can have multiple responses to the same question and that the responses they give will vary with the institutional environment. They have not constructed their questions so as to exact community responses and, not surprisingly, they found none.

A number of years ago I wrote Angus Campbell, then director of the Survey Research Center at the University of Michigan and leader of the group that produced *The American Voter,* asking if his center had conducted any studies in which they sought, by the wording of questions, to elicit two types of responses—self-interested and community-oriented—on the same policy issues. His reply follows:

I think we have always asked our respondents to assess policy proposals in terms of their own preferences. Occasionally they will say that a proposed change might be best for society at large but they would personally not favor it. I recall answers of this sort in response to a question regarding an income tax in Michigan.

With no real evidence at hand, I would guess that from people of some sophistication it would not be difficult to elicit two independent responses of the kind you suggest. People of less complicated intellectual habits would probably tend to have little concept of public interest and, if pressed, would simply identify it with their private interest.[20]

Donald K. Kinder and D. Roderick Kiewiet are the first American students of political behavior to demonstrate that citizens will vote the public interest, as I have defined it, rather than their pocketbooks, when their preferences for the former are elicited effectively.[21] They examined whether citizens, in voting for Congress and for the President, and in their party affiliations, were influenced more by the immediate and tangible circumstances of their private lives, or by their views of the nation's economic well-being. The evidence was much stronger for the second alternative:

> We found that voters' definitions of national economic problems correlated with their political preferences. Moreover, voters' judgments of recent trends in general business conditions, their ratings of the incumbent administration's handling of economic matters, their evaluation of which party was better equipped or more inclined to solve national economic problems, all contributed to their decision about which congressional candidate to support; substantially influenced their presidential voting; and affected even the most central of political predispositions, party identification. Political preferences thus seem to be shaped by citizens' conceptions of national economic conditions, not by the economic circumstances of their personal lives. . . .
>
> We do not mean to imply that personal economic discontents are of little significance. Evidence to the contrary is massive. . . . When asked to name their fondest hopes and worst fears, Americans refer most frequently to their own economic circumstances. To be suddenly unemployed is no doubt a more significant experience in many respects than to notice an increase in the national unemployment rate. Our point here is not that personal experiences are generally unimportant, but that they are, or seem to be, *politically* unimportant. . . . Personal economic grievances are . . . compartmentalized away from political preferences.

Kinder and Kiewiet's findings have not been accepted by some of their colleagues who point out, among other things, that the two K's have not taken account of the tendency for people's personal interests to color their perceptions of the public interest.[22] That this happens is true, of course, but it does not seriously weaken the central argument that one cannot know individuals' political opinions simply by knowing their personal opinions and interests.

As a consequence of the interest that Kinder and Kiewiet have generated, similar findings are beginning to appear for the first time in other studies.[23] Investigators frequently fail to find what they are not looking for, as in the now classic example of published drawings of cell nuclei made from direct microscopic observations dated both before and after the discovery and description of chromosomes. Chromosomes kept showing up in the later drawings, not in the earlier ones. When the ideal for the class "cell nuclei" included chromosomes, chromosomes were perceived as part of the visual input.[24]

Some social scientists have argued that it is best that citizens use narrow, particular preferences in decision making for public policy. Individuals are doing well enough, they argue, if they know what is best for themselves. How can they pretend to know what is best for others? They have a hard enough time acquiring sufficient data to know their own utility functions. How can they possibly know the utility functions of all other actors? This being the case, the only valid decision models—valid in the sense that they operate with sufficient information—are those where individuals vote only their own limited interests, and political institutions aggregate these.

This argument misses the point on two scores. First, the discussion model does not require that each citizen divine the utility functions of all other citizens, rather that each citizen respond in terms of what he or she thinks is best for the political community. When citizens do this they are likely to take a view of the consequences of their voting that is broader than their own economic interests, but their decisions are just as "rational" as when they vote their narrower interests. Each citizen is to vote what *he* thinks, not what he thinks others might think. Citizens are to vote their own preference functions, but it is to be their preferences for the political community.

Second, we are, or should be, concerned about institutions of representative government, not simply the aggregation of individual votes in opinion polls or even in elections. There are, for example, many questions that individual citizens cannot answer in terms of what would be good public policy —for example, the right relationship of corporate to individual tax rates— because the average citizen does not have the capacity to obtain, understand, and use the information necessary for a decision here. To get the "right" response, this question needs to be asked of a smaller group of elected legislators who can carry the discussion to a greater level of specificity. The analysis of alternative institutions and procedures in terms of their capacity to elicit these responses is, or if it isn't it should be, a central concern of political scientists.

Several recent studies of the behavior of voters in congressional elections show that voters' assessments of the candidates competing in each district have a greater direct effect on electoral choices than do national conditions and events, such as recessions, unemployment, inflation, and political scandals.[25] These findings are sensible and consistent with the behavioral assumptions of the discussion model, for they can be understood to mean that voters give attention to choosing candidates who are likely to represent and refine the voters' political views in the subsequent legislative and administrative processes.

Finally, there are social scientists who agree that individuals' preferences depend on their several roles in society, but they go on to say that in making decisions relating to the political community, or to social welfare, each individual uses a composite preference or utility function—a total net position representing a balance of all roles.[26] This last hypothesis is not supported by experimental evidence and seems to me to be unfortunate, for it misses the point that individuals respond differently depending on how the question is asked of them. The hypothesis of a single combined preference function fails to give proper emphasis to the differentiation of institutions for putting the question.

ELECTIONS AND EXECUTIVE–LEGISLATIVE RELATIONS

A final assumption of the deliberative model of executive–legislative relations is that the electoral process creates a sufficiently close connection between the President and Congress to sustain legislative and administrative processes that depend heavily on cooperation between the two branches.

Voting studies have shown a strong disassociation between voting for President and for Congress. Presidential coattails, if they were ever strong, are now so weak that, according to W. Dean Burnham, incumbent congressmen "have become quite effectively insulated from the electoral effects . . . of adverse presidential landslides."[27] Thus it is argued that presidential elections *by themselves* have had surprisingly little influence on congressional responses to the President's initiatives.

The degree to which aggregate national fluctuations in public opinion and voting affect congressional elections has varied over time. But it exists and, as R. Douglas Rivers points out, is something congressmen worry about.[28] These national fluctuations are likely to register public dissatisfaction with the course of governmental policy, in the manner of retrospective evaluations in voting, and for this reason they create a significant electorally-based connection among congressmen themselves and between congressmen and the President. Rivers has called this a "shared fate."

> An unfavorable public judgment will mean a loss of seats for the party which currently occupies the White House but will, to a lesser degree, damage the reelection prospects of all incumbents. . . . Inasmuch as Congressmen share a single 'common fate' it is the same fate that awaits the President, and this connection promotes congressional support for the program of a popular president.

Thus retrospective voting and shared fate, when they are examined closely, contribute to consistency between the electoral process and the legislative and administrative processes as we have modeled them.

27

Consequences of Using *pma* Rather than Discussion Model for Analysis of Institutions

With this understanding of the basic assumptions of the discussion model, we can compare the consequences of using either the *pma* model or the discussion model for the analysis of Congress and executive–legislative relations.

The principal function of governmental institutions in the *pma* model (apart from guaranteeing basic rights and protecting the community from its enemies) is to aggregate particular interests; to coordinate through partisan mutual adjustment the opinions that have been articulated by others in support of their particular interests.[29] According to this model, individuals can respond to public policy issues in terms of their participation in many overlapping groups, but not in terms of the political community. All groups have their unique responses, their standards, and identifiable interests except one, the political community as such. The National Association of Manufacturers (NAM) has a clear "interest"; the United States of America does not. But if individuals are capable of playing many roles, of responding in many ways to choice situations, of multigroup membership, why cannot one of the groups be the political community to which individuals are tied by a response in terms of the communal interest? The NAM has found a way to define a common interest for its many and diverse members. Why can't the political community do the same? Stripped of its adornments, the *pma* model holds that political community does not exist, that there is no such thing as a community response to public policy issues, only individual and lesser group demands.

In the discussion model, representative institutions are used for interest group bargaining, to be sure, but they are also needed for an additional purpose that is at least as important as the first, namely, to elicit community-oriented responses from citizens, by organizing and conducting a continuous discussion through electoral, legislative, and administrative processes. Thus for the *pma* model the principal criterion for evaluating leadership and accountability of governmental institutions is simply how well they conduct partisan mutual adjustment. For the discussion model there are broader grounds for judging representative institutions, namely, how well in each stage of discussion they perform the selective function of taking over from the previous stage and the instructive function of handing on to the next stage.

The fact that the standard for evaluating political institutions is much narrower in the *pma* model than in the discussion model does not mean, however, as some supporters of *pma* believe, that their model is descriptive and inductive, while the other is normative and deductive. In differing degrees both models describe the way it is and the way it should be. Nor is it true that *pma* is value free, whereas the discussion model is value laden. Neither is value free. Nor is it true that the *pma* model is realistic, while the discussion model is idealistic. How realistic is it to pretend that there are no community-wide interests? Furthermore, discussion does not necessarily mean calm, disinterested conversations about what is best. It can mean heated arguments and angry debates in which the opinions of citizens have been formed, at least in part, by their different experiences.

Also, breadth of view, the criterion for the exercise of legislative and administrative discretion, is not always achieved. It would be foolish to deny that bureaucratic politics and legislative–executive relations are conducted frequently on grounds that are narrower and more interest-oriented than this. New values that are agreed upon by the community and the electorate, and by the legislators, may confront bureaucratic inertia and be resisted by special interests. There are in the real world, in other words, a great many imperfections for a discussion model. But so also are there imperfections for an interest group model, in cases where partisan mutual adjustment fails. Admittedly, the criterion for success is much less demanding for the *pma* model than for discussion. Analogously, there are imperfections and "externalities" in the real world for the economic market model, the basic tool of economic analysis. Economists have learned how to deal with these in studying their realm; so can political scientists in theirs.

An adequate analysis of political institutions in terms of interactions among individuals, groups, and their representatives must account, then, for two different but related problems. One concerns the many possible responses of participants in a choice situation and how individual responses are influenced by alternative institutional structures and alternative processes of government. This we can call the problem of dominant loyalties. The second problem assumes that the participants' preference functions are given, and is concerned with factors that determine the relative influence of the various participants on the final outcome. This we can call the bargaining problem.[30]

The group theorists assume that citizens are capable only of limited responses in terms of particular interests; and that preference functions are, therefore, fairly well fixed. Thus they are concerned largely with the bargaining problem, whereas the discussion model attempts to deal also with the problem of dominant loyalties. It rejects the utilitarian view that if each person or each group pursues its own happiness (as Bentham would have put it) the general result will be the happiness of all. Because man's inward-looking actions are performed for limited ends and with limited insight, the general result of a system whose definition of the public interest is the sum of, or the adjustment of, such inward-looking views and actions would be one that no one had willed for the community as a whole.

Provenance of the Discussion and *pma* Models

I should identify, if only summarily, the theoretical progenitors of the two models. For the discussion model there is Rousseau's distinction between the general will and the sum of particular wills. Although scholars continuously argue about it, my understanding of Rousseau is that he thought of individuals as being ambivalent, always subject to conflict between productive and egoistic tendencies, and therefore able to respond to choice situations in terms of either the general will or particular wills. A true law is, according to Rousseau, a rule of general, not particular application, and the great problem for the state is how to procure such laws. Basically the general will is expressed only through deliberation of the citizens.

Modern English liberal thought is a related source, and the most immediate one, of the discussion model presented here, especially the writing of two twentieth-century Oxford political philosophers, A. D. Lindsay and Ernest F. Barker.[31] Like Rousseau they believe that individuals are ambivalent, possessed of both self-centered tendencies and those that motivate them to accept obligations to fellow citizens. And they agree with Rousseau in principle on the need for a deliberative state. Since, however, a modern society is vastly more complex than that described by Rousseau, the translation of the spirit of its common life into collective action, into laws and acts of government, is far more complicated than the process envisioned by the French philosopher. Yet basically, as Lindsay says, "the only satisfactory way of doing that will be by discussion."[32]

These views of twentieth-century English philosophers in support of a discussion model of democratic government were influenced by an analysis of British government, especially the history of parliament, that, although it may be little appreciated today, used to be known by every English schoolchild, according to J. H. Hexter.[33] This relates to the remarkable evolution of the seventeenth-century parliament from a body representing social orders to one representing the whole country, thereby converting local and class privileges into modern liberty and free government. This was accomplished in good part by the development of techniques for government by discussion. As Samuel H. Beer has said: "To put the main point plainly: it was in England during the seventeenth century that the essential mechanisms of government by discussion were invented."[34]

David B. Truman's *The Governmental Process* is the proximate source of contemporary interest group theories.[35] It has had, arguably, as great an influence on contemporary American political science as any book written since World War II. Truman himself documents this influence in the 1970 introduction to the book's second edition. The phrase "partisan mutual adjustment" was used in 1959 by Charles E. Lindblom, who subsequently made additional contributions to interest group theory.[36]

The fountainhead of interest group theory is, however, Arthur F. Bentley's *The Process of Government,* published in 1908.[37] Truman acknowledges it as his model: "As the title of the present volume suggests," he says, "Bentley's 'attempt to fashion a tool' has been the principal benchmark for my thinking."[38] Bentley's concept of the relation between group interests and the public interest of the political community is signified in the following quotation:

> The great task in the study of any form of social life is the analysis of these groups. . . . When the groups are adequately stated, everything is stated. When I say everything I mean everything. The complete description will mean the complete science in the study of social phenomena. . . .
> There is no group without its interest. The interest I put forward is a specific group interest in some definite course of conduct or activity. It is first, last, and all the time strictly empirical. There is no way to find it except by observation. . . .
> As for political questions under any society in which we are called upon to study them, we shall never find a group interest of the society as a whole. We shall always find that the political interests and activities of any given group—and there are no political phenomena except group phenomena—are directed against other activities of men, who appear in other groups, political or other. The phenomena of political life which we study will always divide the society in which they occur, along lines which are very real, though of varying degrees of definiteness. The society itself is nothing other than the complex of the groups that compose it.[39]

The "common good" in the title of this book is derived, of course, from Aristotle's *Politics*.[40] He argued that while associations have ends, the political association has the highest, for it exists "for the sake of the *general* advantage which it brings."[41]

2

What Do Congressional Committees Do?

TO THIS POINT I have defined roles for Congress as a whole and for the Executive as a whole. But what about the relations between the whole and its parts—between Congress and its committees, between the chief executive and the bureaus, and between the committees and the bureaus? To be consistent with the roles defined, the executive bureaus are responsible to the President for leadership in the legislative and administrative processes. The policy emanating from any one governmental bureau needs to be integrated with related policies from others; and the administrative performance of related agencies needs to be coordinated. Since integration and coordination require effective hierarchical organization, and since the Executive intrinsically is better able to provide this than is the legislature, the bureaus will be in a hierarchical relationship to the chief executive.

In like manner, to be consistent with the roles defined, the committees of the legislature are responsible primarily to the whole chamber. The unique contributions of the legislature to democratic government are defined largely from the virtues of the body as a whole, rather than those of standing committees, each with a specialized competence and jurisdiction. At the same time, of course, the standing committees of the Congress are as essential to the legislature's control of both the legislative and administrative processes as the bureaus are essential to the Executive's leadership and implementation. Thus the principal organizational and procedural problems of the American Executive and of the American Congress relate to the effort to insure that the whole is master of its parts.

The formal relations among President, bureaus, whole House, and committees are illustrated by the arrows in figure 2.1. Nonetheless, direct relations between bureaus and committees, indicated by the X's on the bottom line of this figure, occur more frequently than those that follow the arrows. Furthermore, they are inevitable and they are desirable. It would be impossible for Congress to control legislation and administration effectively if all executive–legislative relations had to channel through the whole House and the Executive Office of the President. Normally, direct relations between bureaus and committees do not undermine our model of executive–legislative relations; only under certain circumstances is this the case. What, then, are these circumstances?

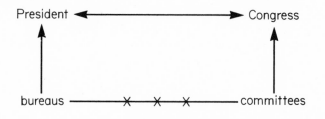

FIGURE 2.1
Executive–Legislative Relations—Normal Form

First is when major conflicts between the two branches are conducted at this lower level rather than between the White House and the whole House.

Example. In the early 1950s the nation was rocked by Senator Joseph McCarthy's charges that the Army, particularly the Signal Corps, had been infiltrated by "pinkos" and "homos." The confrontation was between Senator McCarthy (R. WI), chairman of the Subcommittee on Investigations of the Senate Committee on Government Operations, and Secretary of the Army Robert T. Stevens. It was resolved only after President Dwight D. Eisenhower finally assumed responsibility for Stevens, and the full Senate assumed responsibility for McCarthy by appointing a bipartisan select committee to study censure charges against their Wisconsin colleague.

A second circumstance that raises problems for our model of executive–legislative relations occurs when the relations between bureau and committee are so intimate and so ubiquitous that they preclude the President and the whole House from participating in the legislative and administrative processes when they want to participate. When, in other words, bureau–committee relations are so intimate as to challenge the President's control over bureaus and Congress's control over committees, then the roles as defined are endangered. This latter condition can be called the pathological form of bureau–committee relations, in the sense that it is a deviation from the normal or typical form. It is shown graphically in figure 2.2 and is illustrated by the following example.

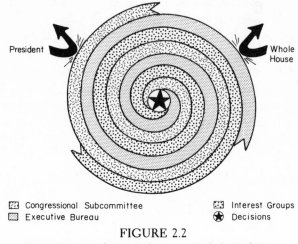

Congressional Subcommittee
Executive Bureau
Interest Groups
Decisions

FIGURE 2.2
Executive–Legislative Relations—Pathological Form

Example. Presidents Franklin D. Roosevelt and Harry S Truman were frustrated in their efforts to adopt national policies for the development and use of water and land resources by the U.S. Army Corps of Engineers and the congressional committees that authorized the planning and construction of water-resources projects. The Corps considered themselves to be "engineering consultants to and contractors for the Congress of the United States," and as such they resisted and ignored directives from the Executive Office of the President and from the President himself. This pathological form of bureau–committee relations was terminated in the 1950s when the Corps and the committees changed their approaches to executive–legislative relations. The Corps began to clear its policies and projects with the President's office before sending them to Congress and to participate actively in interagency committees for the purpose of developing uniform policies for the executive branch. The congressional committees altered their conduct to accommodate the new form of executive–legislative communications.[1]

The purpose of this chapter is to examine the theory and practice of congressional committees. I use the lens of executive–legislative relations, and within this, the finer lens of relations between committees and the whole House. Other investigations have used different lenses. Most important among them are studies that treat congressional committees as self-contained social systems, those that view committees in terms of the goals and perceptions of the committee members themselves, and those that view committees in terms of the organizational needs of Congress, defined in the language of systems analysis and organizational theory.[2] Using these alternative lenses political scientists have in the last fifteen years made significant progress in understanding committees. I shall use many of their findings. The first two alternatives, however, are so inward-looking—they focus so strongly on the committee per se—that those who use them, unless they are extraordinarily attentive to the external environment, give insufficient attention to the broader framework of executive–legislative relations. Thus, for example, they attach too little importance to the fact that on most important issues the committees are dealing with proposals of the President or of a cabinet secretary or agency head. These inward-looking studies may also give insufficient attention to the techniques, both external and internal, by which the whole House controls its parts in the committees.

From the formative years of Congress until about 1840, the role of legislative committees was debated frequently by the members themselves. I shall look briefly at these instructive debates and then construct a framework of analysis for today in terms of history and of our model of executive–legislative relations. The historical material is adapted from the original work of Joseph Cooper.[3]

Theory and Practice of Committees, 1789–1840

The legislative procedures envisioned by Republican (Jeffersonian) theory were these: (1) All important subjects should be referred first to the whole House. (2) Principles should be discussed and determined in the whole House. (3) Thereafter subjects should be referred to a committee to bring in a bill. (4) Subjects were to be referred in the first instance to a committee, rather than to the whole House, only if they were routine—for example, claims— or if they were so complicated that the members themselves could not determine the facts in the whole House—for example, revenue bills.

The underlying premises of these procedures were, first, a profound faith in the diligence and capacity of individual members of Congress, and second, a belief that the ideal process was one in which each member would have his full say and an equal say. Furthermore, spontaneity of discussion in the House was to be limited only by the necessity of its being germane, that is, confined to the broad subject under consideration.

Thus any form of leadership of the House was thought to prejudice the process, whether it was leadership by the Executive, by the Speaker, or by parties. As for executive leadership, Republican theory called for congressional preeminence in both initiation and oversight of the legislative process. The Republicans discussed, but rejected, a procedure for referring subjects first to the executive departments for their views; and they rejected in theory any procedure that would allow the Executive to draft bills and introduce them.

Toward party leadership the Republicans originally shared a deep and basic hostility, identifying parties with factions, with selfish interests, with what by definition was antithetical to the public interest. This hostility to parties was implicit in the practice of referring subjects first to the whole House where discussion was to be nonpartisan. Free discussion and mutual enlightenment, without regard to party, were believed to be the best way to elicit the public interest.

However, this, the Jeffersonian (or Republican) theory, broke down in practice. In practice, standing committees developed. By 1817 more important matters were referred first to standing committees rather than to the whole House, and the standing committees had begun to establish their right to report bills whether or not they had been charged by the whole House with the subject. Furthermore, in practice, whenever possible, the House was closely managed and led by the Republicans through their party caucus and through partisan control of the speakership and of the committees—all of this a far cry from Republican theory.

Why did Republican theory break down with Republicans in control of both branches of the government? In part, this was due to growth in the size and business of the House; the House found it difficult to work effectively under the Jeffersonian rules with so many members and so much to do. But this reason has probably been overstressed; certainly it was not the only one. Jeffersonians began to lose faith in the capacity of individual members to determine and order the facts without first referring subjects to specialized committees. What's more, under Jefferson as President, and contrary to Jeffersonian theory, the Executive led the legislative process, almost as much as previously under the Federalists.

Under Madison, however, a break developed between the Congress and the executive branch, a break that was occasioned both by Madison's weakness as a legislative leader and by the desires of several strong members of the House to gain control. Madison's first Congress, the eleventh (1809–1811), was a shambles. The old Jeffersonian system of leadership and caucus control by the Executive broke down without any other leadership and guidance system arising to fill the gap. However, in the twelfth Congress (1811–1813) Henry Clay became Speaker, and it is Clay who was responsible for transforming the office of the Speaker into a leadership organ and for advancing the position of the standing committees in relation to the whole House. Clay quite rightly perceived that if Congress were to dominate the executive branch, then it must have an adequate, expert leadership and guidance system of its own. This did not mean that the President and the departments would not be relied on.

Rather, it meant that the House would be prepared for all vicissitudes of executive–legislative relations because of the functions to be performed by the Speaker and by the regularly appointed standing committees. In times of executive weakness, the House would have the means for legislating without aid from the departments; in times of cooperation, it would have the means for retaining some policy influence.

Republican theory contained a basic conflict. On the one hand, there was a belief in the whole House as against small committees of the House; on the other hand, a belief in congressional preeminence over the Executive. As it turned out, these were inconsistent. Since the Republicans believed in the preeminence of Congress, they should have recognized the need of Congress to have its own leadership organs. But the Republicans refused to recognize the inconsistency. Instead of going to the theoretical root of their conflict and constructing a revised theory that would deal directly with committees, they made various efforts to rationalize the breakdown. The theory had held that where the subject matter was so complicated that facts could not be set straight in the whole House, the subject could be referred first to a committee. It was not believed that this would be necessary except in a very few cases; but as committees grew, this loophole was enlarged.

The Jeffersonians, then, did not succeed in bringing the standing committees into their theory directly, even after the committees had arrived in practice. It remained for the Jacksonians to develop a theory that accounted for standing committees. Jacksonians readily accepted referring subjects first to committees. Why? Why were they willing to depart from Jeffersonianism in this regard when they were unwilling to do so in many others? The reason is due to the emphasis that they placed on the President as tribune of the people and the President as legislative leader; and to the emphasis that they placed on party as an organization headed by the President which served as an intermediary with the people and with Congress.

With regard to the President, they held that he had higher status as a direct representative of the people than the Congress. There was no question but that he was legislative leader. Party was the agency through which the President was to appeal to the people for support; and once support had been obtained, it was the function of the party to help the President to carry out the people's will. The Jacksonians anchored the presidency in a national party system.

Thus Jacksonians could openly accept prior reference of subjects and bills to committees because of their theory of executive–legislative relations. If primary responsibility for initiation in the public interest was in the hands of the President and the party he headed, there was no longer any strong theoretical argument against giving matters first to committees. The Jacksonians were right in realizing that a theory for congressional committees must be justified in terms of a theory of executive–legislative relations in which presidential leadership of the legislative process is recognized.

At the same time, Jacksonians overestimated the capacity of national or presidential parties to control the conduct of the Congress, and for this reason their theory does not explain adequately the part of committees in the House today. The roles of national parties, congressional parties, and nonpartisan congressional majorities in the organization and operations of Congress are discussed in the next chapter. Let it be said here simply that it may be easier for the President, through party, to influence the whole House than to influence its standing committees. The committees, as small groups concentrating on limited subject matter, frequently develop integrative norms that make them less subject to control by party leaders than is the whole House. The Appropriations Committee, as we shall see in chapter 8, is governed by such norms, principally economy, that lead to integration and cohesion in the committee and frustrate party partisanship. Similar norms operate in many committees, while some are quite partisan.[4]

Example. In a study of the Democratically controlled House Agriculture Committee during the Nixon Administration, committee members were asked: "Do you feel that there is more partisan emphasis on committee oversight when the Executive is not of the same party as the majority of the committee, as during the 80th and 91st Congresses? Do you feel there is a more partisan character to committee decision making because the Administration is controlled by the Republicans and the committee by the Democrats?"[5] Of the twenty-one respondents, only one indicated without qualification that he felt partisanship played an important role in decision making. Four other members gave qualified agreement, and the remaining sixteen members stated that partisanship was no factor at all. Here is a sample of responses:

CHAIRMAN W. R. POAGE (D. TX): "Decisions in the committee are not made on a partisan basis normally. [Secretary of Agriculture] Hardin does work more through [ranking minority member] Belcher than me, even though I am the chairman, and so it is only human nature that I view the Department from a tougher attitude. But this is just because of the way Nixon's people treat us. Inside the committee, we are all dedicated to the best for American agriculture, and we try to decide on this basis, not along party lines. There are enough interests outside the committee hostile to the American farmer already; we cannot afford to break up into partisan lines within the committee."

PAGE BELCHER (R. OK): "When it gets down to it, we are not a partisan committee. Bob Poage and I work well together. We don't always agree, but it is never partisan bickering. I don't think he's out to oversee Nixon more stringently, and I think if he does have disagreements they are policy disagreements, not based on narrow partisan considerations. This attitude is true of all the members of the committee, I think, with only a few exceptions, and these men don't set the tone for the rest of us."

GEORGE A. GOODLING (R. PA): "I don't think the committee is partisan in any real sense. Members may feel it necessary to make a play for political coverage, and so you get Democrats blasting Nixon and his policies, but this is mostly for the folks back home. Basically, members are concerned with the problems facing farmers, and so don't play politics with the issues once they have won their headline in the local newspaper. Everyone understands the needs of politics, but we don't let it spill over into real issues and decisions."

ED JONES (D. TN): "The party factor on this committee is nil. . . . Personal philosophy and one's approach to farm problems are much more important than your party label. Frankly, I was very surprised to discover that this was the case when I got here. But I find that I am in agreement with at least 50 percent of the Republicans on almost all things, and so for me party just isn't an issue. The men on the committee are there, mostly, because they are interested in farm problems and needs. The senior men on the committee and the junior men too are serious and dedicated to the job, and the interests of the farmer are the overriding consideration. As a result, party is just not important."

Thus a new theory of the role of legislative committees is needed.

A Modern Framework for Committees

Fortified with knowledge of the period in our history when the role of legislative committees was debated most seriously, and with a model of executive–legislative relations, we can now derive a framework of analysis that will enable us to describe and evaluate committees in today's Congress. In these terms I treat, first, the justifications for committees and, second, the costs of relying heavily on them.

JUSTIFICATIONS FOR COMMITTEES

The first justification for committees relates to the legislative process. Congress's role of overseeing and controlling the process includes the capacity to offer, debate, and adopt alternatives to the Executive's proposals. The President initiates, to be sure, but Congress is not limited to his proposals in its deliberations. Without committees to examine alternatives and to bring out relevant details pertaining to them, Congress would have to assume, in effect, that the Executive had examined all alternatives and selected the best one. But we have never been willing to assume either of these propositions, necessarily. In comparison, the British Parliament, without an effective system of standing committees, is forced to assume both.[6]

Thus congressional committees hear nongovernment witnesses, in part to see if there are alternatives that the Executive has ignored. They hear a variety of government and nongovernment witnesses, in part to see if the President in his initiative has selected the best alternative.

Also, congressional committees provide cues to noncommittee members on how to vote on legislation that the committees have reported. We no longer assume, as did the Jeffersonians, that each member has the capacity, with the aid of floor debates alone, to reach a decision on how to vote on all the questions that require a vote today. Instead, we assume that members take voting cues from a number of sources: their constituents, interest groups, party leaders, the President, committees.

In a 1976 study Frans R. Bax sought to determine the most important cues for members in their voting decisions. Based on all bills reported by fourteen legislative committees and considered by the House with roll-call votes in two Congresses, 1967–1970, for a total of 662 observations, he found that the most important cues influencing members' votes on the floor were those given by the committees reporting the bills. Cues given by constituents, party leaders, and the President were less influential in the congressmen's voting decisions.[7] This finding does not apply, of course, to each bill individually, or to the most salient bills as a group, for which constituency is a very important cue. But for all important bills taken together members are more likely to take their cues from senior members of the committees that have held hearings on the bills and reported them than from any other source. We shall consider some further implications of this finding below when we discuss the costs of committees.

A second justification for committees relates to the administrative process. We rely heavily on congressional oversight as a means of holding bureaucracy accountable for administrative performance, and for this committees are essential. They can develop the expertise needed for this purpose and they have the time required to oversee. Part 3 of this book illustrates this point in detail.

Again it is interesting to note that Great Britain, without an elaborate committee structure such as ours, cannot rely as heavily on legislative oversight as we can. Traditionally the British have relied more than we on professional standards of the career public service as a means for holding the bureaucracy accountable.

A third justification relates to Congress's reserve capacity to initiate legislation where the Executive has not done so; in this area committees are an essential resource. The activities of committees and committee staffs for this purpose are developed further in chapter 12.

COSTS OF COMMITTEES

Understanding the justifications for committees, in terms of our model, we must recognize that they manifest, also in terms of our model, certain inevitable costs or dangers.

First, committees tend inevitably to lead Congress away from a concern for broad policy and general administrative performance. While committees are needed for the reasons given, their very existence leads to specialization. This situation in the legislative branch has its parallel in the Executive, where the need for expert information and performance is provided by the bureaus. Yet these specialized bureaus always present the danger that executive action will be so narrow in scope or so fragmented that the public interest will not be realized. To combat this danger in the Executive, there is a fairly well-developed system of coordination, involving such procedures as legislative clearance, that is, review and evaluation by the Executive Office of the President of all legislative proposals of the agencies before they are submitted to Congress.

Devices for integration in the legislature are more difficult to realize, simply because the Congress is less hierarchically organized than is the Executive. But there are important mitigating factors here. First, because Congress as a whole represents the nonexpert and the capacity for change, the conduct of its committees is less likely than that of the bureaus to be programmed or predetermined in a highly specialized manner. Also, there is less need for coordination in the legislature than in the Executive. Leadership, which is the Executive's normal role, requires greater coordination than does control, which is Congress's normal role. Although there is less need in Congress than in the Executive for such coordination, certainly there is a requirement, and the tendency of committees to distract attention away from broad policy and general administrative performance is one of their potential costs.

A second cost is that committees tend inevitably to challenge the President for control of the bureaus. Direct relations between committees and bureaus, we have said, are frequent, inevitable, and desirable. They raise questions for the model of executive–legislative relations only when major conflicts between the two branches are conducted at this level, rather than between the White House and the whole House, and when relations between bureau and committee are so intimate that they preclude the President and the whole House from participating in the legislative and administrative processes where they want to participate—that is, in the pathological form of bureau–committee relations.

The question here is: Can committees, alone or in combination with bureaus and interest groups, so frustrate the Executive that executive leadership in policy and administration is made impossibly difficult? Woodrow Wilson, when he wrote *Congressional Government* in 1884, thought yes; he called it committee government. But some years later, in *Constitutional Government*, Wilson said that things had changed and that "the President is at liberty both in law and conscience to be as big a man as he can." On the whole this remains true today.

Some supporters of strong executive power push the panic button when congressional committees become very active in their oversight activities for fear that this will lead to the President's losing control of the executive establishment. There is such a danger in the pathological state of committee–bureau relations, to be sure, but senior executive officers frequently exaggerate the powerlessness of the President in such situations. They are wont to use the influence of congressional committees as an excuse for not doing what they, the Executive, do not want to do. In response to outside proposals for a change in policy, an executive officer will frequently respond: "That's an interesting idea, but the Committee on Appropriations [or some other committee] won't buy it, so we'd better forget it." What he means in all likelihood is either that he does not buy the proposal, or that he is not prepared to make the effort to sell it to Congress.

Finally, committees tend inevitably to challenge the whole House for control of the legislature's business. Committees may, in other words, become master rather than servant of the House. The unique contributions of the popularly elected legislature—institutionalization of the lay mind, and of the open mind, and representation of a different constituency than the President's —all apply to the Congress as a whole, not necessarily to specialized and sometimes unrepresentative committees of Congress. This potential cost, it will be observed, is the one that preoccupied Republican (Jeffersonian) theory on standing committees.

In this context one can ask whether the influence of committees as cue-givers for voting by noncommittee members in the whole House gives the committees a form of mastery over the larger body. Probably not, for it appears that the cues are transmitted from committee to the rest of the House not by the committee as a single unit but by senior, respected committee members of both parties. Thus, when a noncommittee Republican looks for a cue, it is likely to be from a senior Republican on the committee whose views and integrity the noncommittee Republican respects, and analogously for noncommittee Democrats. More specifically, a liberal Democrat is likely to take his cue from a liberal Democratic colleague on the committee.

Where a committee is unanimous in its recommendations on legislation—

where the Democrats and Republicans on a committee agree—then noncommittee Republicans and noncommittee Democrats get the same cues, to be sure, but they get them from different sources. Where a committee is not unanimous, different noncommittee members get different cues. All of this makes the fact that committees are a very important influence on voting decisions in the House less a threat to whole House mastery of its parts than might first appear to be the case.

TECHNIQUES FOR WHOLE HOUSE CONTROL OVER COMMITTEES

Recognizing, then, the reasons for standing committees as well as their costs, we can describe and evaluate the techniques that are used by the whole House to control relations between it and committees. There are two types of techniques. First are those by which the whole House reviews and controls the output of its committees—that is, the bills and other measures that the committees report to the House. I call these external controls, and they are discussed in chapter 5. Second are techniques by which the House controls representativeness and democracy in the committees, so that the committees will act in accordance with the wishes of the whole House. These internal controls are analyzed in chapter 6. The two types of control are obviously related. To the extent that the whole House uses external controls with great effect, there will be less need for internal controls and vice-versa. Furthermore the whole House can and does use these controls selectively. If it believes that the Committee on Education and Labor, for example, is more partisan and less representative of the House than other committees, the House can be more vigilant in reviewing the legislation reported by the committee than it is normally, ensuring that the committee's bills are wide open to amendment on the floor.

A Different Model of Committees in
Executive–Legislative Relations

The analysis of committees presented here is not in vogue with many political scientists, who instead emphasize a "whirlpools" or "iron triangles" theory that goes as follows.[8] For each substantive policy area—agriculture, civil rights, transportation—there is an independent and unique decision-making subsystem, consisting of an executive bureau, a congressional subcommittee, and the relevant pressure groups. The major objective of all participants in each subsystem, according to this theory, is to insure that the subsystem aggregates and retains the political power and influence necessary to make and control public policy in its area. Thus each subsystem should be studied independently, which is done by case studies. In these studies the independence and uniqueness of each subsystem are emphasized, and relatively little attention is paid to the roles of major institutions and their representatives in public policymaking. Policy orbits rather than institutions are separately defined.

This alternative method for studying committees is analogous to the pattern of direct bureau–committee relations mentioned earlier. It describes a great deal of routine governmental activity where the President and Congress as a whole have elected not to intervene, but can do so at any time they choose. Beyond this it describes what we have called the pathological form of bureau–committee intercourse. Indeed, it confuses the pathological and normal forms. Although whirlpools and iron triangles can be found at any time, they do not describe the normal pattern of American executive–legislative relations.[9] Furthermore, the case studies must be used with caution, for they may not be typical of the conduct of American government. Case study writers frequently select subjects in which the pathological form of bureau–committee relations is present. They are easier to organize and write and they are more dramatic. Finally, it will be observed that analysis of committees based on iron triangles is inspired by, if not derived from, the more general *pma* model of American politics, whereas the analysis presented here is consistent with the discussion model of the political system.[10]

3

What Do Congressional
Leaders Do?

WHAT ARE the roles of congressional leaders and political parties in the whole House? In terms of leadership the House could be organized according to one of three archetypes:

Alternative 1: to give effect to the discipline of national parties, the President, as head of one party, controls that party in the Congress.

Alternative 2: to give effect to the discipline of congressional parties, party leaders in the Congress control their respective parties.

Alternative 3: to give effect to ad hoc or nonpartisan and bipartisan majorities in Congress that join together in support of individual bills or classes of bills.[1]

Under the impact of Jeffersonian thought, which was antithetical to giving any members more authority and greater privileges than others, the House postponed as long as it could creating permanent leadership and control groups to manage the House's business. Instead the House adopted stopgap and piecemeal measures, among them, reliance on committees to do the work of the House, even though this too was antithetical to Jeffersonian principles.

In fact, reliance on committees had increased so much that by 1885, by the time Woodrow Wilson wrote *Congressional Government*, responsibility for managing the business of the House was dispersed among the committee chairmen. Wilson called it committee government, and he deplored this diffusion of power. Contending that the legislative process should be "a straightforward thing of simple method, single unstinted power, and clear responsibility," he proposed to strengthen the Executive and give it more positive leadership in the legislative process. Something like the British system of cabinet government should be introduced into the United States, he said. Wilson proposed Alternative 1.[2]

Reforms of 1890

Soon after this, the House finally took action, enacting the reforms of 1890. But it preferred a different remedy. If the House needed a master, it would try to find him among its own members. The House preferred and adopted Alternative 2. It gave the power to its Speaker, so much power that he came to be known as Czar Reed, and after him Boss Cannon.

What were the sources of the Speaker's power under the reforms of 1890? First, the right of recognition on the floor. A resolute determination to use this power to favor those who supported his leadership and to discriminate against those who opposed it, especially those members of his own party who in his judgment should support him, though they might not wish to do so, enabled the Speaker to control the course of business.

A second source of the Speaker's power was the right to interpret the rules. Third, the Speaker became chairman of the Rules Committee. Finally, he had the right to appoint the members of all the standing committees at the beginning of each Congress; and he was not inhibited by any ironbound rule of seniority.

All the Speaker needed for control of the whole House and of its committees was support by a majority of his own party. This he was able to get by appealing to a belief in party discipline, then shared by a majority of members of both parties, supplemented, as needed, by selective use of the formal powers themselves. Thus, when George W. Norris (R. NE) began to oppose the Speaker of his own party, Cannon denied him the committee assignments and a committee chairmanship that Norris wanted and thought he was entitled to.

A major consequence of this radical solution of the problem of legislative management was that the Speaker became almost as powerful as the President in the legislative process. This realization of Alternative 2 was, in other words, a serious challenge to presidential leadership. Yet the Speaker represented only a majority of the majority party in the House.

Furthermore, this realization of Alternative 2 meant a complete frustration of Alternative 3. The various possible majorities of the House, which might have been found for particular measures, were without leadership. It was not only the minority party, but the potential majorities composed of members of both parties that were constantly frustrated under the system of party government instituted in the House in 1890.

As a consequence of this, in part, there was a revolt in the House in 1910 —a revolt against the Republican Speaker by the insurgent Republicans who were, in turn, supported by the Democrats. The direct primary system, introduced in many states in the early years of the century, had rendered ordinary members more independent of the regular party organizations than they had been previously. It had made it safer for discontented members of the majority party to repudiate the House leadership. This accounts for the insurgents.

Reforms of 1910

The objective of the reformers of 1910 was to make way for ad hoc majorities. To this end they adopted the following measures. First, the powers of the Speaker were curtailed. He lost authority to appoint members of standing committees. He lost chairmanship of the Rules Committee. He lost absolute discretion to recognize members on the floor, by virtue of certain automatic procedures and calendars that were instituted. The Speaker remained the foremost leader of his party in the House, but he could act effectively only in cooperation with others—with the majority floor leader, the chairmen of important committees, and the chairman of the Rules Committee.

Second, individual members were freed from undue dependence on the favor of the Speaker for the consideration of private and local bills. Such dependence had been the case because members had to be recognized by the Speaker in order to gain the floor to bring up bills. The reform was effected by two new automatic calendars—the private bill calendar and the consent calendar. Bills reported by committees could be placed on these calendars without the Speaker's intervention, and certain days of each month were reserved for their consideration, the bills to be taken up in the order in which they had been placed on the calendars.

Third, the rules were changed for the purpose of enabling any majority of the House, whatever its partisan composition, to consider and adopt a measure on which that particular majority was agreed. The specific reforms for this purpose were calendar Wednesday, to enable a majority to take up and pass bills that had been reported by legislative committees, and the discharge petition, to enable a majority to discharge a committee. These specific reforms were not successful for they were used infrequently. But the dictatorship of the Speaker was broken.

Development of Leadership in the House Since 1910

Since 1910 the House has been organized according to Alternative 3, but it has required the active participation of congressional party leaders, frequently in association with the Executive, to put together the ad hoc majorities to pass bills. Normally, these have been leaders of the majority party; in exceptional cases they have been minority party leaders, when the minority party controlled the presidency. Action in the House has been partisan action, in the sense that it has not ordinarily been accomplished except under the direction, or at least with the consent, of the majority party leaders. But it has not been partisan in the sense that it is accomplished by the united efforts of the majority party against the united opposition of the minority party. The leadership has been partisan, while the actual majorities have been unstable combinations of national and local interests, frequently with a casual regard for party. Thus party government, as developed in the House of Representatives, has meant a legislative process in which action depends upon the practical capacity of the majority party leaders to find majorities for their measures wherever they might exist, regardless of party.

A brief examination of partisanship in voting on the House floor and of the formation of ad hoc majorities will support this analysis. In years of presidential elections one might expect to find a high degree of partisanship. Yet in 1972 a majority of the Democrats joined a majority of the Republicans on 73 percent of the rollcalls; in 1976, on 64 percent; in 1980, on 62 percent. Or to turn the data around, partisan votes in which the majority of one party opposed the majority of the other occurred on only 27 percent of the rollcalls in 1972; 36 percent in 1976; and 38 percent in 1980. Add to these cases rollcalls on which the majority in the House consisted of a majority of one party and a minority of the other, and one has almost all recorded votes. The only roll-call votes for which party leaders can normally count on the support of all members of their party are those relating to organizing the House at the beginning of each congress—for example, selection of the Speaker and of committee chairmen, fixing the ratios of party members on committees. When the leaders have tried to expand this expectation of unanimous party support from questions of organization to votes on House procedures, they have been rebuffed (see chapter 6).

In discussing committees as cue-givers to Congress, we said that a Republican is likely to look to a senior Republican on a committee for his advice, and a Democrat, to a senior member of his party; but this influence of party is different from control by party leaders. Indeed, partisanship on the floor is determined, to a greater extent than some have believed, by the way committees do their work, and different committees work in different ways. If a committee is bipartisan, so in all likelihood will be the whole House, because noncommittee Democrats and noncommittee Republicans will get the same cues.

In recent years there has been a remarkable increase in the number and influence in the House of informal caucuses of members, most of which are bipartisan. Prior to 1970 there were only three of these, two of which were partisan—the Democratic Study Group and the Republican Wednesday Group. Of twenty-two additional caucuses organized formally since then, most of them with staffs and offices in Capitol buildings, only three are partisan. The remaining nineteen have a bipartisan orientation which underscores regional, economic, or social considerations—New England Congressional Caucus, Congressional Steel Caucus, Congressional Black Caucus. To the extent that these caucuses have become cue-givers, too, they are likely to promote ad hoc rather than party partisan majorities.

The point here is not that party has been unimportant in influencing members' votes. Party affiliation is indeed important. The point is rather that for a great number of important issues, the majorities of both parties have agreed; that on no important issue could one party expect to pass a bill without some support from the other; and finally that the majorities that form to pass bills differ for each issue, they are ad hoc majorities.

Responsibility for mustering the ad hoc majorities for major bills rests primarily on the Speaker and majority leader. They work with the chairmen of the committees reporting the bills, with the ranking minority members if they support the legislation, and with legislative liaison officers in the White House and Executive departments if the bills are part of the President's program.

When a committee votes to approve a major bill, the chairman will normally report this to the majority leader and Speaker who will ask him if the bill is likely to command a majority of votes on the floor. The committee chairman frequently will not know with any certainty, and the Speaker and majority leader, if they choose to do so, will agree to find out and to help build a winning ad hoc coalition. For this purpose the House leaders are assisted by party whips, who serve both as an intelligence network, counting noses, and as vote-seekers. The leadership's decision on scheduling a bill for debate is based largely on intelligence gathered in whip polls. In recent years Speaker Thomas P. O'Neill, Jr., has introduced the additional practice of appointing ad hoc task forces, charged with passage of specific bills. These groups, which include many junior members, are designed to help build winning coalitions as well as to satisfy junior members' desires to participate in party leadership.

If the bills are in the President's program, the legislative liaison officers of the White House and of the Executive departments will aid in mustering votes. They search for support in both parties, for ad hoc majorities, and they consider party discipline to be none of their business. Bryce N. Harlow, who was White House liaison officer for President Dwight D. Eisenhower and briefly for President Richard M. Nixon, has said that the techniques for legislative liaison are not much different when the majority party in Congress is not the President's party than when the two are the same.

Given the need to rely on the majority party leader and the Speaker, is this a return to Czar Reed or Boss Cannon? No. Whereas, with his formidable formal powers, the Speaker of 1909 needed only the support of a majority of the majority party to be czar, the new leader has to put together a bipartisan ad hoc majority on each issue or set of issues. He is a broker, not a dictator.

There are many misconceptions about legislative liaison. The job of White House and departmental liaison officers is to create a receptive environment for the President's program in the Congress and to bring the nuances of congressional reactions back to the Executive. They sense when the mood of Congress requires compromise, and they learn with whom agreements can be reached. Liaison involves very little coercion, not even very much arm-twisting, and considerably less offering of special privileges than frequently is reported. Instead the liaison officers try to convince members that it is good for them to support the President, and they provide certain services to any member who wants to use them, principally up-to-date information on activities of the government that affect the members' constituencies.

As for special privileges, the authors of many introductory textbooks in American government tell their students how the President wins support for his program by buying congressmen's votes with projects and jobs. One text is entitled *Who Gets the Cookies?* Another text asserts that pork is "the daily bread of most congressmen . . . juicy tidbits are gratefully received in dozens of congressional districts." Even the respected political scientist, Clinton Rossiter, has said: "It troubles many good people, not entirely without reason, to watch the President dabbling in politics, distributing loaves and fishes. . . . Yet, if he is to persuade Congress, he must put his hand firmly to the plow of politics." Yet all of these rich metaphors are spoken in the face of abundant testimony to the contrary by successive White House liaison

officers who have served under presidents from Eisenhower to Reagan.[3]
Two examples from the Reagan Administration illustrate the point:

Example. Between May and July 1981 President Ronald Reagan won two
stunning victories in the House on his economic program. In one, relating to the
Budget, he had the support of sixty-three Democrats on one crucial vote and twenty-
nine on another, although Speaker Thomas P. O'Neill, Jr., and the Democratic leadership made extraordinary efforts to keep all Democrats in line. In the critical vote
relating to taxes, the President had the support of forty-eight Democrats. In reporting
these events, the major media gave great attention to bargains and deals that the
President and his assistants had made to keep individual Republicans in line and to
win over Democrats.

The *Washington Post*, in an article appearing on June 27, 1981, in major papers
all over the nation through the *Post*'s syndicated news service, said: "In a flurry of
last-minute arm-twisting, President Ronald Reagan and his White House lieutenants
cut deals right and left to win House approval of their Budget alternative, in some cases
reversing their crusade to cut spending. The high-level horse-trading for Democratic
votes included concessions by Reagan on sugar price-support legislation, federal aid for
Conrail, medical aid for the poor, student loans and the Clinch River fast-breeder
reactor in Tennessee, among other items. The Administration was putting a different
spin to it yesterday—Office of Management and Budget Director David A. Stockman
said there were no deals, only 'accommodations'—but the outcome was the same.
Reagan's stunning victory was clinched by White House largesse." *Congressional
Quarterly Weekly Report* carried bylines reading "Wheeling, Dealing, and Accommodation" (July 4, 1981) and "Dispensing Favors" (August 1, 1981), although its full
reports were more balanced than the eye-catchers.

For some of these so-called deals, the issues had not previously been presented to
the President for his decision; the White House and Executive departments were still
working on them. Had they been presented, the President might well have made the
same decision as when he was confronted with the issues by congressmen. The Administration agreed to reexamine other issues and reach decisions before details of the
programs would have to be written into authorization and appropriation bills, but it
did not necessarily make commitments on what the decisions would be. For some
programs previously scheduled for termination, the Administration agreed to short-
term funding while it reexamined the issues, again making no commitments on final
decisions. And on some issues the President and his aides did accommodate the
congressmen, especially to win over at the last minute undecided votes.

This helps to set the record straight, but it still misses the big story. The firm
foundation for the President's victories was not so-called deals but the remarkable
popularity of the man and his ideas among voters and legislators. Members heard from
their constituents. The Capitol switchboards were jammed with calls supporting the
President. The President's principal arguments in his phone calls to members were that
the election had given him a mandate for the general substance of his program and
that he believed there was popular support for it in the members' districts—shared fate.

The following dialogue between Sam Donaldson, television reporter for ABC news,
and Edwin Meese III, the President's counsellor, on the evening of Reagan's budget
victory illustrates the point:

DONALDSON: "Mr. Meese, the President had to lobby hard personally. What did he promise some of these Democrats who voted with him?"

MEESE: "He promised that they would be recognized as doing the will of the American people."

DONALDSON: "Well now, that sounds like a Boy Scout, if you'll forgive me. And I was one myself once, believe it or not."

MEESE: "Seriously, that's what the President did talk to them about. He said the people realize that in order for the economy to be restored to the position it used to be, we need to have cuts in the increase in federal spending as well as tax cuts, which of course occurred in the House. And that's really the basis on which he discussed these matters with the congressmen and I think why they responded."

Example. On October 28, 1981, President Ronald Reagan won another stunning victory in the Senate, when it failed to veto the President's plan to sell AWACS airplanes to Saudi Arabia, by a vote of 52 (41R., 11D.) to 48 (12R., 36D.). Before the vote it was widely predicted that the President's plan would fail. When the White House pulled it out, the mass media were again filled with stories of arm-twisting, wheeling, and dealing. There was arm-twisting of a sort, to be sure, much of it by the President, but it related to the substance of the issue. It was when the President himself took over the lobbying that the Administration began to close the gap. Tom Pettit and John Chancellor of NBC's "Nightly News" got it right this time, immediately after the vote:

PETTIT: "The big victory [was] preceded by a crucial presidential letter, a letter dated today, for a reluctant Gordon of Washington, Quayle of Indiana, and others. The letter was conclusive. It promised extensive U.S. involvement in security of the planes, and it addressed the Israeli lobby objections directly. We will continue to make available to Israel the military equipment it requires to defend its land, and people, with due consideration to the presence of AWACS in Saudi Arabia. That assurance persuaded Cohen of Maine to shift, though he said Saudi Arabia is about as immoderate as Yasir Arafat. Cohen had been reassured that the President could always cancel before the planes arrive in '85.

CHANCELLOR: "Earlier this year the President was credited with performing miracles in getting the Congress to approve his economic program. Now he's done it again on a significant issue involving foreign affairs."

I asked a colleague and former president of the American Political Science Association why so much of the media missed the big story and instead played up wheeling and dealing in the face of this evidence. His response was: "That's what these reporters were taught when they took college political science in the 1950s."

I should not be misunderstood to claim that the Executive never offers appointments or projects to influence congressmen's votes, but rather that this is not a primary tool of legislative liaison. It is not the way in which majorities are put together for the President's program, and it is done very much less frequently than is suggested in most textbooks and mass media reports on

Congress, which give the impression that wheeling and dealing are an important, even the dominant, characteristic of executive–legislative relations.

APSA Proposals of 1950

We have been discussing legislative liaison in the context of leadership in the House as it has developed since 1910 under the impetus of the reforms of that year. In the late 1940s there was a great deal of criticism of Congress resulting from the bitter conflict between Democratic President Harry S Truman and the Republican Eightieth Congress. In response, the American Political Science Association appointed a blue-ribbon Committee on Political Parties. The committee's report was critical of congressional organization.[4] It was, they said, disintegrated; and this disintegrated organization made it difficult for the President to be an effective leader. The political scientists' focus was on the President, on Truman's problems with the Eightieth Congress. More responsible party organization in the Congress was to be the answer, to be accomplished by tightening up the internal organization of each party, merging its various leadership committees and groups into single and powerful party policy committees. The party policy committees were to plan and control the legislative agenda; to make committee assignments; to select committee chairmen; to issue leadership directives. The parties were to hold frequent party caucuses under the leadership and control of the party policy committees. The caucuses were to adopt party standing orders. These orders and the policy committee leadership directives were to be enforced by party discipline, which was to be effected by a combination of sticks and carrots: the skillful use of patronage; promotions for the faithful and committee demotions for the disloyal; and the expulsion of serious offenders from the congressional parties.

When the committee's report was published, a good number of political scientists opposed it.[5] The proposals, they said, assumed a degree of party homogeneity that did not exist in Congress, and without this, party discipline might be impossible to achieve, or possible only at great costs, one of which might be a breakup of the two-party system. That is, under strict party discipline, southern and northeastern Democrats, and eastern and midwestern Republicans, might not be able to hold together in a single party.

Furthermore, attempts to impose party discipline might promote special interests rather than the public interest. The necessary discipline might be won by party leaders' making bargains with special interests in exchange for support, as, for example, party discipline had been purchased in the past in Great Britain. Such a method of coalition building would be much less likely to approximate the public interest than the method used in Congress of bipartisan and ad hoc majorities for individual programs. Also, the imposition of party discipline might stamp out statesmanship among individual members, and Congress relies on this heavily for its leadership reserve. Could Senator J. William Fulbright (D. AR) have become national leader of antiwar sentiment in the late 1960s if he had been subject to discipline of his party in the Senate?

The principal objective of the reformers was to increase the powers of the President—to make presidential leadership more effective than it was with a fragmented Congress. Indeed, their report, although it ostensibly supported Alternative 2, was more consistent with Alternative 1 for organizing the whole House. But it is not at all clear that their reforms would have achieved this. Disciplined parties in the House could be anti-presidential, as well as pro-administration. It is not clear that tightly disciplined congressional parties are compatible with a strong presidency. In any case, the scholars' reforms were not acceptable to the Congress.

Reforms of 1970s

Congress itself fashioned and adopted a large body of reforms in its organization and procedures in the early 1970s, which are the most important reforms since 1910.[6] They were the culmination of a momentum for reform that had built up in the late 1960s. The reforms in the House were contained in four measures: (1) Legislative Reorganization Act 1970, which was the result of the work of the Joint Committee on the Organization of Congress—the Monroney-Madden committee; (2) House Committee Reform Amendments 1974, which were the result of the work of the House Select Committee on Committees—the Bolling committee; (3) Budget Control Act 1974; (4) House Democratic Caucus reform of rules and procedures for the Ninety-fourth Congress, approved in 1974. Since 1975 the House has received reform proposals from two additional select committees, the Commission on Administrative Review, chaired by David R. Obey (D. WI), reporting in December 1977; and a second Select Committee on Committees, chaired by Jerry M. Patterson (D. CA) and reporting in April 1980. Although I shall refer to these latter reports occasionally, the House did not adopt major reforms in response to them.

OBJECTIVES

The reformers had multiple objectives. One was to enable Congress to develop and pass alternatives to the President's programs—that is, alternative legislative programs and alternative expenditure programs or budgets. This was to be accomplished under the direction and leadership of the majority party in Congress. As such, this objective was consistent with Alternative 2 for organizing the House, and it represented a dramatic reversal in Congress's thinking about its role in executive–legislative relations.

The Executive had for a long time, probably from the beginning, dominated the legislative process; the President set the legislative agenda. Congressmen assented to this by their actions—that is, they reviewed, modified, and adopted or rejected the President's proposals—but they failed to admit it in theorizing about themselves. Members kept talking about "regaining" their traditional and rightful powers as a legislature to initiate legislation. By 1970, however, most members had begun to talk like they had been acting. When one reads the testimony of members in the *Congressional Record,* and before the Monroney-Madden committee, and even before the Bolling committee, one finds few claims that Congress should be the great initiator of the nation's legislative programs.

By 1974, however, many members had reverted to earlier talk about Congress's role as initiator of legislation. This was due to a combination of motivations and frustrations. There was a Democratic Congress and a Republican President. But this was also true in six of the eight years of Eisenhower's presidency. The difference was that Nixon was an activist; he had proposed programs that challenged those of the Great Society—for example, the new federalism and block grants. Also, there was a general reaction in Congress against the growth of executive power, manifested in the Vietnam War and such issues as executive privilege and the President's impounding of appropriated funds. And finally there was Watergate.

To be sure, some members were skeptical of this objective. Barber B. Conable, Jr. (R. NY), testified:

Now, the issue of competing with the Executive I think is a false issue. We are not a collective presidency and we are never going to be and it does not serve the Congress well to assume functions for which we are ill-equipped.

I think the whole issue of competing with the Executive is one that needs rethinking. We are not going to achieve the same degree of expertise, or the same degree of oversight that the executive branch is going to have. It would be far preferable for us to be effective legislators than to try to constitute of ourselves a collective presidency.

55

Yet I find lots of people who think that somehow, if we are not able to compete with the President in direct and absolutely identical ways, that the Congress is somehow subservient. I think that is a misunderstanding of our function.[7]

Nonetheless, one objective of the congressional reformers was to enable Congress to develop and pass alternatives to the President's programs.

A second and closely related objective was to enable Congress to monitor the Executive, to make sure that the President and the bureaus did not exceed the powers and authority that were rightfully theirs, and that they would carry out the alternatives that Congress enacted and correct any deficiencies in them—in other words, systematic oversight by Congress of Executive implementation. The Democrats in the House, especially the liberal Democrats, realized that President Nixon, in his efforts to dismantle some Great Society programs, had a telling argument about the programs' failures. They concluded that Congress needed a greater capacity to identify problems that developed in the implementation of programs and to correct them, or require the Executive to correct them, so that the programs might succeed.

There were two other objectives of the reformers, and, as we shall see, these were not necessarily consistent with the first two. A third objective was to increase the power and the influence of individual members, especially the junior ones. This objective was enhanced by the attention given in the media and in Congress to the seventy-four freshmen elected to the Ninety-fourth Congress in 1975 in the wake of Watergate. It was enhanced also by the favorable public image of the House Judiciary Committee, sitting on the impeachment of President Nixon, where every member had his equal say, the most junior as well as the most senior: Wayne Owens (D. UT) as well as Robert McClory (R. IL).

The fourth objective was to let the sun shine on all of Congress's work; to increase opportunities for public accountability by requiring that Congress operate in the open, with no secrecy allowed in legislative procedures. This was a strongly held objective with a broad spectrum of members of both parties.

MEASURES

To achieve the first two objectives, development of alternative programs and systematic oversight of implementation, the following reforms were enacted. First, the capacity, authority, and power of committees were strengthened. Committee staffs were increased in size and pay. General support organizations for all committees, such as the Congressional Research Service, General Accounting Office, Congressional Budget Office, Office of Technology Assessment, were strengthened. Committee jurisdictions were realigned. To concentrate the attention of members on committee work, their committee assignments were to be limited. Basically, each member was to serve on no more than a single major committee, although this rule, adopted by the Democratic caucus rather than by the whole House, has been disregarded on numerous occasions. New rules required committees to conduct oversight of agencies within their jurisdiction. Committees were given the option of establishing oversight subcommittees or directing their regular legislative subcommittees to do the job. All committees were given power to issue subpoenas. (For further analysis of reforms relating to committees, subcommittees, and committee staffs, see chapter 6.)

Second, legislative procedures were devised to control the President's impoundment of appropriated funds and to control backdoor spending by placing it under limitations similar to those that apply to appropriated funds.

Third, since the objective was to substitute congressional leadership for executive leadership, a congressional leadership organization was needed. The overall instrument was to be the majority party in Congress. But who in the majority party? The leaders among congressmen who supported the objective of substituting congressional for executive leadership—including Richard Bolling, John C. Culver (D. IA), Paul S. Sarbanes (D. MD)—wanted to strengthen the Speaker as leader of the majority party in Congress, and for this purpose to provide him with an organization and staff. The Democratic reformers created, therefore, a new Democratic Steering and Policy Committee in 1973, with the Speaker as chairman. It was strengthened in 1974 and again in 1981. The Committee has twenty-nine members: the Speaker, majority leader, caucus chairman, and caucus secretary, all elected by the caucus; nine members appointed by the Speaker, including the whip and deputy whips; twelve members elected by Democratic congressmen from their regions, each region including approximately an equal number of Democratic members; and the chairmen of four major committees—Appropriations, Ways and Means, Rules, and Budget. The Speaker controls the Steering and Policy Committee: he is its chairman; he appoints nine members and can influence the selection of many more; he controls the staff.

The Steering and Policy Committee was designed to perform several specific functions. It was to develop the policy alternatives, which were then to be presented to the Democratic caucus for approval by that body. Also, it was to make Democratic committee assignments and to select Democratic committee chairmen, subject to confirmation by the caucus. These powers were taken from the Democratic members of the Ways and Means Committee and given to the Steering and Policy Committee which the Speaker controls.

In addition to creating the Democratic Steering and Policy Committee, the reformers increased the Speaker's powers by giving him more latitude in referring bills to committees. Under the new rules he could refer a bill simultaneously to more than one committee or sequentially to more than one. Also, the Speaker's formal power over the Rules Committee was increased. He personally, not the Democratic Steering and Policy Committee, could nominate all Democratic members of Rules, subject, again, to caucus approval.

To achieve the third objective—to increase power and influence of individual members, especially junior ones—the following reforms were approved. First, subcommittees, in which junior members would have greater influence and control, were strengthened. Each committee was required to have at least four subcommittees. Previously the important Ways and Means Committee, for example, had no subcommittees; it did all of its work in full committee. The number and jurisdiction of subcommittees was now to be determined by a majority of all members of the full committee, not by committee leaders, as had been the case in some committees. As for membership on subcommittees, the Democrats provided that senior committee members be limited to two subcommittees. All remaining vacancies were to be distributed among junior members. No member was to serve as chairman of more than one legislative subcommittee, thereby dividing up leadership positions among as many members as possible. Subcommittees were given staffs of their own. Previously staffs were often assigned to the full committee and then lent to subcommittees as they needed assistance. All subcommittees were, like the full committees, given power to issue subpoenas.

Reforms to strengthen committees were adopted in support of the first and second objectives—to enable Congress to develop and pass, and oversee the implementation of, alternatives to the President's program. The strengthening of subcommittees, adopted in support of the third objective, weakens the full committees, however. Different objectives can lead to different institutional reforms that are in conflict.

In addition to strengthening subcommittees, those Democrats who sought by reform to increase the power and influence of individual members acted to strengthen the Democratic caucus. Some members who voted to strengthen the caucus did so because they believed that a strong caucus, as well as a more effective Speaker, were needed if the majority party was to pass legislative and budget programs that were alternatives to the President's. But many members who voted to strengthen the caucus did so because this was a means for giving more power and influence to individual members, since all Democratic members have an equal vote in the caucus.

The caucus was provided with a staff of its own, and an aggressive chairman was elected. According to the reform plan, the caucus was to be called frequently by the leaders to vote on legislative policy, as well as party rules and procedures. Also, any fifty Democratic members could by petition call the caucus into session, whether or not the leaders wanted it. Votes in the caucus were presumed to bind members unless they had made contrary campaign promises, or questioned the constitutionality of a caucus action, or opposed it as a matter of conscience. But there were to be no disciplinary actions taken against members who refused to follow the caucus's votes.

The caucus was given power to vote separately and secretly on the appointment of each committee chairman, rather than vote on all chairmen en bloc, as had been the case in the past. Since nominations for these positions are made by the Democratic Steering and Policy Committee, which is controlled by the Speaker, increasing the power of the caucus to vote against the nominations amounts to increasing the power of the caucus to override the Speaker.

At the same time that the Speaker's control over the Rules Committee was enhanced by allowing him to name its Democratic members, the power of the caucus over that committee was increased by providing that a majority of the caucus could vote to "direct" the Democratic members of Rules to vote for an open rule, under which amendments may be offered to a bill, rather than a closed rule.

Thus both Speaker and caucus were strengthened, and, not surprisingly, conflicts have developed between them.

To achieve the fourth objective—to let the sun shine—it was provided that all House committee meetings were to be open to the public unless the majority of a committee voted to close a meeting. This would apply to meetings at which committees mark up bills as well as to those in which they hear witnesses. Conference committee meetings between the House and Senate were also to be open unless the whole House voted to close a particular meeting. House committee meetings and floor debate could be televised. Prior to 1970 the names of members were not recorded in teller votes, only the numbers of yeas and nays. Since then any twenty members can require that names be recorded on such votes in the Committee of the Whole House. Also, roll-call votes in committees are now recorded and made available to the public.

EVALUATION

Have the reforms of the 1970s succeeded in terms of their objectives? The House has not been successful in drafting and enacting alternative legislative programs to the President's. (The effort to develop alternative budget programs is evaluated in chapter 9.) The failure by the Democrats in 1975 to draft and enact an alternative to President Gerald R. Ford's energy program was mentioned in chapter 1. The same was true for congressional alternatives to President Richard M. Nixon's economic programs in 1974 and President Ford's in 1975. There are several reasons for this. First there are the difficulties associated with congressional initiation of complex policies that involve the jurisdiction of more than one committee.

Second, the House, and particularly the Democrats in the House, created institutions and procedures that were in part contradictory. Certainly not all of the reforms could succeed. Has the Speaker, supported by the Democratic Steering and Policy Committee, or the Democratic caucus led the majority in the House? To this day the answer is not entirely clear. There have been conflicts between these leadership groups on both policy and committee appointments.

Example for policy. In 1974 the House Democratic caucus recommended an eight-point economic program as an alternative to President Nixon's economic program and urged the legislative committees to enact it. However, the Democratic Steering and Policy Committee had on the previous day rejected four of the eight points. In the end very little of the program was approved.

Example for committee appointments. In 1975 the Democratic Steering and Policy Committee recommended to the Democratic caucus that all chairmen be re-appointed with two exceptions: Wayne L. Hays (D. OH) was to be replaced as chairman of the Committee on House Administration by Frank Thompson, Jr. (D. NJ); and Wright Patman (D. TX) was to be replaced as chairman of the Committee on Banking and Urban Affairs by Henry S. Reuss (D. WI). The caucus then proceeded to reject four of the Steering Committee's nominations: Thompson, Reuss, W. J. Poage (D. TX) as chairman of Agriculture, and F. Edward Hebert (D. LA) as chairman of Armed Services. The Steering Committee then had to make new recommendations for these committees. They proposed Hays for House Administration, Patman for Banking and Urban Affairs, Thomas S. Foley (D. WA) instead of Poage as chairman of Agriculture, and C. Melvin Price (D. IL) instead of Hebert for Armed Services. This time the caucus rejected Patman and finally agreed to Reuss, whom they had previously rejected.

Several keen observers of the House have concluded that the modern caucus is a product of tensions rather than unities within the majority party. "It provides an arena for conflict and not an instrument for integration, thus threatening leadership power more than reinforcing it. In truth, the caucus has a life and a politics of its own and the hold of the leadership over it is often quite tenuous."[8] A task force of the Patterson committee, composed of three Democrats and one Republican, which was assigned to review congressional changes in the 1970s, concluded that "the Democratic caucus reforms of the past decade have yet to prove themselves as something more than the instruments of factional advance by the liberal block," which have reduced the influence of congressional leadership.

Third, some of the reforms were a reaction to a then current situation, where a heavily Democratic Congress faced an activist and increasingly unpopular Republican President. What would happen when the Democrats controlled the presidency and the House, as they came to do in 1977–1981? In this situation, could an alternative legislative program to that of the Democratic President be developed and enacted by a partisan Democratic majority in the House? No. In the early 1970s, when Nixon was President, there were a number of Democratic caucus votes dealing with legislative policy, but during Jimmy Carter's presidency, only one.

Example. In 1978, an election year, many Democrats wanted the House to approve a bill that would roll back prospective increases in Social Security taxes. The Democratic caucus by a vote of 150 to 57 urged the Democrats on Ways and Means to report the bill. However, President Carter opposed this proposal, and he was supported by the Speaker as well as by the majority of the Ways and Means Committee. Ways and Means rejected the bill; it didn't reach the floor.

Fourth, some of the reforms envisioned a degree of party homogeneity that had existed in the House only on rare occasions since the early century. Discussing his party in 1980, Speaker Thomas P. O'Neill, Jr., said:

"We're five parties in one. We've got about 25 really strong liberals. A hundred and ten progressive liberals, maybe 60 moderates, about 45 people just to the right of the moderates, and 35 conservatives. We have 10 fellows who haven't voted with us 10 percent of the time. We have 13 who haven't voted with us 20 percent of the time."[9]

Furthermore, the reforms sought to strengthen party in Congress at the same time that the influence of party on voters' decisions was declining in the nation.

Finally, and most fundamentally, Congress continues to operate to this day under Alternative 3, ad hoc majorities. The extraordinary Democratic majority of the Ninety-fourth Congress—seventy-four Democratic freshmen—led the Democrats to adopt reforms consistent with Alternative 2. But no important bills would have passed even in that Congress without some support from Republicans. Ad hoc majorities were required in the legislative process. Thus even if one agrees with some of the 1970s reformers that Congress was so decentralized that it could not be an effective check against an overgrowth of presidential power, or with the 1950s reformers that congressional decentralization meant that the President could not be an effective leader, or with both groups, one needs to ask if there are techniques other than party to achieve an acceptable degree of coordination in the House and of congressional control over, or cooperation with, the President. Are there techniques that are within the compass of Alternative 3 and that will not break down when the presidency and Congress are controlled by the same party?

So much, then, for evaluation of measures designed to implement the objectives of drafting and enacting alternative legislative programs to the President's and improving congressional oversight of program administration.

The reforms enacted for the objective of increasing the power and influence of individual members, especially the junior ones, have been remarkably successful. The number of standing subcommittees in the House increased by 33 percent between 1971 and 1981. In the Ninety-fifth Congress (1977–1979) roughly 80 percent of all committee meetings were subcommittee meetings. By 1979 over 50 percent of Democratic members held chairmanships of standing committees and subcommittees. The relative influence of subcommittees on legislation has grown greatly. Action by full committees has more and more meant ratification of previous action taken by subcommittees. Subcommittee chairmen have gained influence on the House floor, as floor managers of certain bills heard by their subcommittees and as cue-givers to noncommittee members.

These recent developments have been characterized as the rise of "subcommittee government" and of a "juniority system" in the House. With perhaps some exaggeration, a 1981 analysis by *Congressional Quarterly* said: "This year's House and Senate newcomers are about to learn an exhilarating and troubling truth about life in a modern Congress: Power is theirs for the taking. If at the end of next year, no one has heard of them, it will be essentially their own doing."[10]

The larger number and greater autonomy of subcommittees has resulted in a greater decentralization of authority in the House and greater burdens on the House leadership in trying to make a whole out of the parts. As one senior congressman has said: "We are going the way of the Senate," which in the language of the House means going to the dogs. "We've spread the action by giving subcommittees more power and making it possible for members to play more active roles on them. But there's nothing at this point to coordinate what all these bodies are doing and to place some checks on their growing independence."[11] Based on a survey of members and other sources, the Patterson committee found that there was agreement among a large majority of members of both parties that the House committee system was "in disarray," and that the proliferation of subcommittees had weakened the capacity of the House for coherent and coordinated policymaking and administrative oversight. A reaction may have set in. The Patterson committee recommended that the number of subcommittees that could be established by standing committees (except Appropriations) be limited to six. In 1981 the Democratic caucus adopted a rule with a limit of eight, or the number then established, whichever was fewer.

Finally, opposition has developed in Congress in recent years to the reforms enacted to achieve the fourth objective—sunshine—especially to the rule that all committee meetings be open. A task force of four members of the Patterson committee has reported that this rule has unnecessarily slowed the legislative process; inhibited the range of discussion in committee meetings and the willingness of members to explore controversial issues; made it more difficult for members to change their positions; subjected members to undue pressure from lobbyists and representatives of special interest organizations; and inhibited the discussions and compromises which are an essential part of House-Senate conference committee meetings.

Ad Hoc Majorities and the Public Interest

Does the dominance of ad hoc majorities in the House contradict our basic discussion model and lend support instead to partisan mutual adjustment? At first it might appear so. The Speaker and majority leaders act as brokers in assembling ad hoc majorities for their bills. Yet this brokerage politics does not necessarily involve the trading and exchanging of private interests and those of narrow pressure groups, although some of this is involved. The previous discussion of the Executive's legislative liaison activities has its counterpart here. Much of the work of House and committee leaders involves educating noncommittee members about the reported bills that are to be debated and convincing them that the bills are good legislation—good for the country and for the congressmen's districts. Too frequently this basic fact gets lost in investigative reporting and analysis of House operations. I shall have more to say on this subject when discussing congressional voting in the next chapter.

4

What Do Congressmen Do?

IN the last chapter we examined how the whole Congress is organized to control its parts, that is, its special interests in the standing committees and in other groups. We shift now to the individual members of Congress: how they define their roles and whom they represent.

The Members and Their Job

Political scientists used to say that there were two types of congressmen: (1) those, the great majority, who take instructions from their constituents, who find out what their constituents want and give it to them in the constituents' terms; and (2) those members who serve their constituents in the manner in which they, the members, in their judgments believe to be the best. We called this latter group the congressional statesmen—the Burkeans.

Recent studies of the performance of congressmen show that these categories are deceptive. Even if members see it as their job to follow the instructions of their constituents, this is seldom what happens. They are of necessity more free agents than many had believed. Like it or not, they probably lead their constituencies as much as they follow them.[1] There are several reasons for this.

First, it is in fact impossible for members to ascertain their constituents' views on any large issue with sufficient precision to obtain for themselves a clear set of instructions. In terms of the issues with which congressmen are faced, there is nothing like a clear mandate from the people. This is due in part to the complexity of most congressional districts, to their multiinterest character. The district rarely broadcasts clear messages to the congressman. The members must choose which advice of their constituents they should follow. Communications from the districts are usually so muddled that congressmen can do anything they choose while still believing they follow the districts' wishes.

Furthermore, the key to members' behavior is not their constituencies as single entities defined by demographic characteristics, but rather their constituencies as they perceive them, which may be something very different. Richard F. Fenno's recent study, based on the activities of eighteen members in their home districts, concluded that these members perceived four concentric constituencies: geographic, reelection, the congressman's primary or principal strong supporters, and personal. Since members make their own estimates of the relative importance of each of the four constituencies, as they perceive them, they are likely to have great degrees of freedom in responding to their constituencies by their activities in Congress.

A second reason why members are more free agents than has generally been believed, and less simply servants of the interests of their constituencies, is that the members create many of the voices to which they then respond. If in 1980 voters had favored a new civil rights measure, they might well have written to Senator Jacob K. Javits (R. NY). If, on the other hand, they had opposed such legislation for fear that it would further weaken states' rights, they might have written to Senator Strom Thurmond (R. SC). When two members on opposite sides of an issue meet in the cloakroom before a vote and each says to the other that 80 percent of his mail supports the position that he plans to take, this is likely the case. People write more to senators and congressmen with whom they agree. Thus, members select the problems and pressures to which they respond, and consciously or unconsciously they determine what they hear and what they do.

At home in their constituencies, each member creates for himself a particular "home style" which involves a "presentation of self," as Fenno has called it.[2] Members are able to interpret their voting and activities in Washington in the context of their home styles, and this gives them an independence that has sometimes been overlooked. For some members, in Fenno's words, "the search for political support at home is not just a matter of winning reelection. It is also a matter of winning voting leeway [in Washington]." And even for members who may not consciously pursue this leeway, "when we combine presentational and explanatory activity at home, it appears that members of Congress are much less constrained by their supportive constituencies and have much more voting leeway on the House floor than they believe or will admit."

These findings with regard to members in Washington and at home call for a reinterpretation of the familiar pressure group theory. Interest groups and the general public exert pressure, to be sure, but members usually do not respond to these efforts as raw pressure. Furthermore, they generate many of the pressures they feel, although they may in the future find that they are constrained by such self-generated pressures. As Lewis Dexter has said, "The application of pressure is conspicuously less effective than might be assumed if one did not take an exceedingly close look at what actually happens."[3]

A third reason why members are so much free agents relates to their job, which is so multifaceted—the demands on congressmen are so great—that they are faced with the necessity of making choices on how to allocate their time. Congressmen must organize their offices, which, with the staff increases of recent years, are large member-centered enterprises. They must provide constituency service. They have committee work to do, and work on the floor. They must return to their districts periodically. All members do some of each of these categories of work, and each member decides how much of each he needs to do or wants personally to do and how much he can delegate to his legislative and administrative assistants. Some members spend a great deal of time in their offices greeting constituents. Others leave much of this to carefully chosen administrative assistants and receptionists, and instead devote a great deal of time to committee work.

In 1977 a select committee of the House, the Commission on Administrative Review, chaired by David R. Obey (D. WI), made a survey of House members to determine, among other things, their views of the proper functions of the House and of individual members. As it was sponsored by a House committee, one can assume that members responded to this survey more thoughtfully than they sometimes do to the surveys conducted by outsiders.

One question related to the role expectations of members. They were asked: What are the major kinds of functions that you feel you are expected to perform as an individual member? The question was asked of 146 congressmen, and they could answer with one (but not more than four) functions. There was a total of 278 responses, and these responses demonstrate unquestionably the multiple roles of congressmen. (see table 4.1)

As for committee work, studies have shown that one significant variable for classifying committees is the goals of the members—the goals that congressmen want to achieve through membership on a committee. In these terms, Fenno found three types among the six committees that he studied in the early 1970s. The primary goal of members of the Appropriations and Ways and Means committees was achieving influence in the House; they were insiders. The goal of members of the Interior and Post Office committees was to help constituents and thereby insure members' reelection. Members of the Education and Labor and the Foreign Affairs committees emphasized strong subject

TABLE 4.1.

Representatives' Perceptions of Roles They Are Expected to Perform

	Number of Responses
legislative role	87
constituency service	79
education/communication—educate and inform constituents and others	43
representative role—represent the district; be a spokesman for the district	26
political role—getting re-elected, campaigning, party work	11
other	32
	278

matter interests; they wanted to make good public policy. The point here is that congressmen join a committee of one type or the other principally because of their own preferences; or having joined one, they become socialized so that their preferences are similar to those of their fellow congressmen. And choice of committee is only one of several choices that representatives must make in deciding how to fulfill their roles as members of Congress. The recent proliferation of subcommittees, their greater independence, and the larger freedom of junior members to select the subcommittees on which they serve give additional support to this element of choice.

Finally, members cannot pay an equal amount of attention to all of the important issues that come before them, nor even all of those that are of direct concern to their districts. They must decide with which issues they want to identify themselves and to which issues they want to give only marginal attention.

Legislators and Constituency Service: Policies and Projects

With this understanding of the job of congressmen, we can examine the question of whether they are more concerned with national policy or with projects and services for their districts and constituents. An example illustrates the issue.

Example. In a seminar some years ago on congressional supervision of the Executive, I stated that Congress's principal concern in legislation for the Federal Aid to Airports Program was not with project grants to individual airports, but with standards and criteria for the program as a whole—for example, size of airports that should qualify for various categories of grants; types of buildings and structures—runways, control towers, reception halls—that should qualify for grants; state and local matching funds for each grant category. A mid-career student contradicted me. Congressmen were principally concerned, he said, with project grants for airports in their districts. He knew this, for he was the legislative liaison officer for the airport division of the Federal Aviation Administration. He received calls daily from members inquiring about projects in their districts and urging action on them. I requested him to look further into the matter by reading the full legislative histories of all of the short-term authorization and annual appropriation bills for the program for a period of eight years (1963–1970)—House and Senate hearings, reports, floor debates.

In thousands of pages of these documents, the student found only four incidental references to specific projects. I was right; he was wrong. What then were the frequent calls that he received from congressmen? After the authorizations had been enacted and after the lump-sum appropriations had been voted, members called, as servicemen for their constituents, to see if projects in their districts qualified under the legislation. It is these calls that he had believed to be the major legislative activity of Congress in this program. What he had failed to see, until he did his study, is that in legislation for airports, Congress's major concern was standards and criteria.

All members are constituency servicemen and all members are legislators, and although different members place greater or lesser emphasis on one role or the other, they all play both roles. As constituency servicemen, members are indeed interested in securing authorizations and appropriations for projects in their districts, and as legislators they have a broader interest in national program standards. The roles are different ones and they are played with different institutions and different resources. The legislative role is performed through committees and floor debate, and in the members' offices, with the assistance of legislative assistants. Constituency service is performed principally through members' offices, with the assistance of administrative assistants, sometimes called case workers, and of district offices. As one member has said: constituency service is performed by members "as individuals, not as the House."[4]

It is true, of course, that when members in their legislative capacity vote on a program, they will have in mind how the program affects their districts, and how alternative changes in the program's standards and criteria would affect the allocation of funds to their constituencies, but this is a different level of generality than the authorization of individual projects. (The use of constituency service to provide information to Congress on executive performance is discussed in chapter 13.)

Failure to understand this distinction between members as constituency servicemen and as legislators is probably a major reason for the misrepresentations of the textbooks from which several examples were quoted in the previous chapter.

If members were more project-oriented in their legislative roles, they would name individual projects in the authorizing statutes and allocate funds to them in the appropriations statutes. But they don't do this. For the vast federal programs in housing, education, health, welfare, environment, many of them involving the construction of projects—sewage plants, housing units, classrooms, laboratories, hospitals—the authorizing statutes contain standards and criteria for allocating funds, and the appropriations are large lump sums to be assigned by the Executive in accordance with the standards.

The question remains why? Why does Congress favor formula grants over project grants? First, formula grants are likely to be more equitable, and in their legislative roles members are preeminently concerned with equity, especially among congressional districts, and with making sure that the Executive does not have discretion to favor some districts and groups over others.

Example. During the 1960s the House and Senate Committees on Appropriations were concerned that the Soil Conservation Service and the Budget Bureau were favoring some regions over others in the allocation of funds for watershed projects. The chairman of the House Appropriations Subcommittee, Jamie L. Whitten (D. MS), said in the hearings that the committee did not want to designate individual projects, but that if the SCS and the Budget Bureau, in exercising their discretion, were not more equitable among regions, "we might be forced to deal with these projects on an individual basis so that all sections would be dealt with alike."

Second, formula grants, more than project grants, help to build majorities for programs in Congress. Congress is terrible, unbelievably bad, at logrolling and porkbarreling. It tends to generalize every program so that all states and all districts participate in some way, and for this reason it prefers fixed allocation formulas that are more general and widespread in their impact. All districts do not have the same problems, to be sure, but they all have the same number of citizens. Having approved such formulas in authorizing legislation, members, as constituency servicemen, press the administrators for allocations under the formulas; and in newsletters to their constituents they frequently will personalize the national policy in terms of projects for their districts.

In 1965 President Lyndon B. Johnson appointed a Task Force on Urban Problems to propose new programs to reverse the deterioration of neighborhoods in large cities. The task force proposed a program for sixteen demonstration cities, costing hundreds of millions of dollars. In the process of legislative approval first in the White House and then in Congress, the formula for selecting cities was modified to accommodate sixty to seventy cities, and the number grew in later years.

This tendency to universalize the particular does not necessarily result in good public policy.[5] It might have been better to limit the model cities program to sixteen demonstrations in large cities, as recommended by the President's task force, rather than to include more than sixty cities as was done in authorizing the program. But a word of caution is needed here.

Our definition of public interest, which was derived, you will recall, from the process of decision making in national government, emphasizes breadth of view. The process should result in a very broad view of the incidence, effects, and consequences of any governmental action. From this point of view one can raise a question of whether it is better policy to spend hundreds of millions of dollars on an experiment in sixteen cities, or to increase the amount somewhat and spend it in more than sixty cities. By diluting the funds, the experiment, as conceived, was never conducted, to be sure. But, as it was conceived, it was a mighty expensive experiment, whose benefits, if the experiment worked, would have been concentrated fairly narrowly. It is arguable that the public interest, defined in terms of breadth of view, was better served by the alternative program covering more cities.

A third reason for Congress's preference for programs over projects is related to the way the whole House is organized. If one wanted to insure that an Administration proposal to spend hundreds of millions of dollars on a few cities, or a proposal to appropriate even more than this for New York City alone, for example, would pass the Congress, then the Congress would have to be organized differently than it is, with much more party discipline—in accordance with Alternative 2 rather than Alternative 3.

These three factors—the meaning and role of equity in deliberations of Congress, how the concept of breadth of view is used, and the importance of ad hoc majorities in organizing the Congress—should be considered in evaluating Congress's poor adaptation to porkbarreling, its propensity to universalize the particular.

Reelection and Other Roles

I have discussed the roles of congressmen as constituency servicemen and as overseers of legislation and administration. What about their activities in seeking reelection? Some observers would have us believe that the electoral connection is the most important variable in understanding the organization and operations of Congress.

Obviously all members, except those who are retiring from Congress, seek reelection. But reelection is not likely to be a member's single objective. It is a goal to be achieved, or "satisficed"—a constraint that must be met if the member's career is to continue. Once it is achieved, however, the member can and does pursue other goals. Members have multiple objectives among which reelection is a necessary one; but there is considerable covariation among the several objectives. Legislative work, administrative oversight, constituency service all influence the electoral performance of incumbents, although political analysts dispute the relative importance of each. Morris P. Fiorina and others have found a strong relation between constituency service and reelection. Constituency-oriented activities, are, he says, "an uncontroversial means of securing a reliable base of local support. . . . Legislators have a substantial incentive traceable to the electoral system [to engage in such activities]." John R. Johannes and John McAdams, on the other hand, have found a weak relation between constituency service and votes for incumbents. They have estimated the comparative influence of three election strategies: constituency service; general "ideological positioning to represent the policy preferences of the district"; and legislative activism, defined in terms of floor speeches and bills introduced. Constituency service, as it turned out, had no statistically significant effect on reelection prospects, whereas ideological positioning had an effect large enough to substantially influence these prospects, and legislative activism had some pay-off in these terms.[6]

Based on case histories of the success or failure of incumbents in the 1980 congressional elections and on interviews with congressmen, rather than on statistical manipulation, *Congressional Quarterly* has concluded that district outreach, as they call it, is necessary but not enough to insure reelection. It may fail for any number of reasons, they have said, principally national trends, like the 1980 shift to the right which placed many members out of synch with their constituencies, and the caliber and campaigns of opponents. Also, voters in most districts have come to expect that their congressmen, whether re-elected or newly elected, will provide constituency service. Thus, constituency service is likely to have a significant influence on elections only where voters believe that an incumbent has failed to provide the service expected.[7] This evidence supports Johannes and McAdams, but we shall have to await the results of further studies, currently underway, before we can be more definite about the relation between the several facets of congressmen's work and their reelection. Johannes and McAdams, for example, do not address the possibility that congressmen may perceive that constituency service is more important than shown in their findings. Clearly, however, the electoral connection cannot be used exclusively nor even principally to explain the congressman's job, the operations of Congress, or the relations between Congress and the Executive.

Congressmen's Votes and Constituency Opinion

In recent years political scientists have invested a tremendous amount of time and effort in analyzing the relations between members' votes in Congress and the characteristics of their constituencies. The first studies correlated gross demographic characteristics with members' votes on the floor—for example, the relation of their votes to the number of Polish Americans in their districts, or the number of Jews, or the number of blacks, or the number of elderly. But these studies were crude and deficient in several respects. For one thing, gross characteristics of groups of individuals serve as an adequate indication of their attitudes only when the issues affect directly and clearly the members of the group. Later studies rejected demographic traits of voters and used instead opinion polls to determine directly constituents' attitudes. Correlations were made of the constituents' attitudes on the one hand and members' roll-call behavior on the other. But such correlations, too, were unreliable, and as a result efforts were made to refine them by introducing intervening variables from which causes of voting could be inferred. This was called causal analysis. Models were constructed to test several possible alternative paths for the connection between constituency opinions on the one hand and members' roll-call behavior on the other. The intervening variables included opinions held by the members themselves and their perceptions of constituency attitudes. First results indicated that the path varied with the issues. No single, generalized configuration of attitudes and perceptions linked representatives with their constituencies, but rather several distinct patterns developed, and which path was used depended very much on the issue involved.[8]

Alternative path analysis was more sophisticated than predecessor techniques, but it too had methodological problems, principally that causal orderings could not be inferred from path analysis and the ubiquity of multicollinearity, that is, the explanatory variables were highly intercorrelated so that it was difficult to estimate their individual effects on any variable of interest. Political scientists continue to search for a convincing model that explains the relation of constituents to the votes of their representatives. Such a model must give full credit to the several factors that make members more independent of their constituencies than are instructed delegates, with special reference to the fact that the districts' voters seldom transmit clear mandates to their representatives. A recent model that appears to do this is one based on cue-giving and cue-taking. When members vote on the floor, it asks from whom do they take cues or advice—from constituency, from party, from the Administration, from other members, and if other members, which ones? I have discussed previously two studies of this type. Both of them report that members take their cues more readily and more directly from other members than from constituents, party leaders, or the Executive. These recent studies, when compared to the earlier ones, are consistent with the theme that members' voting behavior derives from their multiple roles as congressmen and the freedom they have to choose among them.

A Theory of Representation

This analysis of the roles played by individual members leads us to a brief examination of the theory of legislative representation. The theory that is most familiar in America, which I shall call the traditional theory, holds that the proper system of representation is one that insures the choice of representatives who will reflect as completely as possible the variety of interests and opinions among the people. This theory, however, is unable to answer some of the difficult questions about representation, and on some questions it leads to answers that those who accept the theory are hesitant to embrace.

Take, for example, the grouping of voters into representative districts. The traditional theory leads to a preference for minority representation over single-member districts, such as those used for the election of members of the House. The single-member district falls short of the requirements of traditional theory since only a majority or a plurality is represented, leaving substantial minorities without a direct voice in government. Thus if a congressman is elected by 51 percent of the vote, presumably 49 percent remain unrepresented.

As a matter of fact, proportional representation (PR) with multimember districts would appear to be the only logical conclusion of the traditional theory of representation. Yet the proponents of traditional theory are usually hesitant to opt for PR as a reform in national politics, indicating that they have some reservations about their theory.

A second question that the traditional theory cannot answer very well relates to the nature of representatives' responsibilities to their constituents. Should they vote according to their judgment, or should they seek to obey the wishes of their constituents? The traditional theory, with its emphasis on mirrorlike representation, points to the latter. Yet members cannot avoid judgment. Recognizing this, should they take into consideration only or principally the interests of their constituencies as they perceive them to be, or the interests of the entire nation as they perceive those? The traditional theory points to the former, but it never comes to grips with this problem, nor perhaps can it, the way the theory is formulated.

73

An alternative theory is one that focuses on the functions of the electoral process in a democratic system, in relation to the functions of community discussion, and those of the legislative process and of the administrative process. Government is conducted in these several related stages of discussion, so that the electoral process is one of the parts of the system. It cannot be regarded by itself, in isolation, as is done in the traditional theory. The electoral process takes over from the community and its groups, performing a selective function; and it hands on to the President and Congress in the legislative process, performing an instructive function. It provides discussion and, at the moment of choice, selection of citizens as representatives.

Now, some of the problems that were difficult to resolve under the first approach to representation can be resolved under this one. As for proportional representation, it is aimed at perfection in recording the voice of the electorate, but it gives little or no attention to excellence in choosing units of government that are capable of conducting an effective legislative process and an effective administrative process. Under PR the constituency of each representative is so homogeneous that representatives have little room to focus on the broader public interest and to exercise the discretion that should be theirs if the legislative and administrative processes are to fulfill their responsibilities. Legislative bodies selected by PR usually don't work very well.

Turning to the nature of representatives' responsibilities to their constituents, in the discussion model the electorate will both guide the representatives and vest them with the exercise of their own deliberative discretion. If it did not guide, the representatives would not carry on a further stage in the governmental process of discussion, but an entirely new and disconnected stage. If the electoral system did not vest the representatives with deliberative discretion, they would not be able to carry discussion to a genuine further stage. Thus one can say that the electorate does not necessarily give detailed instructions or specific mandates. It elects a President and a Congress, but it neither participates directly in, nor dictates, legislation. The voters elect a President and a Congress for the purpose of doing something different from and beyond what they can do themselves.

This, I submit, is different from traditional theory. Whereas traditional theory has only one criterion for judging an electoral system, namely, how accurately its results mirror divisions in the electorate, the discussion model has two criteria: the system's representativeness in reflecting the body politic, and its responsiveness in creating institutions that can perform their roles. The discussion model treats the legislature not only as a representative body, but as a deliberative body as well. Furthermore, it is consistent with recent empirical studies of elections and of voting in Congress.

PART II

Relations Between the Whole House and Congressional Committees

5

External Controls over Bills

Reported by Committees

RELATIONS between congressional committees and the whole House are managed by two types of techniques. First are those used by the House to control legislative action on the bills, reports, and other measures that are produced by the committees' work. These external controls are the subject of this chapter. Second are techniques by which the whole House controls representativeness and democracy in the committees, so that the committees will act in accordance with the potential wishes of the House. Such internal controls are discussed in chapter 6. The two classes of techniques are related in ways that we can examine after we know more about the techniques themselves, but it is obvious that to the extent that Congress uses external controls with great effect there will be less need for use of internal controls, and vice-versa.

Scheduling Debate on Bills Reported by Committee

The whole House decides which of the bills that its committees have approved should be debated on the floor, and under what conditions. There are six alternative ways for bringing public bills reported by committees to the House floor for debate (and an additional procedure for private bills). These are: (1) a rule recommended by the House Rules Committee; (2) privilege to report at any time, which is given to certain committees for specific purposes, including the Appropriations Committee for all general appropriations bills, Budget Committee for budget resolutions, Ways and Means Committee for revenue bills; (3) suspension of the rules, a procedure that requires a two-thirds vote for legislation to pass; (4) calendar Wednesday, an infrequently used procedure in which committees are called in alphabetical order on Wednesdays to debate bills they have reported; (5) consent calendar, under which bills can be debated providing no more than two members object to doing so; and (6) unanimous consent.

The House considers on the average 800 to 900 public bills per session. Of these 100 to 150 are debated under rules, the remainder under the alternative procedures. Most bills dealing with major new programs and with periodic renewals of controversial programs are considered under rules, while those debated under the several other procedures are generally less important and less controversial. Nonetheless, important and controversial bills can and do come up under these other procedures. In the Ninety-sixth Congress, 1979–1981, approximately 350 bills were considered under suspension of the rules and 200 under unanimous consent or the consent calendar. A number of the suspension bills were important in terms of their subject matter and some of them were controversial, although only 4 percent failed to gain the two-thirds majority required for passage. Suspension was used, for example, to debate and pass bills that authorized the appropriation of funds for operations of the federal personnel system, the Federal Elections Commission, child nutrition programs, the Civil Rights Commission, most intelligence activities of the government including the CIA and FBI, international programs of the Treasury Department, development of deepwater ports to accommodate supertankers; and programs for research on aeronautics, oceanics, and environmental protection. It was used also for legislation that continued the President's authority to propose plans for reorganizing the federal bureaus, enlarged the jurisdiction of federal magistrates, and extended for two years the statute that restrained the Department of Health and Human Services from putting into effect a proposed regulation banning saccharin because it was found to cause cancer in animals. Nonetheless, the focus in the analysis that follows is on the rules procedure.

Once a committee votes to report a bill to the House with a recommendation that it pass, the committee decides whether to seek a rule or to bring it up under an alternative procedure, although this decision is sometimes left to the committee chairman in consultation with the senior minority member. If the decision is to proceed under a rule, the chairman requests the Rules Committee to grant one. The Rules Committee holds a hearing on this request and votes whether to recommend a rule to the House. If the Rules

Committee reports a rule, the House votes on whether to approve it. Once the rule is approved, the House can proceed to debate the bill.

The rule, then, schedules the bill for debate, but it does more than this. It allots time for floor consideration of the bill and divides this between proponents and opponents, and between general debate and debate on amendments. The rule also regulates which amendments may be offered on the floor. The Rules Committee can propose an open rule under which all amendments that are germane to the bill can be considered. It can propose a closed rule under which no amendments may be considered. In this case the House must approve the bill as the legislative committee has reported it or reject it; but it cannot amend it. Or the Rules Committee can propose a restricted rule that specifies which amendments may be considered and in what order. Finally, a rule can sanction what are normally irregular and prohibited procedures; it can provide for circumventing the regular House rules. House rules provide that all amendments to a bill must be germane, and that consideration and debate on a nongermane amendment will be disallowed if any member makes a point of order against it. A rule, however, can provide that points of order may not be made against certain nongermane amendments so that they can be considered on the floor.

In exercising its discretion in fashioning rules, the Rules Committee normally works with the House leadership. Its members may also seek to promote their own policy preferences, but in the end the committee must satisfy a majority of the whole House which in each case approves or rejects the rule that the committee proposes.[1]

ALLOTTING TIME

Rules of necessity restrict discussion in the full House, and occasionally there is opposition to a proposed rule on this ground. But rules are rarely used to choke off discussion on pertinent topics or to gag individual members.

Example. In the late 1960s members of Congress who had become opponents of the Vietnam War and of high military spending sought to limit the military and the President by offering amendments to the annual bills which provide authorizations and appropriations for weapons systems. The annual authorization bills were normally debated under rules that allow a maximum of three hours of general debate, equally divided and controlled by the chairman and ranking minority member of the Armed Services Committee, with amendments considered subsequently under a five-minute rule. In 1969 Armed Services requested such a rule. Opponents of the war and military spending, led by Donald M. Fraser (D. MN) of Armed Services and Thomas P. O'Neill, Jr. (D. MA), of the Rules Committee, proposed instead a rule allowing ten hours of general debate, divided equally between majority and minority parties, with each side pledging one-half of its time to the opponents of the bill, since the ranking Democrats and Republicans were equally strong in their support of it. At the Rules

Committee hearing, O'Neill argued that in the preceding five years, the committee had allowed more than four hours of general debate on ten bills—Civil Rights Act, 1964, ten hours; Housing Act, 1965, six hours; Medicare, 1965, ten hours; Elementary and Secondary Education, 1965, six hours; War on Poverty Amendments, 1966 and 1967, eight and six hours, respectively; Model Cities, 1966, six hours; Law Enforcement, 1967, five hours; Extension of Surtax, 1969, five hours; Reform of Electoral College, 1969, six hours—and that this military bill was equally or more important than many of them. "The destiny of this great nation cannot be considered and disposed of in three hours." The Rules Committee responded by proposing four hours, equally divided, and the whole House, after debating the rule, approved it overwhelmingly, 324 to 61.

The scenario was repeated in 1970, Fraser requesting eight hours, with two hours reserved for his group of opponents. The Rules Committee again allowed four hours, and their rule was approved by voice vote.

CLOSED RULES

In general, members do not like closed rules, and the Rules Committee is reluctant to grant them. In recent years, on the average, one rule in fourteen has been closed, although the percentage of closed rules granted varies from Congress to Congress. Thus the Rules Committee frequently turns down committees and committee chairmen who request closed rules, thereby protecting the right of members of the House to work their wills on committee bills.

Over the years, tax and related bills of the Ways and Means Committee have frequently been given closed rules under the assumption that they are so complex and integrally balanced that amendments to individual items, if adopted on the floor, could result in an incoherent tax policy. Nonetheless, the Rules Committee has failed to grant closed rules on such bills where it believes that the whole House should have greater freedom to decide.

Example. The Debt Ceiling Bill of 1972, as reported by the Ways and Means Committee, included a provision setting a $250 billion limit on federal spending and allowing the President, then Richard M. Nixon, to make any cuts in programs necessary to bring expenditures within this limit. Ways and Means requested a closed rule. Except for Ways and Means Chairman, Wilbur Mills, the House leadership—the Speaker, majority leader, and chairman of the Appropriations Committee—objected to giving the President such broad authority. They requested an open rule, so that they could offer an amendment to strike this provision, and the Rules Committee reported an open rule, turning down Ways and Means. As it turned out, the leadership's amendment was defeated on the floor, 167 to 216. Subsequently, however, the Senate refused to go along with the Ways and Means provision, and as a result no spending ceiling was adopted in 1972.

Even though the Rules Committee has turned down Ways and Means and other committees on their requests for closed rules, certain liberal Democrats in

Congress have sought procedural reforms that would reduce the committee's discretion to grant them, especially on revenue and tax bills. In February 1973 the caucus of all Democratic members adopted a caucus rule, not a House rule, requiring committee chairmen, who were, of course, Democrats, to give advance notice in the *Congressional Record* if they planned to ask the Rules Committee for a closed rule. Thereafter, any fifty Democrats who wanted to offer amendments to a bill, which they could not offer under a closed rule if it were granted, could call for a meeting of the Democratic caucus. If a majority of the caucus voted to support one or more amendments, then the caucus was to instruct the Democratic members of the Rules Committee to fashion a rule that would allow a House vote on the amendments. Such caucus instructions were not binding, so that any Democratic members of the Rules Committee could disregard them if they wished. This procedure has been tried only twice, both times regarding depletion tax allowances for oil.

Example. In May 1974 the Ways and Means Committee reported a bill that would have increased taxes on the oil industry by phasing out over several years the so-called depletion allowance. Representative William J. Green (D. PA) had offered an amendment in the Ways and Means Committee that would have ended the depletion allowance immediately, rather than over several years. His proposal was defeated 19 to 6. Green, however, wanted to offer the same amendment on the House floor, which he could not do under a closed rule. He therefore called for a meeting of the Democratic caucus which supported him. It was the time of the Arab oil embargo, and oil companies were especially unpopular in the nation. But Ways and Means thwarted the challenge by withdrawing its request for a rule and dropping the bill. There was no test.

The same scenario was replayed the next year, in 1975. This time Rules Committee Democrats approved a rule that allowed a House vote on the Green amendment, which passed in the House but subsequently did not carry in the Senate.

The liberal Democrats who supported this reform spoke in elevated tongues of the need to open up the legislative process and to have open rules. In all fairness, however, it should be pointed out that these very same members have demanded closed rules where such rules suit their policy preferences.

Example. When Ways and Means in November 1975 was working on a bill to reduce personal and business income taxes, President Gerald R. Ford insisted that the bill include a limit on federal spending, so that reduced spending would accompany reduced taxes. The Ways and Means Democrats voted against any spending ceiling and they voted further to insist on a closed rule so that the President's proposed spending ceiling could not be considered as an amendment to the bill on the House floor. The Rules Committee granted a closed rule. The most ardent advocates of the closed rule had been the most liberal of the Democrats.

Again in 1981, liberal Democrats sought to deny the whole House an opportunity to vote on the President's budget proposals as a whole. In this case, the budget reconciliation bill, they designed a complex restricted rule that would allow the House to vote on those parts of President Ronald Reagan's budget which the Democrats thought would be most unpopular and deny the House a vote on the proposals as a whole. The Democratic members of the Rules Committee, especially its chairman, Richard Bolling (D. MO), were involved actively in the strategy of this intensely partisan move, and the President lobbied actively for his proposals. Under these circumstances, the whole House defeated the rule, and the House went on to pass the President's bill.

RULES SANCTIONING IRREGULAR PROCEDURES

Members are especially critical of rules that sanction irregular procedures. The House Rules Committee is reluctant to grant them, and in cases where they have done so in recent years, members frequently have opposed the rules on the floor.

Example. The General Revenue Sharing Act of 1972, as reported by the Ways and Means Committee, provided that $30 billion over five years be distributed to state and local governments by the Secretary of the Treasury directly, without any necessity for its being appropriated. Ways and Means asked for a closed rule and one sanctioning irregular procedures—that is, waiving points of order that could otherwise be made against the bill because it violated the House rule against appropriating money in an authorization bill. The Chairman of the Appropriations Committee and others opposed to this form of backdoor spending were prepared to make the point of order. In this case the House Rules Committee granted the rule as requested, by a vote of 8 to 7. The rule was challenged on the floor, but approved by a vote of 223 to 185. The nation's mayors and governors, especially the most liberal ones—John Lindsay of New York, for example—had lobbied intensively for a closed rule that also sanctioned irregular procedures.

RULES COMMITTEE HEARINGS

The Rules Committee normally holds hearings before it votes on a rule, a practice that has been criticized in the mass media as being conservative and redundant, since legislative committees will have held extensive hearings before voting to report bills. Such criticism, however, stems from ignorance. The Rules Committee's hearings are to enable it to fashion a rule that is responsive to the desires of the House and the leadership, to decide on whether to allow two or four hours of general debate, for example, or to approve a closed rule or one allowing only certain amendments. The committee's witnesses are members of Congress, not representatives of the Executive or the public.

REASONS FOR DENYING A RULE

In addition to determining the conditions of debate, the Rules Committee decides whether or not to grant a rule in the first place, and in doing so, it plays an important role in the relations between legislative committees and the whole House. The Rules Committee will reject a legislative committee's request for a rule for one or more of the following reasons. First, the committee will deny a rule if it believes that a bill has not been properly prepared—that is, that the procedures followed in the legislative committee were incomplete or improper.

Example. In 1972 the Housing subcommittee of the House Committee on Banking and Currency reported a bill to the full committee after lengthy hearings. The full committee then held more hearings and considered the bill in executive session over a period of six weeks from late July to mid-September. This long deliberation was due in good part to a conflict within the committee between the full committee chairman, Wright Patman (D. TX) and the chairman of the Housing subcommittee, William A. Barrett (D. PA). Patman and others offered dozens of amendments in the full committee. Finally the bill was reported three weeks before Congress was to adjourn by a vote of nineteen yes, three no, six voting present. However, twenty-five of the committee's thirty-seven members wrote supplementary views in the committee report.

The committee formally requested a rule. Before the Rules Committee William B. Widnall (NJ), ranking Republican on the Housing subcommittee, said that Patman had made a mockery of the legislative process by his dilatory handling of the bill during full committee sessions. Patman, although he formally requested the rule, said to the Rules Committee: "It's a good bill in many ways. You do what you want." Faced with this intramural squabble, the Rules Committee voted 9 to 5 against a rule. It was protecting the House from incompetent work in the legislative committee.

Second, the Rules Committee holds bills if it believes that more time is needed for members to digest their provisions and their consequences. As a past chairman of the committee has said: "One of our functions is to give Congress a breathing spell to find what's involved rather than running it through."

Third, and most important of all, the Rules Committee delays granting rules for bills until the bills' sponsors in the House have been able to put together majorities to pass their legislation. By doing this, the committee performs an important supporting role for the legislative committees.

Example. Representative Harold D. Cooley (D. NC), chairman, Committee on Agriculture, said on the House floor: "The Land and Water Conservation Act was reported from the Committee on Interior and Insular Affairs in November 1963, and the chairman of that committee promptly sent a letter to the chairman of the Rules Committee asking for a rule on the bill. For many months the bill lay dormant before the Rules Committee because the chairman and members of that committee knew there was so much opposition to it in its existing form that its enactment by the House was very doubtful.

"It was precisely for the purpose of removing a large body of opposition to the bill that my amendment was drafted and it was not until my amendment was drafted and thoroughly discussed by all the groups interested in this bill that a hearing was scheduled by the Rules Committee.

"My amendment did remove the opposition to the bill of the largest and most important single group which was dissatisfied with its provisions—the private timber industry of the United States. When this opposition was withdrawn, the Rules Committee scheduled hearings on the bill and very quickly reported it for floor action."

Legislative committees frequently report bills that were amended in the committee markup. In a loud voice a committee chairman may ask for a rule, while sotto voce he asks the Rules Committee to hold the bill while he and other supporters attempt to determine whether or not the legislation, as amended, is likely to command a majority on the floor. The point is that committee chairmen and others may not be able to determine this until the bills have been reported and noncommittee members have been informed on exactly what is in the legislation.

Fourth, the Rules Committee may hold bills that members do not want to vote on.

Example. In 1968 the Committee on Un-American Activities (since abolished) reported a bill to create a Freedom Commission and a Freedom Academy to counteract Communist propaganda and Communist psychological warfare. The academy was to be modeled on West Point and the Naval and Air Academies, with cadets nominated by members of Congress. Most members, probably, opposed this preposterous proposal, but preferred not to have to vote on it for fear that unscrupulous opponents in the next election might use their votes as evidence that they were pro-Communist. The Rules Committee protected them—it failed to give the bill a rule.

Finally, the Rules Committee may defer bills that are opposed by substantial numbers of members from both parties, frequently including the leadership. In fact, it is difficult to find bills supported by a large majority of the House and by the majority leadership which the Rules Committee has held up for any great length of time. Members of the Rules Committee, to be sure, have definite views on much of the legislation that comes before them. They express these views in the hearings and often they vote consistently with them. If they believe, however, that a clear majority of the House wants to vote on a measure, they will report it. Richard F. Fenno, Jr., said in 1973 that the Rules Committee will stop a bill if its members do not think the bill is good public policy. This was true to some degree in the 1950s and 1960s, but it would be so today only if the policy views of Rules Committee members were reinforced by the leadership and by large numbers of House members.[2]

On those few occasions in the past when a majority of the House have felt that the Rules Committee has not represented them, that majority has not hesitated to reform the committee. The House has altered the composition of the committee, as it did in 1961, increasing its size from twelve to fifteen. It has required that the committee follow certain procedures, as it did in 1967 when William Colmer (D. MS) was in line to become chairman. Liberal Democrats opposed Colmer, and House leaders sought to mollify them by exacting from Colmer, as a condition of supporting him as new chairman of the committee, agreement that the committee would adopt certain rules limiting the chairman's discretionary powers. Colmer agreed, the rules were adopted, and he was selected as chairman. Furthermore, the House has provided means for bypassing the Rules Committee. A great part of the annual legislation necessary to carry on the business of government—appropriation bills and budget resolutions—is privileged and not subject to any interference by the Rules Committee, unless the bills' sponsors seek the protection of closed rules or rules sanctioning irregular procedures. Under suspension of the rules an extra-ordinary majority, with support of the Speaker, can bypass the Rules Committee. And there are the automatic calendars—consent, Wednesday, and private bills.

There remains the question of whether the Rules Committee should be a tool of the House majority leaders, reporting any and all rules that they wish. Or of the majority party caucus? Or should the committee be an instrument of the whole House? The extent to which the Rules Committee has served as a tool of leadership has varied, although all Rules Committee chairmen in recent years have cooperated closely with the majority party leaders. Today, indeed since 1973, the committee has been more a tool of the House leadership than at any time in recent history. The majority party has a better than 2:1 ratio on the committee (11D.–5R.), although its ratio in the whole House and on most legislative committees has been much lower—for example, 3:2 in the Ninety-sixth Congress (1979–1981) and 5:4 in the Ninety-seventh (1981–1983). This 2:1 ratio, which has been in effect since the early 1960s, has not assured leadership control of the committee in all cases, since some of the committee's majority members have on occasion been unwilling to follow the leaders. Thus, to consolidate further the Speaker's control, the Democratic caucus in 1975 gave him personal authority to nominate Democratic members of Rules, subject to caucus approval. In recent years the Speaker and majority leader have been able to command a majority on the committee on almost all issues.

These developments have meant trouble for the Rules Committee, however. In the first session of the Ninety-third Congress (1973), the committee lost thirteen rules on the floor—that is, the House defeated thirteen rules that the committee had reported—an unheard-of situation. In the previous forty-four years, on the average, the committee had been overruled by the House less frequently than once per year. For many of the rules defeated in 1973, the committee majority was following the commands of the Democratic leadership, proving, of course, that the leaders did not command a majority in the House. The result was a loss of prestige for the Rules Committee, and a reduced capacity of the committee to be responsive to the House in setting the conditions of debate. The committee, however, regained some balance and prestige thereafter. In the Ninety-fourth Congress (1975–1977), only three of the 301 rules recommended by the committee were rejected by the House. The House continues to discipline the committee, however, when it becomes involved in shaping highly partisan strategy, as in the case of the 1981 budget reconciliation bill cited earlier.

Discharge of Bills from Legislative Committees

If a legislative committee fails to report a bill that a sizable number of the whole House wants to consider, there are several techniques by which the whole can discharge the bill from the committee.

The Rules Committee can report a rule to the House which, if adopted, discharges the committee and schedules the legislation for House debate. Although it is used rarely, this power, and the threat that it may be used, is significant as a means of whole House control over its so-called little legislatures—its committees.

Examples. In 1964 the Rules Committee discharged the Judiciary Committee of a bill proposing a constitutional amendment that would block the Supreme Court from ordering reapportionment of state legislatures. The amendment would overrule the Court's decision in *Baker* v. *Carr.* When brought to a vote, the bill was supported by a substantial majority in the House, 210 to 175, but not by the two-thirds required for a constitutional amendment.

In 1972 the Rules Committee discharged the Education and Labor Committee of a bill to establish a board to settle a West Coast dock strike by compulsory arbitration. The rule was adopted by a vote of 203 to 170, over the vigorous opposition of Speaker Carl Albert, and the bill became law.

Second, suspension of the rules can be used by the House to discharge a committee. It requires a two-thirds vote and support of the Speaker, who has full discretion on whether or not to recognize a member proposing a suspension motion.

Third, in certain cases the Speaker and the whole House can instruct a committee to report a bill by a certain date when the bill is referred to the committee in the first instance. The Speaker's power relates to so-called multiple referrals where several committees have jurisdiction over a bill. If legislation is referred sequentially to one committee and then another, the Speaker invariably imposes time limits for reporting. If it is referred simultaneously to more than one committee, he may also set a reporting deadline.[3]

Example. On May 2, 1977, the majority leader, James C. Wright, Jr. (D. TX), introduced a bill to establish a comprehensive national energy policy. It was divided and referred simultaneously to five standing committees, with instructions to report not later than July 13.

In addition to the Speaker, the whole House has used the referral technique to instruct committees to report bills, this in connection with the budget process.

Example. The House in May 1981 passed a budget resolution that directed sixteen committees to report to the House by June 15 legislation that would reduce authorizations of a large number of programs. Although many committees were reluctant to do so, fifteen of the sixteen complied. The sixteenth was in organizational disarray, without effective leadership.

Finally, there is the discharge petition by which any 218 members (an absolute majority) of the House can, by signing a petition, bring to a vote in the House the question of whether or not to discharge a committee of a bill that the committee has failed to report. If a majority of those voting in the House then approve a discharge motion, the bill will be taken up. This procedure is considered to be clumsy by House members and subject to abuse if it leads them to take up bills that have not been considered in committee. Thus the discharge petition is used infrequently. From 1909, when the petition procedure was initiated, to 1980 approximately 865 discharge petitions were filed in the House, twenty-six bills were actually discharged, and twenty of these passed the House. Nonetheless, the procedure is an important means of whole House control over its committees. The threat that it will be used can move a committee to give serious consideration to a bill that it has neglected or to report one that it has rejected.

Example. The House Judiciary Committee had refused to report the Equal Rights Amendment. On June 11, 1970, Representative Martha Griffiths (D. MI) introduced a discharge petition. By July 20 it had obtained 218 signatures. On August 10 the House agreed to a discharge motion, 333 to 22, and then passed the legislation by more than the two-thirds vote necessary for a proposed constitutional amendment.

Amending Legislation Reported by Committees

The House can amend bills reported to it by its committees, unless it is working under a closed or a restricted rule, or under an alternative procedure, such as suspension of the rules, that limits amendments. But the House need not ever work under these limitations if a majority objects, since a majority can reject a rule that provides for them, and one-third of the members can defeat a motion to take up a bill under suspension.

The power to amend is manifest. Not so obvious, perhaps, is the impact of this whole House power on committee performance. As we shall see in chapter 8, the Appropriations Committee is ever fearful of being overriden on the floor, fearful that the House may acquire an easy habit of amending individual appropriation accounts, thereby impairing the internal integrity of the bills as a whole. To avoid this, the committee is especially sensitive to the expressed preference of any potential majority of the House. Committee members' antennae are finely tuned which is true also of other committees. At the same time there are committees that do not draft their bills with a special eye to avoiding House amendments or even House defeat. Their members would rather present the House with good policy, as they have defined it, than insure that the committees' bills are adopted as proposed.

In 1973 Richard F. Fenno, Jr., reported on his study of six House committees in this context, although his perspective was committee behavior, determined by the different goals of the members of each committee and the different environmental constraints in which they operated, rather than House control over committees, which is our focus.[4] The Ways and Means Committee fashioned its bills so that they enjoyed overwhelming success on the floor. Many of the bills, to be sure, were protected by restricted or closed rules or by the suspension procedure under which amendments cannot be offered, but the House would not have abided these procedures if it had not been satisfied that the committee was sensitive to its views.

Influence and success in the House were not the most prominent goals of members of the Foreign Affairs Committee, and as a consequence of this, in part—there were other reasons—the committee's bills were heavily amended on the floor. From 1955 to 1966 the committee confronted 286 proposed amendments to its annual foreign aid authorization bills of which 114 passed. The comparable figures for appropriation bills were 75 amendments proposed and 31 passed.

Members of the Education and Labor Committee were motivated, more than members of the other committees, by a desire to recommend "good" public policy, even if this resulted in amendments or defeat on the floor. But the committee did not have a united opinion of what was good public policy. Members perceived the issues as partisan and ideological, and they dealt with them accordingly in their committee, making only feeble efforts to achieve strategic policy accommodations. "More often than the other five, they will prefer a live political issue to a passed compromise bill."[5] Of bills reported by committees between 1955 and 1966, the House passed 59 percent for Education and Labor, 94 percent for Ways and Means. Of twelve major bills reported by Education and Labor during this period, seven passed, but of the seven two were completely rewritten on the floor and others were amended.[6]

The committees studied by Fenno do not necessarily make decisions the same way today, ten years later. The environmental constraints under which each committee operates have changed, particularly in response to congressional reforms of the 1970s; the committee members' goals, less so. But something like the variety of behavior that he described is present and influences the House's use of its power to amend as a technique for controlling its committees.

House Control over Nonlegislative Committee Actions

So far I have discussed techniques of House control over committees where bills are involved. House control over other forms of committee activity is much more difficult to effect. Take the case of investigations, which are the subject of chapter 12. Here committees and subcommittees can operate substantially without review by the whole, although, through investigations, the committees can have substantial influence on policy and administration. Subcommittees hold investigative hearings and prepare reports which are issued as congressional documents, accompanied frequently by considerable publicity. Yet the reports will not have been considered and debated by the whole House and frequently not even by the full committees. They may represent the opinions and conclusions of very small groups, while the form in which they are prepared gives the false impression that they are more general actions of the Congress. Congress might require committees to report findings of investigations to the floor, with time allotted for discussion, so that a floor record could be made. However, the most effective means for whole House control over committees where committees use nonstatutory devices, such as investigations, may be the techniques of internal control, to insure that the committees operate democratically and that they represent in some way the whole House.

6

Internal Controls over

Committee Operations

THERE ARE three levels of rules by which either the whole House or congressional parties in the House control committee organizations and procedures. The first level comprises the more or less permanent rules of the House relating to jurisdiction and composition of committees, their organization into subcommittees, and their procedures for conducting hearings and reporting bills to the House. The second level relates to temporary features of House and committee organization which are approved at the beginning of each Congress and terminate two years later at the end of the Congress, unless they are reenacted. These cover such matters as election of committee chairmen and members, party ratios on committees, and they may authorize temporary changes in the permanent rules. The third level covers rules adopted by party caucuses. They may relate to numerous features of committee organization and procedures, but caucus rules apply only to the conduct of members of the party in question.

Rules at the first level are approved by the whole House, normally as the result of a strongly bipartisan decision-making process. Those at the second level are also approved by the whole House, but in this case the House simply confirms decisions that have been made by party caucuses and leaders. By custom the leaders can count on the unanimous support of their party members on votes relating to the temporary organization of a single Congress, so that in this area House control means in effect control by the majority party. Level-three rules are not approved by the House, only by a party caucus. Although they are intended to control the conduct of party members, they are not binding, as we observed in the previous chapter with regard to the Democratic caucus instructions to Democratic members of the Ways and Means and Rules committees. Members are generally free to disregard caucus instructions.

These distinctions are based on certain generally accepted principles for organization and conduct of the legislature, principally that it is not the majority alone, but the majority and minority together, that represent the nation; that ad hoc majorities should be free to organize, support, and adopt any measures on which they agree; and that congressional parties should be the means for organizing each Congress so that it can do its work. Although they are legislative norms, not constitutional law—since one Congress cannot bind another—the distinctions are generally respected. Recently, however, the Democrats in the House have on several occasions introduced considerable partisanship into the decision-making process for level-one rules; and where they have done this, rulemaking has faltered or failed.

An analysis of the provenance of several congressional reform measures of the 1970s serves to illustrate the decision process for level-one rules. The Legislative Reorganization Act of 1970 is a classic example of rulemaking at this level. The process by which it was drafted and debated followed closely that which had been used for the Legislative Reorganization Act of 1946, the last previous reform act.

Example. In response to many statements in Congress in the mid-1960s on the need for congressional reform, the House and Senate established a Joint Committee on the Organization of Congress, with six members from each House equally divided between Democrats and Republicans (the Monroney-Madden committee). This committee, in its 1966 report, was unanimous in support of recommendations for major changes in congressional organizations and procedures, although six of the twelve members filed supplemental views. Only one of the supplemental views, signed by four Republicans, was in any way partisan, and it was unusually restrained, saying that the committee "did not delve deeply enough" into one matter, that it "might have looked more closely" at another, and that the four members "would have preferred" a somewhat different recommendation on a third issue.

The joint committee's recommendations were then referred to separate committees in each House with authority to report bills. The Senate committee reported a reorganization bill similar to the joint committee's proposals, which passed the Senate in 1967, by a roll-call vote of 75 to 9, after seventeen days of debate and the consideration of numerous amendments. On only one amendment was the vote partisan, in the sense that the majority of one party opposed the majority of the other. The floor proceedings were overwhelmingly nonpartisan.

The Democratic House leadership deferred action on the reorganization bill until 1970. In that year a subcommittee of the House Rules Committee, with three Democrats and two Republicans, drafted a bill and report that they approved unanimously. On the floor Barber B. Conable, Jr. (R. NY), and Sam M. Gibbons (D. FL) led a successful bipartisan effort to strengthen this bill and enact it. It was approved, as amended, by a vote of 326 to 19.

The House Committee Reform Amendments of 1974 are also an example of level-one rulemaking, but in this case attended by greater partisanship than the 1970 act.

Example. In 1973 the House created a Select Committee on Committees of ten members, five Democrats and five Republicans (the Bolling committee). Its proceedings were bipartisan and its final report was unanimous. The Democratic leaders then referred the Bolling committee recommendations to their caucus for consideration, while urging the caucus to approve them. The caucus voted instead, 111 to 95, to send the recommendations to a caucus committee on Organization, Study and Review, chaired by Julia B. Hansen (D. WA), with instructions to report back to the caucus in two months. The consequent Hansen committee proposals were much less ambitious than those of the Bolling committee, and the caucus voted to "direct" the Rules Committee to send both the Bolling and Hansen resolutions to the floor under an open rule, allowing the House to decide between them. This was done, and the House in 1974 adopted the Hansen plan, 203 (150 D., 53R.) to 165 (67D., 98R.). Although a majority of the Democrats supported the Hansen plan and a majority of Republicans the Bolling plan, the vote was not strongly partisan. The Hansen plan would not have been adopted without Republican support, and almost one-third of the Democrats supported the Bolling plan.

In reviewing this history, a task force of the Patterson Committee (see next example), comprised of two Democrats and one Republican, concluded that: "Reform, to be successful, must be bipartisan in scope. . . . The Bolling committee was able to avoid partisan conflict until mid-1974. However, the emasculation of the Bolling committee resolution by the Democratic caucus sparked considerable negative Republican reaction."[1]

In 1979 the House created another Select Committee on Committees, chaired by Jerry M. Patterson (D. CA), to reform committee organizations and procedures. Unlike the previous two examples of level-one rulemaking, the Patterson committee was marked by partisan conflict from the beginning, and as a consequence it was a failure.

Example. The conference of all House Republicans voted on January 15, 1979, to ask the House Rules Committee to send to the floor a resolution establishing a new Select Committee on Committees, and the Democratic caucus made a similar request two weeks later. Such a resolution was reported by the House Rules Committee, but it included two provisions to which the Republicans objected. First, the committee was to be partisan in composition—ten Democrats and five Republicans. Republicans had offered an amendment in the Rules Committee to make the select committee bipartisan—eight Democrats and eight Republicans—but this was defeated. Robert E. Bauman (R. MD), a member of the Rules Committee, objected in the committee's report that the resolution "establishes a partisan committee to deal with nonpartisan issues.

Not only is the select committee membership not equally divided between the minority and the majority, as was done in the past, it does not even accurately reflect the makeup of the membership of the full House."

Second, recommendations of the select committee concerning such matters as optimum size of committees, appropriate number of committee and subcommittee assignments per member, and number and jurisdiction of subcommittees were to be made to the party caucuses and not to the whole House. Thus, on these matters decisions for the House would be made by the majority party. A Republican amendment in the Rules Committee to strike this provision was defeated, and Bauman complained in the committee's report that the resolution "contains an unprecedented provision which gives the Democratic caucus the privilege to make decisions which will affect the entire House. The right to make these decisions . . . should be the domain of the full House, not of a party caucus." The House approved the select committee by a vote of 208 (187D., 21R.) to 200 (74D., 126R.).

Not surprisingly, this attempt to use a strongly partisan decision-making process for level-one rules came to little. Lacking support in the House, the committee hesitated to make recommendations on many controversial questions, and of the few recommendations they made, only one, relating to the number of subcommittees of legislative committees, was adopted, in a much modified form. It is questionable that the Democratic leaders wanted reform in the first place. In addition to imparting a highly partisan flavor to the committee's membership and procedures, they selected a little-known third-term Democrat to be its chairman. The Republicans, on the other hand, were serious, but to no avail. Their caucus first proposed the select committee; and even though they voted against setting it up under the conditions dictated by the Democrats, a senior Republican, James C. Cleveland (NH), was appointed as ranking minority member.

Turning next to level-two decision making, the party loyalty that leaders can expect to receive from their members is limited to matters of temporary organization of the House, and does not extend necessarily to parliamentary procedures, as the following example illustrates.

Example. In 1980 John Ashbrook (R. OH) offered an amendment to the Treasury Department appropriation bill to prevent the Internal Revenue Service from formulating or carrying out rules that would withdraw tax-exempt status from private schools found to have discriminated against minorities. A similar amendment had been included in the appropriation bill for the previous year. The presiding officer ruled the amendment out of order, as legislation in an appropriation bill. Ashbrook appealed this ruling of the chair to the full House. The Democratic leaders supported the chair's ruling and tried to make the vote on it a matter of party discipline, as in votes on temporary organization of the House. The ruling was upheld, 214 to 182, but forty-four Democrats, fifteen northern Democrats and twenty-nine southern Democrats, voted against their leaders. Speaker Thomas P. O'Neill, Jr., subsequently sent them all letters criticizing them sharply for deserting the party on an important procedural vote. He argued, among other things, that a vote on a procedural motion in the House compares to a vote of confidence in a parliamentary system, and that in such a system the government would fall if a vote to sustain the chair were to fail. The dissenting

Democrats were angered by the Speaker's reprimand and unimpressed by his arguments.

With these distinctions in mind, we can turn to the principal subject of this chapter, the specific techniques for whole House control over congressional committees, each of which involves one or more of the three levels of rulemaking.

House Control over the Numbers of Committees and Subcommittees and Their Jurisdictions

The whole House can and does control the number of committees and their jurisdictions. Thus in the 1946 Legislative Reorganization Act, Congress reduced the number of House committees from forty-eight to nineteen, combining their jurisdictions, and the number of Senate committees from thirty-three to fifteen. In 1975 there was a modest reshuffling of committee jurisdictions in the House as a result of the Committee Reform Amendments of the previous year.

Until 1970 the whole House exercised little control over how committees organized themselves into subcommittees, and there was considerable variation among committees. Thus the House Committee on Agriculture had ten subcommittees, whereas Ways and Means had none. Although the Committee on Foreign Affairs had ten subcommittees, most committee actions on legislation were taken in the full committee, whereas the Committee on Public Works had decentralized its decision making considerably among subcommittees.

There were several factors that determined the degree of centralization or decentralization of legislative committees, that is, the number of their subcommittees and their autonomy.[2] Workload was not one of them, however, for Ways and Means, with no subcommittees, had one of the heaviest assignments in the House. The principal factor was the compatibility of the interests of committee members and their views of the breadth and intensity of work the committee should pursue. Where there was a high degree of compatibility, there would be a number of subcommittees; for there was less resistance to creating them and, as in the case of the Committee on Public Works, to giving them considerable autonomy. Where, on the other hand, the interests of committee members conflicted on vital issues, the members were likely to prefer to do a good part of their work through the full committee. In that case, there had been few or no subcommittees, as in Ways and Means, or the subcommittees had little autonomy, as in Foreign Affairs.

The personality of the committee chairman was also a factor. A weak chairman was likely to be saddled with subcommittees that had some autonomy. A strong chairman might prefer weak subcommittees or none, because he believed that this was the best way to avoid committee splits that could be damaging to the committee's legislative proposals, or because he believed that this was the best way to insure that the substantive results of committee work would be to his liking. On the other hand, a strong chairman might prefer strong subcommittees, because he believed the committee should have a broad scope and intensity in its work.

Many of these considerations remain relevant for committees and subcommittees today, but they have been overridden in some degree by actions taken since 1973 by the Democratic caucus and the whole House to assert, for the first time, control over the number of subcommittees and their jurisdictions. The Democratic caucus in 1973 adopted a so-called bill of rights for subcommittees as part of its caucus rules. The rights were designed principally to reduce the autonomy of committee chairmen and senior members. There was to be a Democratic caucus in each committee with authority to determine the number of subcommittees and their jurisdictions, to select subcommittee chairmen, and to fix party ratios in the subcommittees, which were to be no less favorable than the ratios on the full committees. In 1974, the whole House, in the Committee Reform Amendments, provided that each committee (except Budget) must have at least four subcommittees.

By these actions the majority party and the whole House asserted control over subcommittees, but the result of this reform has been to make it more difficult for the whole to control its parts. In most cases it is easier for the House to control its committees if the committees, in turn, control their subcommittees—easier, that is, than if the subcommittees have a great deal of independence. The reforms of 1973–1974 strengthened the subcommittees and gave them that independence. Some of the consequences of this have been discussed in chapter 3.

Subsequently a limit was imposed on the number of subcommittees that could be organized by a standing committee. Congressional concern about the excessive proliferation of subcommittees had been confirmed by a survey of members made by the Patterson committee in 1979. Of 184 respondents (122D., 62R.), 81 percent (80 percent D., 82 percent R.) believed that the number of subcommittees should be reduced; the remainder were equally divided between those who answered no or were undecided. The Patterson committee considered two alternatives: to require approval of the whole House for any new subcommittee proposed to be established by a committee; or simply to limit the number of subcommittees that could be established by any committee. They chose the second by unanimous vote, proposing a limit of six. In response, the House Democrats in 1981 adopted a caucus rule limiting the number of subcommittees of most legislative committees to eight or the number then existing, whichever was fewer. The Republicans favored a limit of six and held that the maximum number, whatever its size, should have been adopted by the whole House, as was the 1974 rule on the minimum number of subcommittees, not by the Democratic caucus alone.

House Control over Size and Party Ratios of Committees

In varying degrees the whole House controls the size and party ratios of committees. Before 1974 the number of members on each committee was set by the House in its rules, although these could be altered temporarily at the beginning of each Congress. The Committee Reform Amendments of 1974 eliminated these numbers from the permanent rules, leaving it to the House to establish the size of committees by the number of members elected to each one. Thus committee size is presently a level-two decision. The party leaders seek agreement when a Congress is organized, but if this is not reached, the majority can impose its will on the minority, for this is the type of organizational issue on which party leaders can count on the unanimous support of their members on the floor.

The size of committees will be controlled in part by limits on the number of committees on which members may serve. The Bolling committee proposed a House rule that would limit all members to one major committee. This was dropped in the substitute Hansen resolution which was adopted by the House. Subsequently, however, the Democrats approved a similar limitation as a caucus rule, although it has been disregarded on several occasions.

When the whole House votes on the membership of committees at the beginning of each Congress, it approves in effect the committees' party ratios, but the whole House in this context means the majority party, for committee ratios are presently considered to be a question of short-term organization—of level-two rulemaking. For most committees the ratios correspond to the party division in the House. However, the majority party generally maintains extra-ordinary majorities on the three money committees—Appropriations, Ways and Means, Budget—and on the Rules Committee.

Until recently negotiations between majority and minority leaders have achieved generally accepted accommodations on the ratios. Since 1975, however, the Democratic caucus has sought to mandate ratios, thereby limiting the discretion of their leaders in negotiations with the minority party, and more sharply politicizing the apportionment process. The Republicans on the Patterson committee, in their minority report, complained about these recent developments and suggested as a remedy "that merits scrutiny" incorporating in the House rules a requirement that the allotment of committee seats reflect, to the closest degree possible, the proportional ratio of the parties in the House as a whole, thereby making party ratios level-one decisions rather than level two. "We submit that the question of committee ratios should not be read in partisan terms. Rather, equitable committee allocations are an assurance that committees fairly reflect and represent the substantive views of both parties in the process of policy deliberation."

Example. Between 1941 and 1981 the party ratio on the Ways and Means Committee has been 3:2 except when the majority's numbers in the whole House have exceeded this ratio. During this forty-year period the Democrats have had a better than 3:2 majority in the House in four Congresses, and for these their ratios on Ways and Means have equaled those in the House as a whole. The Eighty-ninth Congress (1965–1967), elected when Lyndon B. Johnson swamped Barry M. Goldwater for President, gave the Democrats a 7:3 majority in the House and a 7:3 majority on Ways and Means (17D., 8R.). In the following Congress, when the Democratic House majority dropped to just under 3:2, Ways and Means reverted to its traditional 3:2 ratio.

The Democrats enjoyed another big victory in the 1974 election, in the wake of Watergate. Their majority in the Ninety-fourth Congress again equaled 7:3, and this ratio was used for Ways and Means. In that year, however, the large class of freshman Democrats joined liberal incumbent Democrats in promoting congressional reform, and one of their targets was the Committee on Ways and Means, whose long-time chairman, Wilbur Mills (D. AK), was ill. As a result the committee was increased in size from twenty-five to thirty-seven (25D., 12R.). Since thirteen incumbent Democratic members of the committee had been reelected, this gave the Democrats twelve new seats to be filled by members more liberal on the average than the incumbents, according to the reformers' plan. House and committee ratios remained the same in the next Congress (1977–1979), but the Democrats lost a few seats in the Ninety-sixth Congress, resulting in a House ratio of just over 3:2, and Ways and Means was altered accordingly to twenty-four Democrats and thirteen Republicans.

Ronald Reagan's victory in 1980 was accompanied by an increase of Republicans in the House. The Democratic majority was reduced to approximately 5:4, and the Republicans, therefore, expected the House to restore the traditional 3:2 ratio on Ways and Means. The Democratic caucus and leadership balked, however, insisting on a better than 2:1 ratio on the committee; and to establish this ratio, with their shrunken numbers in the House, the Democrats proposed to reduce the size of the committee from thirty-seven to thirty-five, with twenty-three Democrats and twelve Republicans.

The issue was especially important for Republicans, since Ways and Means had responsibility for a good part of the newly elected Republican President's economic program; and it was, indeed, to thwart this program on a partisan basis that the Democratic leadership wanted to have an extra-ordinary majority of more than 2:1 on the committee. A 3:2 ratio would not have been sufficient for this purpose, since the leaders could not count on the support of all Democratic committee members on questions of substance.

The Republicans tried to negotiate with Speaker Thomas P. O'Neill, Jr., but to no avail. They took their grievance to the House floor, proposing, first, the traditional 3:2 ratio on Ways and Means, but this motion was defeated 180 (179R., 1D.) to 220 (all D.). The Republicans then moved to keep the committee at thirty-seven, assigning the two additional seats to their party. This motion, too, was rejected 179 (all R.) to 221 (all D.). On questions of impermanent House organization, the parties were unified.

Although Speaker O'Neill opined that only "a couple of windbags" practicing "picayune politics" were behind the Republican objections, Republican resentment that they had been treated unjustly ran wide and deep. Minority leader Robert H. Michel (R. IL) said on the floor that "The Democratic caucus, in an obvious attempt to reverse the election mandate, has packed the key committees." Republican leaders announced that they would try to write tax legislation on the floor, a most unusual procedure, since they had so little influence in the committee. And they were successful in doing this. Subsequently a floor majority of Republicans and some Democrats substituted President Reagan's tax proposal for the committee's bill. Thereafter, Ways and Means chairman, Dan Rostenkowski (D. IL) sought to sweep behind him these unordinary events, promising that the committee would "return to bipartisan tax-writing."

House Control over Membership of Committees

The whole House approves the membership of committees. As in questions of committee size and party ratios, however, the House has, almost invariably, confirmed decisions made by the congressional parties; and in 1974 the House rules were amended, in the Committee Reform Amendments, to require that the House elect committee members from nominations submitted by party caucuses.

For the Democrats, committee assignments are approved by the Democratic caucus. Although contests develop in the caucus occasionally, for the most part it approves assignments that are recommended to it by the Democratic Steering and Policy Committee, whose origins and composition were discussed in chapter 3.

Republican committee assignments are approved by the Republican Policy Committee, which in turn confirms decisions made in the Republican Com-

mittee on Committees, composed of one member from the Republican delegation of each state. This group, being too large for decision making of this
type, delegates its authority to an executive committee which consists of one
member from each state having seven or more Republican congressmen, these
elected by the state delegations, five to six members chosen by the party leader
to represent states with six and fewer Republicans, and two additional members chosen by the Republican leader to represent freshman and second-term
Republicans. Committee members have weighted votes depending on the
number of Congressmen they represent. Thus, in the Ninety-seventh Congress (1981–1983), Clair W. Burgener of California had twenty-one votes and
Edwin B. Forsythe of New Jersey, seven.

What considerations do these groups take into account in making assignments? For committees, other than the four senior or exclusive committees
of Ways and Means, Appropriations, Rules, and Budget, two determinants
dominate the selection process. First, the structure of the committee system
and the logistics of the assignment process—that is, the numbers of vacancies
on committees, the numbers of applicants for these vacancies, and an informal
rule that states with large party delegations, or regional zones, are normally
entitled to representation on all major committees. The second determinant
is members' preferences. A recent study of Democratic committee assignments from 1958 to 1974 found that over 80 percent of committee assignments were in response to the expressed preferences of rank-and-file Democrats.[3] By comparison, the members' personal characteristics were insig-
nificant as determinants of committee assignments, party leaders did not play
a major role in the process, and seniority made little difference. As a member
of the Democratic Committee on Committees said in 1973, "If we tilt at all,
we tilt towards the freshman."[4] Dividing the committees into two groups,
those populated by new members who were drawn chiefly from the pool of
requesters, and those populated by new members who had been assigned or
co-opted for service on a committee, the study found that all major committees but one, Foreign Affairs, were in the first category. The assigned committees were typically minor or second committees.

Example. Shirley A. Chisholm (D. NY) and Allard K. Lowenstein (D. NY), both
freshmen in 1969, were assigned to the Committee on Agriculture. Representative
Chisholm objected to the assignment in the Democratic caucus. "No tree grows in
Brooklyn." Her talents would be wasted. She had requested Education and Labor.

Why was she assigned to Agriculture? New York had twenty-six Democratic members and by custom there had been one or more on each of the major committees. In
the preceding Congress there had been three Democrats from New York on Agriculture, two with rural constituencies and Frank J. Brasco from Brooklyn. The two

upstaters were not returned and Brasco wanted off. He was shifted to Banking, Finance and Urban Affairs. This left no Democrats from New York on Agriculture.

The Committee on Education and Labor in the preceding Congress had three New York Democrats: Adam Clayton Powell, Hugh L. Carey, and James H. Scheuer. They all returned to the committee.

There were four freshman Democrats from New York to be given committee assignments. Mario Biaggi of the Bronx was assigned to Merchant Marine and Fisheries, and Edward I. Koch of Manhattan, to Science and Astronautics, neither of which interested Chisholm. Chisholm and Lowenstein were selected for the New York vacancies on Agriculture, which the Democratic Committee on Committees believed was not inappropriate, since Agriculture considers distribution of food to the poor, food stamps, and problems of migrant farm laborers, in which they thought Chisholm and Lowenstein would be interested.

Having protested in the Democratic caucus, Chisholm was told that she need not accept the assignment. She didn't, and subsequently was assigned instead to the Committee on Veterans' Affairs.

At the beginning of the next Congress, the Ninety-second, in 1971, Carey left Education and Labor to serve on Ways and Means, and Powell was defeated for reelection, leaving only Scheuer as a New York Democrat on the committee. Chisholm was then moved to Education and Labor, as was Biaggi, where she served until 1977 when she was chosen by the Speaker for a seat on the Rules Committee.

As for Agriculture, Lowenstein was not reelected to Congress, again leaving the committee without New Yorkers. The Democratic Committee on Committees assigned John G. Dow from Newburgh, previously a member of the committee, who had been defeated for reelection in 1968 and regained his seat in the 1970 election, and Herman Badillo of the Bronx, a freshman. Badillo wanted Education and Labor and, like Chisholm before him, asked the caucus to change his assignment. His request was supported by the Speaker who persuaded Teno Roncalio of Wyoming, who had been selected for Education and Labor, to step down and accept a seat on Public Works. Some caucus members objected to giving New York Democrats four seats on Education and Labor while no other state had more than two, but with the Speaker's support, Badillo's appeal was sustained.

Only twice in recent history have Democratic freshmen challenged committee assignments in the caucus, and in this respect the example relating to Chisholm and Badillo is abnormal. I use it, nonetheless, because it illustrates the committee assignment process for most committees.

In assignments to the senior or exclusive committees, however, members' preferences do not have as much force. In the Appropriations Committee, for instance, a substantial number of assignments are prearranged by party leaders and senior members of the committee. While they take preferences into account, they look for new members who are "responsible" as legislators and who are likely to support the economy norm of the committee, about which more in chapter 8. Party leaders intervene actively in recruitment for Ways and Means, and they control assignments to the Rules Committee. The situation on the Budget Committee is different, since its members are chosen for limited terms, while they serve on other committees; but party leaders are active in making assignments.

The result of this assignment process is that some committees are fairly representative of the House as a whole and some are quite unrepresentative, perhaps none more so than the Committee on Education and Labor. In terms of regional representation this committee had two southerners among its thirty-three members in the Ninety-seventh Congress (1981–1983). This is 6 percent of the committee, while representatives from the southern states make up 26 percent of the House. (The percentages are 9 and 28 if Kentucky is included as a southern state.) Furthermore, Education and Labor members are on average more liberal than the House as a whole, especially the Democratic members. Using the 1980 support scores compiled by the Americans for Democratic Action (ADA) and published in *Congressional Quarterly*, the whole House scored 44 percent support for liberal measures; the Committee on Education and Labor, 54 percent; Democrats in the House scored 57 percent; Democrats on Education and Labor, 71 percent; Republicans in the House, 21 percent; Republicans on Education and Labor, 24 percent.

The whole House could require that the committees have a diversity of interests representing those in the House as a whole.[5] It could by resolution fix the criteria to be followed by the parties in selecting committee members, and one of these could be representativeness, assuming the House were able to define this criterion in a way that would be acceptable to a large majority of its members. In addition, or alternatively, the House could limit membership on committees to a fixed number of years, with the idea that enforced rotation would increase representativeness.

Some scholars find little reason for concern about the unrepresentative character of committees, holding that committees should be principally arenas for the accommodation of particular interests *(pma)* or advocates of the interests and programs within their jurisdictions (whirlpools). From our perspective, with its emphases on breadth of view and the functions of Congress in legislation and administration, there is reason for concern. On the one hand, there are advantages of the committees as presently constituted. Members are interested in committee work and many of them work hard at it. They have sufficient interest and knowledge to evaluate alternatives to the President's proposals and to oversee administrative performance. If rigid criteria for representativeness were adopted, the principal current criterion for selection, the members' preferences, would have to be downgraded. The result would be, in all likelihood, a decline in members' interest in committee work—they would give more attention to the other facets of their job—and a reduction in the capacity of committees to fulfill their functions, as defined by our model.

On the other hand, unrepresentative committees present a danger that narrow interests will dominate the legislative and administrative processes. The important question is whether or not there are means, other than trying to make the committees themselves representative, to avoid this. Certain techniques of whole House control are especially relevant in this context. The House can shift jurisdictions among committees if it is dissatisfied with any of them, as it has done between the Committees on Agriculture and on Education and Labor with respect to food programs for children in schools. It can refer certain bills to several committees and, by the order and terms of reference, control their relative influence on the legislation. Indeed, overlapping committee jurisdictions, whatever their disadvantages in terms of coordination of the House, can reduce the cost of unrepresentative committees. The whole House can require committees to follow certain procedures—for example, open hearings, provision for the minority members on committees to select some of the witnesses in hearings, standards for the recruitment and assignment of committee staff—that are likely to make committee members more responsive to diverse policy viewpoints. And there are the external controls over consideration and passage of committee bills, discussed in the previous chapter, which the whole House can use selectively. It is, in part, because the Committee on Education and Labor is unrepresentative that the whole House scrutinizes carefully legislation that the committee reports and amends it frequently.

Whole House Control over Committee Procedures

Until the 1970s each committee set its own rules to a significant degree. There were so-called reformed and unreformed committees. On an unreformed committee, the chairman, frequently with the cooperation of the ranking minority member and other seniors on the committee, was able to frustrate the will of a majority of committee members as well as the freedom of action of minorities and of individual members. The names and numbers of reformed and unreformed committees were always changing, depending on the personalities and policy orientations of their chairmen and on the resolve of committee majorities to challenge them. To reform all committees the House at any time could have imposed standard operating procedures on them, including procedures that would insure that any majority could work its will. Congress did just this in the Legislative Reorganization Act of 1970, which included a bill of rights for committees. By putting uniform procedures into law, the whole House elected to exercise considerable control over its little legislatures.

The most important provisions of the committee bill of rights are these: (1) A majority of committee members can by written request require the chairman to call a committee meeting. If the chairman absents himself, the senior member of the majority party present shall preside. (2) Committees are to include in their reports on bills the results of each committee roll-call vote, including how each member voted. There are limitations on proxy voting in committees; no general proxies, only proxies for specific votes. (3) A majority of a committee can by written request require the filing within seven days of a committee report on a legislative measure that has been approved by the committee. All committee members are to be given an opportunity to review and approve the text of committee reports, and, if they request it, three days in which to file minority, supplemental, or additional views in the reports. (4) All committee meetings, including business meetings, are to be open unless the committee by majority vote determines otherwise. (5) If a majority of the minority requests to do so, they can select witnesses to testify during at least one day of the hearings on any measure. (6) Committee minorities can, if they wish, hire a percentage of the committee staff to serve themselves.

The House Rules Committee, in reporting the proposed committee bill of rights, said that there were two major goals of these provisions. First, to strike a more judicious balance between the prerogatives of the majority and minority parties, while at the same time preserving the legitimate rights of individual members; and, second, to give the public a better opportunity to observe the operations of Congress. However, the most important provisions—those for calling committee meetings, voting in committees, reporting approved bills— relate to a different objective, namely, to allow any majority in a committee, regardless of its partisan composition, to work its will. The principal objective of the committee reforms of 1970 was, in this sense, the same as that of the House reforms of 1910.

House Control over Selection of Committee Chairmen

The whole House elects committee chairmen, but House control in this context means control by the majority party. Indeed, the House has staunchly resisted efforts to set the whole against parties.

Example. In 1971 a group of liberal Democrats, led by Brock Adams (D. WA) and Jerome R. Waldie (D. CA), tried to block the appointment of the very conservative John L. McMillan (D. SC) as chairman of the District of Columbia Committee. They failed in the Democratic caucus, and Waldie took their fight to the floor. The leaders of both parties opposed this effort to challenge the tradition of party control over committee membership. The majority leader, Hale Boggs (D. LA), warned that "if a minority on the Democratic side and a majority on the minority side get together they could take over control of the entire committee system in the House." Waldie responded that he would not find that objectionable, "if by doing so the national interest were advanced." But many liberal Democrats who had voted in the caucus to boot McMillan opposed the Waldie motion. Minority leader Gerald R. Ford (R. MI) said that "the matter was one for the Democrats to decide and not for us. The Democrats ought to have the right to choose their own chairman in caucus." In the House 172 Democrats voted against Waldie; 63, including Adams, abstained: and 1 voted present. Only 17 Democrats supported him. As for the Republicans, 86 voted against the Waldie motion; and 78 followed Ford's advice by voting present or abstaining. Fifteen Republicans supported Waldie.

In 1974 the House rules were amended to provide explicitly that the House elect committee chairmen from nominations submitted by the majority party caucus at the commencement of each Congress. Parties, then, while they do not by themselves control the policies that a Congress enacts, nor the administrative oversight that it exercises, are the instrument by which each Congress is organized.

The selection of chairmen is made for the Democrats by their caucus on the basis of recommendations by the Steering and Policy Committee, and for the Republicans, by their conference (the name given their caucus) on the basis of recommendations made by the party's Committee on Committees. In both cases the dominant criterion for choice is seniority; it is followed almost always, as it was in the example of McMillan above.

There have been over the years various proposals to change the seniority rule, most important among them these: (1) Each committee should vote for its own chairman from among the top three in seniority on the committee. Amendments to this effect were defeated in both the House and the Senate in debate on the Legislative Reorganization Act of 1970. (2) The party caucus should choose committee chairmen from the top three in seniority on each committee, using a secret ballot. An amendment to this effect was defeated in the Senate in the 1970 debate. (3) The Speaker should choose committee chairmen with caucus approval. Congressman Bolling made this proposal but it was not put to a vote.

None of these proposals has been adopted principally because there has been no agreement on the objectives of reform of the seniority rule for selecting committee chairmen. Some have wanted to achieve greater democracy in the committees—to terminate the dictatorship of the chairmen of the so-called unreformed committees. Some have wanted to change seniority in order to strengthen party leadership and control of the House. They want to co-opt committee chairmen into a new pattern of strong party control. Some have had a more limited objective, wanting liberal leadership in certain committees. They believe that less senior members will be more liberal.

After the House in 1970 defeated several proposals to change seniority, each party's caucus appointed a task force to examine the problem again. As a result certain changes in procedures for selecting chairmen and ranking minority members were adopted at the beginning of the Ninety-second Congress (1971–1973). First, the Democratic and Republican committees on committees are to recommend to their respective caucuses the names of chairmen and ranking minority members of all committees, as they have done in the past. But the caucus rules have been amended to state explicitly that the recommendations they make need not necessarily follow seniority. However, in all Congresses since then, except one, all recommendations of both parties have been based on seniority. In the Ninety-fourth Congress in 1975, the Democratic Steering and Policy Committee recommended the second senior member, rather than the senior, for one committee, and the fourth in seniority for another.

Second, whereas previously recommendations for committee chairmen were voted en bloc in the caucuses, the new party rules provide for a separate vote on each chairman, and this vote must be a secret one. In the Ninety-second Congress there were no challenges in either caucus. In the Ninety-third there were several challenges in the Democratic caucus, but none were successful. In the Ninety-fourth Congress there were two successful challenges in the Democratic caucus. There have been no successful challenges since.

Thus the parties have changed their procedures for selecting committee chairmen, but, lacking consensus on the objectives of reform, they have adopted no alternative criterion for choice, and without this, seniority continues to be respected, although it has now been breached. Seniority is, after all, a rule that is pervasive in American institutions—the rule of first come, first served. This was the rule used, for example, in settling the public lands, appropriating water holes, and locating mining claims. It is the rule used to determine who gets into a movie theater; we queue up. It is pervasive, perhaps, because it is a rule that can be applied when there is no consensus on any other rationing rule. In that situation seniority is a conflict-reducing mechanism. And this has been to a significant degree the case for its use in selecting committee chairmen.

Insofar as reform proposed in methods for selecting committee chairmen is motivated by a desire for greater democracy in the committees, it is related closely to the question of House control over committee procedures—to the capacity of the majority of a committee to control the committee. If committee procedures insure that a majority can work its will, then the question of seniority becomes less important, because the chairman will have less discretionary power. Thus the solution to the problem of seniority in this context is to adopt committee rules that reduce the chairman's authority. Even before the general reform of committee rules by the whole House in 1970, individual committees had put unpopular chairmen under control.

Finally, insofar as proposed reform in methods for selecting committee chairmen is motivated by a desire to tighten party control over the House, it is related to the character of the whole House as a political institution—how the House is managed, the roles of congressional party leaders and caucuses and ad hoc majorities.

House Control over Committee Staffs

In terms of committee staffs, there were until the middle 1970s two types of committees in the House.[6] In the first category the staffs were relatively small in size and highly professional. In staff recruitment professional training was emphasized over political considerations. Staff members had almost permanent positions—there was little turnover when the majority of the committee changed from one party to the other. In these committees the staff provided services to all members of the committee regardless of the members' rank or party; and the staff served as a central unit for the committee as a whole and for its subcommittees. Examples were the Committees on Armed Services and on Foreign Affairs.

On these committees of the first category, staff were concerned primarily with analysis of facts, appraisal of consequences, and advice as to the best way to attain any given objectives. The staff members were passive, rather than active, in the process of formulating policy, and they avoided involvement in formulating or carrying out political strategy.

In committees of the second category the staffs were typically larger in size than those in the first group. Furthermore, grounds for recruitment were more political and personal. Professional training was a criterion, but it might be second to others. As a result, staff turnover was higher and tenure was lower. In these committees the staffs were divided, the greater part of the staff working almost exclusively for the majority, and the remainder, exclusively for the minority. Furthermore, the staffs were not concentrated at the full committee level, but divided among the committees and their subcommittees. Examples were the Committees on Education and Labor and on Banking, Finance, and Urban Affairs.

On these committees of the second category, senior staff members participated actively in the formulation of policy and in political strategies. They frequently contributed ideas and proposals that became key features in the positions adopted by the members whom they served.

Finally, some committees had staffs with characteristics of each of these two types.

Similar differences can be found among House committees today, as illustrated in table 6.1. Armed Services has a small staff, with low turnover and no employees assigned permanently to subcommittees. Education and Labor, and Energy and Commerce (formerly Interstate and Foreign Commerce) have large staffs, high turnover, and large percentages assigned to subcommittees, almost 70 percent in the case of Energy and Commerce. At the same time, substantial changes in committee staffs have occurred in the last decade, and these changes have important consequences for whole House control over its committees and for executive–legislative relations. The staffs of committees are on average larger, more decentralized, more partisan, and more professional and specialized today than they were in 1970.

The staffs of all House standing committees grew by 179 percent between 1970 and 1979, due principally to growth in committee workload. The data on workload, some of them summarized in table 6.1, show more committee and subcommittee meetings dealing with both legislation and administrative oversight and more amendments to the President's programs considered in committee. These increases in committee activity are due to several causes which have operated with different consequences in different committees. Most important, they represent Congress's response to the vast increase in the number and complexity of governmental programs in recent years. One frequently used index of governmental activity is the number of pages in the *Federal Register*, which publishes agency rules and administrative decisions, both proposed and final. Between 1970 and 1979 there was a 280 percent increase from 20,000 pages to 77,000. Had congressional workload and staffs not increased, Congress's control over the legislative and administrative processes would have diminished markedly relative to the Executive's. Growth in workload and staff is due also to certain developments in the techniques that Congress has used for legislative and administrative oversight, most importantly to the remarkable increase in annual and short-term authorizations, to be discussed in chapter 7. The congressional reforms of the 1970s are another important source of increased workload and staff, most especially the proliferation of subcommittees, which was a response to the reform objective of

TABLE 6.1

Data Relating to Staff of Certain House Committees

	1. Staff Employees		2. Workload Committee & subcommittee meetings		3. Decentralization Staff permanently assigned to subcommittees	4. Tenure
	1979 (no.)	1970 to 1979 (% growth)	1979–81 (no.)	1969–71 to 1979–81 (% growth)	1979 (%)	1962–1978 (index[a])
All House Committees	1959	179	n.a.	n.a.	n.a.	n.a.
Armed Services	47	27	619	63	0	7.7
Public Works & Transportation	82	105	263	49	37	6.4
Education & Labor	120	56	353	−16	50	3.9
Energy & Commerce[b]	154	267	645	52	68	4.5

SOURCE: Column 1: John F. Bibby, Thomas E. Mann, and Norman J. Ornstein, *Vital Statistics on Congress, 1980* (Washington, D.C.: American Enterprise Institute, 1980), tables 5.5, 5.6.
Column 2: *Congressional Quarterly Almanac, 1971;* House Committee Activity Reports, 1980.
Column 3: Charles B. Brownson, ed., *1980 Congressional Staff Directory.*
Column 4: Robert H. Salisbury, and Kenneth A. Shepsle, "Congressional Staff Turnover," *American Political Science Review* 75 (1981): 381–395, table 9.

NOTES: n.a.: not available.
[a]Mean half-life: That is, for each yearly staff cohort by committee, the number of years required for 50 percent turnover was computed and then averaged over all yearly cohorts, 1962–1978.
[b]Formerly Interstate & Foreign Commerce.

increasing the influence of individual members. Finally, there has been Congress's desire to achieve a greater measure of independence from the executive bureaucracy by broadening its own issue expertise.

Three characteristics of these new larger staffs deserve further attention—their professionalism, decentralization, and partisanship. When Congress was considering the Legislative Reorganization Act of 1946, it was concerned about the fitness of committee employees—their lack of professional qualifications and the fact that many of them were political patronage hacks. The LaFollette-Monroney committee proposed standards for the hiring of professional employees on the basis of fitness and nonpartisanship, and the creation of an Office of Congressional Personnel to refine and enforce the standards. Congress approved the standards, but rejected the organization to enforce them. They were wary of creating a centralized professional bureaucracy for the legislative branch. Thus the committees individually were left to enforce the standards, and their performance was uneven at the beginning.

Over the years since then committee staffs have, nevertheless, become increasingly professional, so that reformers today are no longer much concerned about unqualified, patronage appointees. A survey conducted in 1976 by the House Commission on Administrative Review (the Obey committee) found that over 40 percent of committee staffers had come to their present employment directly from other jobs on the Hill. Seventeen percent had come from executive duty in the federal, state, local, or military services, and 26 percent had come from the private sector. Sixty-four percent of committee staff directors had had previous experience in the House or Senate.

Those recruited from the private sector in recent years have included a group of young professionals, most frequently lawyers, who have come to Washington because they want to do a tour of public service, and in some cases to make their mark on the political system, before they settle down to private practice, or they may want to use public service as a steppingstone to good positions in private practice. There is nothing new in this career pattern; what is new is the number of talented professionals who have taken positions on congressional committees and subcommittees rather than in the executive establishment.

Staff growth and committee decentralization have gone hand in hand, so that a significant proportion of the committee staff increases have been at the subcommittee level, and many of these employees owe their principal loyalty not to the House as a whole, nor to its committees, but to subcommittees, and frequently to subcommittee chairmen who may be fairly junior members of the House. This individual loyalty, especially among the young professionals recruited from outside government, is a remarkable feature of the growth of staffs of certain committees, Energy and Commerce, for example. Michael J.

Malbin, in a recent study of congressional staffs, has called it a new system of "personalized committee staffing."[7]

As for partisanship of committee staffs, the Republican minority in the House has argued since the 1960s that a fixed proportion of the professional staff on each committee should be hired by, and assigned to, the committee minority. In response, the Legislative Reorganization Act of 1970 provided that no less than one-third of the committees' staff funds should be used for minority staff. But the Democratic majority ignored this requirement in organizing the House in 1971 and in subsequent years. The provision was revived in the Committee Reform Amendments of 1974, but Democrats again, in organizing the Ninety-fourth Congress (1975–1977), watered it down, denying the one-third guarantee for committee investigative staffs. As of 1980, the positions that had been designated for the minority were about 19 percent of all staff positions on standing committees, with considerable variation among the committees. Armed Services had no designated minority staff, Energy and Commerce 14 percent, Small Business 41 percent.

But these data are not a reliable measure of staff partisanship, for the problem is more complicated than is suggested by analyses or solutions that rely on fixed percentages. While it is true that Armed Services had no designated minority staff, all of its staff professionals were nonpartisan and available to members of both parties. The 14 percent of Energy and Commerce's staff designated for the minority were all grouped at the full-committee level. Thus 46 percent of the full-committee staff was assigned to the minority, while zero percent of the much larger subcommittee staffs were so designated, and these subcommittee staffs included some of the partisan, personalized staffs on which Malbin has reported. Recognizing some elements of this greater complexity, a task force of the Patterson committee recommended in 1979 that the committee review the merits of instituting "tripartite committee staffing," where committee staff would consist of majority-assigned, minority-assigned, and nonpartisan personnel categories. The full committee did not follow through, however.

Is Congress well served by these developments in committee staffing? As a result of staff activities committees have been able to manage a heavier workload than would have been possible with smaller, more centralized staffs. At the same time, the character of the staffs of some of the committees has contributed to the greater workload. Staffs that are personalized tend to be entrepreneurial as well. They are not just passive representatives of their subcommittee chairmen; they are expected to go out and drum up new business.

We are especially interested in the impact of these staff innovations on control by the whole House over its committees and on executive–legislative relations. We can examine the question of whole House control at two levels. First is the relation between staffs and their immediate employers, be they committees or subcommittees. Large professional staffs, whether they are in executive bureaus or congressional committees, tend to develop parochial and professional interests of their own. In the Executive the most divisive consequences of this are mitigated by hierarchical organization and procedures for review. Since Congress lacks effective hierarchy in its organization, one might presume that congressional staffs are highly autonomous, out of control. While there is ample room for argument about this, there is evidence that committee staffs are constrained by the need to satisfy the interests of their bosses. The principal reason is that congressional staffers do not have tenure as do civil servants; they can be fired on short notice.

A 1963 study of the Joint Committee on Atomic Energy, after documenting the crucial role played by the committee staff, asked whether the committee had surrendered a portion of its prized independence to its own staff.[8] After examining this possibility, the authors concluded that this was not the case. The influence of staff, they found, depended largely on the staff's ability to produce results that satisfied committee members; and this, they said, "is a far cry from staff control of the committee." This continues to be the case. A recent study concludes that it is very doubtful that much staff activity exceeds the bounds of member acceptance; and Malbin finds that on subcommittees where a personalized staffing system has developed, the subcommittee chairman is willing to give a great deal of authority to the staff because he can count on their loyalty. "The staffs, acting as surrogates for their 'bosses,' do as creditable a job of representing their interests as any attorney would for a client in a parallel situation outside Congress."[9]

A second level for considering the impact of staff on relations between the whole House and its committees focuses on the decentralization of committees. We have said that greater independence of subcommittees has made it more difficult for the House to control its parts. There is no question but that new staffing patterns have strongly reinforced this independence. The Patterson committee in its survey of members asked if committee staffs generally were too big, and if large committee staffs have contributed to fragmentation and unmanageability in the House. To both questions approximately 63 percent of the 184 members interviewed answered yes, 57 percent of Democrats and 73 percent of Republicans. Twenty-two percent said no and the remainder were undecided. Eighty percent approved of some kind of overall ceiling on committee and subcommittee staffs.

Finally, we can take another look at staff partisanship, in terms of its impact on the relations between committees and the whole House. We have observed that while the House relies on parties for organization in each Congress, it

relies on ad hoc majorities for policy and administrative oversight. Furthermore, that the degree of partisanship on the floor in questions of policy and
administration depends significantly on the degree of partisanship in committees. Different committees have responded in different ways to these environmental conditions, Armed Services, for example, by promoting nonpartisanship to the point of having a highly professional nonpartisan staff. The
question here is whether House rules that require or encourage committees
to designate staff members as majority and minority are likely to influence
committees toward practicing greater partisanship than they would otherwise.
On the one hand, minority staff, to earn their pay, may manufacture divisive
issues that make it more difficult for committee and floor leaders to put
together ad hoc majorities. An intrusion of sometimes artificial party partisanship on a great many issues in all committees would be out of synch with the
way Congress has operated since 1910. On the other hand, partisan staffs can
help to forge the compromises that are needed to assemble ad hoc majorities.
If committee staffs are under the control of their bosses, as we have said they
are, then presumably they will emphasize one or the other mode of conduct
depending on the committee members' preferences. Despite recent studies,
we do not presently have enough information on committee operations to be
more definitive on this important issue.

Turning next to committee staffs in the context of executive–legislative
relations, large professional committee staffs can lead to direct negotiations
between professional committee staff and professional bureau staff, especially
where the employees of the two branches are of the same profession—air
quality engineers, for example. In this case executive–legislative relations are
conducted at a third level, illustrated by figure 6.1. As in the case of committee–bureau relations in general, relations between the staffs of committees and
bureaus are frequent, inevitable, and desirable. They present a problem only
when they result in excluding the whole House and the President, and sometimes the full committee and the department secretary or agency head, from
control over policy and administration. The problem is not so much that
committee staffers will agree with the Administration too readily—some of
them are likely to be disaffected executive employees and others are out to
reform the system; but that, agreement or not, executive–legislative relations
will be conducted in a narrow, rather than a broad, perspective by participants,
none of whom have been elected. This result becomes more likely as the House
becomes more bureaucratized by the increase in size and professionalism of
its committee and subcommittee staffs.

Dubitable staff relations between the legislature and the Executive are more
likely to develop where committees and bureaus have already adopted a pathological form of executive–legislative relations than otherwise. The following

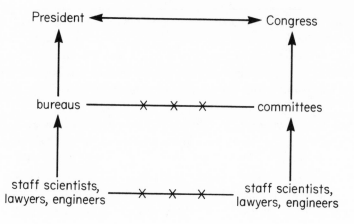

FIGURE 6.1

Executive–Legislative Relations with Strong Professional Staffs

example relating to the Environmental Protection Agency (EPA) and derived from a Brookings Institution study by R. Shep Melnick illustrates the point.[10]

Example. In 1974 the Administrator of EPA, Russell E. Train, acted deliberately to set his agency apart from the President and the Executive and to form an alliance with congressional committees that were in control of the opposition party and were opposed to the Administration's views on the air pollution control program and other programs as well. This can be seen in the legislative history of two proposed amendments to the Clean Air Act of 1970.

In the early 1970s, EPA proposed to allow polluters to use dispersion techniques in addition to constant control techniques to meet air quality standards. Constant controls, such as stack scrubbers and precipitors and the use of low-sulfur coal, reduce the amount of pollution sent into the air. Dispersion techniques, such as tall stacks and varying pollutant output according to meteorological conditions (otherwise known as intermittent control systems or ICS), do not by themselves reduce emissions, but instead reduce local concentrations by spreading the pollutants over wider areas.

Environmentalists challenged in federal courts the use of dispersion techniques on the basis that they were not authorized by the Clean Air Act. The courts supported the challengers, and as a result the Nixon Administration proposed an amendment to the act that would specifically authorize dispersion. Russell Train refused to accede to the President's request that he support the amendment. While he transmitted it to Congress, Train called the amendment "legislative language which would implement the views of other federal agencies."

The Environmental Pollution subcommittee of the Senate Committee on Environment and Public Works, chaired by Edmund S. Muskie (D. ME), was strongly sympathetic with the views of the environmentalists and failed, therefore, to report the Administration's proposal to the Senate. Train later told the press that he had scored a "great and glorious victory" in resisting White House pressure, and thereafter EPA's political executives chose to throw their lot with Muskie rather than with the Administration—a pattern of executive–legislative relations that continued during the Ford Administration.

The Clean Air Act required that EPA set and enforce uniform national standards for air quality. Environmental groups sought to require EPA also to adopt procedures that would prevent any significant deterioration of air quality in areas where it was already purer than required by the national standards (otherwise known as prevention of significant deterioration or PSD). The EPA initially held that the statute did not require such higher standards and that any effort to implement them would have enormous policy consequences, for it would oblige the agency, in effect, to replace uniform national standards with hundreds of localized ambient air standards based on existing levels of pollution.

Nonetheless the Sierra Club sued EPA in federal courts, and the environmentalists' position was upheld. As a consequence, President Nixon and after him Ford proposed to amend the Clean Air Act to eliminate PSD. But Senator Muskie's subcommittee was strongly favorable to the concept, and EPA turned tail. Train refused to endorse the President's initiative. Instead he submitted a set of proposed amendments to the act which was radically different from those submitted by the White House. Train's assistant administrator for air claimed that Train survived "only because Richard Nixon did not."

The abnormally close relations that developed between the agency and the Senate subcommittee tended to exclude from decision making on environmental policy not only the White House but also the full Congress. Indeed, EPA and the subcommittee did not even try to build congressional support in some cases, relying instead on direct relations with each other and on the courts. In this context they used a number of decision-making techniques that required unusually heavy participation by the staffs of the two units. Muskie expected EPA to consult with him or his staff on major policy decisions. Muskie's staff, under the leadership of Leon G. Billings, held frequent meetings with EPA officials—assistant administrators, directors of divisions and offices in Washington, regional directors, laboratory chiefs, and lower-level personnel—where important policies were discussed and sometimes negotiated and agreed to.

Under Muskie's direction the committee staff, with the aid of agency personnel, drafted statutory language of extraordinary detail and specificity with the results that the full House and Senate had difficulty comprehending what was being done and the agency's top administrators ended up with relatively little discretion to make their programs consistent with the policies of the President and the programs of other governmental agencies.

On at least one occasion the staff drafted language that may have been intended to mislead the Congress. In response to overwhelming public, state, and local opposition to EPA's efforts to reduce air pollution in major cities by restricting parking facilities, the House in 1977 undertook to repeal authority for EPA to require such action (otherwise known as independent source review, or ISR). The conference report on the 1977 amendments of the Clean Air Act stated that "the administrator would be prohibited outright from requiring indirect source review, either directly or indirectly." But Senate staff members who favored parking restrictions were able to draft the amendment's language so that it failed to shut the door on regulation of independent sources and, therefore, did not match the legislative intent stated in the conference report.

Faced with public, presidential, and congressional opposition to ISR, the EPA administrator was understandably cautious about proceeding with such regulations. But a federal court, with an eye on the statutory language, ordered him to do so. This result was, indeed, what the staff had in mind in drafting the language. In this case and others committee staff and those within the agency who cooperated closely with them have relied heavily on the eagerness of federal courts, especially the Circuit Court of Appeals for the District of Columbia, to interpret environmental statutes and to issue "action forcing" decisions. As Melnick says: "While Congress as a whole shouted out its opposition to ISR, the court heard only the congressional insiders who wrote—one is compelled to say surreptitiously—the purposely convoluted wording of the statute."

In addition to drafting detailed, little noted, and complex statutory clauses with large policy implications, the Muskie committee staff wrote statements interpreting the clauses, which they published in histories of legislation that were intended for use by the agency and the courts as well as the Congress. Courts, thus, have formed a "critical link between [certain] congressional committee members and their eager staffs, on the one hand, and those [staffers] within the agency willing to take risks for which they can evade responsibility, on the other."

Finally it should be observed that the pathological relations in this example between committee and agency and the staffs of the two units matured at the time of Watergate, under a crisis-ridden presidency. Once established, however, they continued under the next President.

PART III

Relations Between the Executive and Congress

7

Authorization Procedures

Section 834 of the House Rules, first adopted in 1837, provides that: "No appropriation shall be reported in any general appropriation bill . . . for any expenditure not previously authorized by law"; and Section 846 that: "No bill carrying appropriations shall be reported by any committee not having jurisdiction to report appropriations. . . ."

THESE RULES (there are similar Senate rules) are the basis for a fundamental distinction between authorization procedures on the one hand and appropriation procedures on the other. Although there are exceptions, government programs must be authorized before money is appropriated, usually in annual appropriations bills, to carry them out. These rules are also the basis for an important distinction between two types of congressional committees: legislative committees, with responsibility for authorizing programs; and the appropriations committees, for providing funds. Finally, the Budget Control Act of 1974 inaugurated certain preappropriation procedures which have their own work groups, budget committees, in the House and Senate.

This chapter covers authorizations; the next one appropriations; and chapter 9 reports on the new budget procedures. In all chapters we pay special attention to the techniques devised by Congress to control the Executive's initiation and implementation of authorizing legislation and of the budget; and, within this context, to reciprocal relations among the three procedures and the three types of committees.

Control Techniques in Authorizing Legislation

Several techniques of control are available to Congress in authorizing programs. The first is control over the policies that are to be pursued—the standards and criteria to be followed by administrators. Normally the President proposes these and Congress approves, modifies, or rejects them.

A second technique is control over the duration of programs. Programs can be authorized without limit of time, in which case they remain in effect until repealed, or for a fixed number of years, as few as one, after which they terminate unless they are reauthorized.

Third, there is control over the amount of money that can be appropriated. Programs can be authorized without money limits, in which case the statutes provide that "such funds as may be necessary are hereby authorized to be appropriated," or with limits that can take many forms. For example, a program of research and development on converting salt water to fresh water might be authorized for five years with a money limit for the full five-year period, or with individual limits on how much can be spent in each of the five years, or with limits for each component of the program, such as research, demonstration, and the building of pilot plants. Money in the amounts of these limits need not be appropriated, for the right of Congress not to appropriate for a program that is authorized in law is considered to be a fundamental part of the appropriation power of the legislature. At the same time, the money limits cannot be exceeded unless the statute is amended.

The fourth technique is control over administrative organization, personnel, and procedures for implementing programs. Personnel controls and the legislative veto procedure are treated in chapters 10 and 11.

Use of the last three types of control depends on how the first one has been employed. If the policy standards in authorization statutes are specific, Congress will have less incentive to adopt time, money, and administrative controls. At one extreme are the so-called entitlement programs, in which the statutes state explicitly the conditions for performance—for example, a 10-percent disabled veteran is entitled to X dollars per month, to be adjusted annually according to the cost-of-living index. For such programs money limits are scarcely relevant. Except for administrative costs, the only way to control expenditures is to change the definition of the entitlement.

The specificity of program standards in authorization statutes also affects the relative influence and control of legislative and appropriations committees over governmental programs. If the standards are so specific as to constitute entitlements, little discretion remains available for appropriation procedures. The money for veterans' benefits needs to be appropriated, to be sure, but the amounts are fully predetermined. In the language of budgeters, entitlement programs are "uncontrollables."

The growth of entitlements in recent years has been a remarkable feature of American government. Whereas entitlement payments to individuals for such programs as social security, military and civil service retirement, unemployment assistance, medical care, veterans' benefits, student assistance, food stamps and other nutrition programs, housing assistance, welfare and public assistance amounted to less than one-third (31.7 percent) of total federal outlays in 1970, the percentage had risen to almost one-half (48 percent) by 1981, due to: demographic changes; liberalization of entitlement standards in the authorization statutes of existing programs, including cost-of-living escalator allowances; and the authorizing of new entitlements. Although this development is in no way the result of a conspiracy of the legislative against the appropriations committees to control governmental policies, not even necessarily of competition between them, it nonetheless has had profound effects on appropriation and budget procedures, as we shall see in the next two chapters.

For many other programs the standards in authorization statutes are broad and general, which may be due to the nature of the subject matter, or to lack of consensus among legislators on what the specific standards should be, or to some other reason. Whatever the cause, Congress sometimes resorts to spelling out administrative details in the statutes in order to control what would otherwise be a very wide executive discretion. A study of consumer legislation enacted between 1966 and 1973 has shown a strong inverse correlation between specificity of standards and statutory provisions relating to administrative organization and procedures.[1]

In addition, Congress practices a continuing influence over programs that have broad legislative standards by means of annual appropriation procedures and, if the authorization statutes include time limits, by means also of periodic reviews by legislative committees. Before 1960, programs were authorized generally without limits of time, so that Congress relied principally on appropriation procedures to control them. Since then Congress has been intent on authorizing programs for short periods, so that today a very large proportion of the expenditures proposed in the President's annual Budget for controllable programs (that is, excluding entitlements and other fixed expenditures like interest on the national debt) cannot be approved in appropriation bills until Congress has passed and the President has signed legislation authorizing these expenditures for the one year, or in some cases for several years.

The foreign aid program has been subject to annual authorizations from the beginning in 1948[2] and the space program (NASA), from its initiation in

1958, but the most significant development came in 1961 when for the first time Congress required that expenditures for the procurement of weapons systems—missiles, aircraft, and ships—be authorized annually. Previously the military departments had had permanent, open-ended authorizations to purchase any weapons they needed, and congressional control over this important activity had, therefore, been limited to annual appropriation procedures.[3] Soon after the Armed Services Committees had begun to consider annual authorizations for weapons systems, they realized that they had not achieved effective control by attending to procurement alone; that the vast expenditures for research, development, test, and evaluation of weapons systems, which preceded procurement, pretty well determined which weapons would be bought. They therefore extended the annual authorization requirement to these antecedent activities as well. Thereafter Congress progressively broadened annual authorizations to cover all research, development, test, and evaluation carried on by the Department of Defense (to commence in 1964); procurement of tanks and other tracked combat vehicles (1966); personnel strengths in each of the reserve branches (1967); procurement of other weapons (1969); personnel strengths of the regular forces (1970); operation and maintenance expenses (1982); ammunition and communications and supply equipment (1983). In addition, expenditures for nuclear weapons produced by the Department of Energy (formerly Atomic Energy Commission) are authorized annually. Congressional jurisdiction over this program was transferred in 1977 from the Joint Committee on Atomic Energy, which was abolished, to the committees on armed services.

Annual authorizations have also been adopted in recent years for most or all expenditures of the Departments of State, Justice, Energy, Transportation, Housing and Urban Development, and those of other agencies, including the National Science Foundation, Environmental Protection Agency, and the CIA.

This remarkable development in American government has increased the influence of legislative committees vis-à-vis appropriations committees and also the influence of Congress vis-à-vis the Executive. The move toward annual authorizations represents in part a move by Congress's legislative committees to gain oversight responsibilities which they had forfeited to the committees on appropriations by enacting permanent, open-ended authorizations previously. As for the Executive, President Dwight D. Eisenhower, in his last budget message, objected to all annual authorizations and recommended that Congress eliminate the requirement from all statutes. The Office of Management and Budget (OMB) has argued consistently that questions of time, money, and administration be omitted from authorization procedures and considered only in connection with annual appropriations. In 1971 the OMB stated in a report to the Joint Committee on Congressional Operations that: "All authorizations should be removed from the annual cycle and be made effective for longer periods of time, at least two years, and *preferably* five years, or *an indefinite period.* A greater portion of the authorization legislation [should] be stated in program terms instead of in dollar amounts, leaving the amount of dollars to be determined by the Congress when it acts on appropriations" (emphasis added).

Although OMB has argued its case largely in terms of efficiency—for example, annual authorizations take too much time of executive officers who must testify each year before two sets of congressional committees—its real concerns have been based more broadly on executive–legislative relations. Two annual reviews by Congress are likely to result in more restrictions on executive freedom of action than one. But more than this, the legislative committees are likely to be less sympathetic to the point of view of OMB than are the appropriations committees. OMB and the appropriations committees share a preoccupation with economy in government and cutting back the spending proposals of the bureaus; whereas the legislative committees are likely to be more sympathetic to the programs that they have authorized and more supportive of the bureaus that implement them. Indeed, the legislative committees have used annual authorizations in some cases to enable them to serve better as Congress's interpreter of programs that they believe to have suffered unduly in the hands of OMB and the appropriations committees.

Evaluation of Short-term Authorizations

To evaluate this turn to short-term authorizations we should examine it in terms of Congress's role in oversight and control and the Executive's in initiation. For Congress, annual and other short-term authorizations provide oversight from the legislative committees' point of view, which is likely to be different from that provided by the appropriations committees. Although the legislative committees are frequently more favorable to the agencies and their programs, this is not necessarily so; and in any case, the active exercise of oversight by legislative committees is unexceptionable in terms of our analytical model.

Example. Prior to 1977, operations of the FBI were reviewed regularly only by the appropriations committees, which were uniformly favorable to the agency, frequently approving more money for the FBI than the President had proposed in his

123

budget, that is, restoring cuts that had been made by OMB in the Bureau's initial requests for funds. The appropriations committees were unresponsive to the considerable public criticism that surfaced in the late 1960s and 1970s over the FBI's operations in domestic political surveillance, and it was in part in response to this that Congress initiated legislative provisions requiring annual authorization of all expenditures of the agency. At the subsequent authorization hearings before the Judiciary committees the Bureau's activities were scrutinized and questioned as never before.

Example. For many years, during the 1950s and 1960s, the House Appropriations Committee was unusually critical of the foreign aid program, consistently reducing the President's budget. However, the program was subject to annual authorizations, in which the foreign affairs committees were more supportive; and as a result the House Appropriations Committee was constrained in its efforts to slash it. If the House passed an authorization of $4 billion in March, it would be perverse for the Appropriations Committee to recommend only $2 billion in April, whereas this would not be so if the program had been authorized permanently and without short-term money targets. The director of the foreign aid program didn't complain at all about having to testify before four committees instead of two. He relished the opportunity to establish a strong case for foreign aid with the foreign affairs committees prior to having to appear before Appropriations. But, of course, this worm can turn, and it did. In the early 1970s Senator J. William Fulbright (D. AR) and the Senate Foreign Relations Committee which he chaired became more critical of foreign aid than the House Appropriations Committee.

Continuing with an evaluation of annual and short-term authorizations from the point of view of Congress, they may provide an opportunity for Congress to watch and guide new programs in their developmental and experimental years. The House Committee on Education and Labor has in the past followed a policy of authorizing new programs for very limited periods of time, progressively lengthening these as the programs have proved themselves.

Annual and short-term authorizations can also lead to changes in the policies and procedures of programs where such changes may be hard to achieve through appropriation procedures because of the rules prohibiting legislation in appropriation bills. It was by means of provisions added to the annual authorization bills for weapons systems and for foreign aid that Congress limited the President's authority in military and foreign policy near the end of the Vietnam War, not by provisions in the annual bills appropriating money for these activities. The principal reason that Senator Fulbright and the Senate Foreign Relations Committee initiated the provision in 1972 to require annual authorization of all Department of State expenditures was to control foreign policy, not money.

Annual and short-term authorizations provide an opportunity to educate members who are not on the appropriations committees and to educate the public.

Example. When annual authorization of weapons systems was initiated in the early 1960s, Carl Vinson (D. GA), chairman of the House Armed Services Committee, said on the floor:

"I am afraid that the end result of the procedure [which we have followed in the past] was that members of the Appropriations Committee were the only ones in Congress who actually had very much knowledge of the tremendous programs and expenditures which the Congress was called upon to pass on each year. . . . But, it is my intention, and the intention of the Armed Services Committee, to have [this new provision for annual authorization of weapons systems] mean a great deal more than merely bringing the members of the committee into this area of knowledge. It is our firm intention that this law will mean that the members of the House itself will have the very maximum amount of information which is possible to reveal concerning these programs, and be afforded some opportunity to express agreement or disagreement with the course being pursued in our defense and offensive capabilities."

And indeed this is what has happened. Since 1960 the most important issues relating to weapons systems have been revealed and debated in connection with annual authorization bills, not appropriation bills—for example, manned bombers versus missiles, nuclear versus conventional power for warships, missile defense, the ABM, the MX missile.

In this connection annual and short-term authorizations may increase the power of the whole House over its committees. There is more debate on authorization bills than on bills making appropriations, so that the whole House gets to say more. As we shall see in the next chapter, certain norms that operate in appropriation procedures, most notably the norms of economy and unity, impose a consensus and discourage dissent. These norms do not operate in authorization procedures. Thus there have been more significant dissents in reports of the armed services committees on authorizing weapons systems than in those of the appropriations committees in providing funds for the same. Also, it is easier for dissenting members to offer floor amendments to authorization bills than to appropriation bills, since points of order can be made against amendments to authorization bills only if they are nongermane, whereas in appropriation bills many amendments can be ruled out as legislation.

At the same time, annual authorizations have crowded the legislative calendar. Jamie L. Whitten (D. MS), chairman of the House Appropriations Committee, believes that: "the system just cannot digest the increased legislative volume represented by the proliferation of annual authorizations."[4] In some instances they have prevented timely action on appropriation bills which cannot be passed until the authorizations have been enacted (unless the House agrees to suspend its rules against unauthorized appropriations). This timing problem was addressed in the Budget Control Act of 1974, which requires that legislation providing new budget authority for a given fiscal year (the fiscal year begins on October 1) be reported to the House and Senate by their legislative committees before May 15 of the preceding fiscal year. But since there is no time limit on full House consideration and enactment of authorizations proposed by committees, this provision has not solved the timing problem. An alternative proposed by some members, including the chairman of the House Appropriations Committee, would require that authorizations take effect in the fiscal year after the one in which they are enacted. This would solve the timing problem; and it would also require the Executive to cast the annual budget in accordance with authorization statutes that have been approved by Congress. As Chairman Whitten has testified: "Enactment of authorizations prior to submission of the Budget would accomplish maximum congressional impact on the Budget, permit timely consideration of appropriation bills, and would reduce the extensive use of continuing resolutions, which further tends to diminish the influence of Congress on policy."[5]

Turning next to annual and short-term authorizations from the point of view of executive leadership, there is no question but that they reduce administrative efficiency. There is more time spent by executive officers before committees of Congress. Because appropriations are not available for expenditure until the annual authorizations have been passed, governmental agencies have been held in limbo and forced to operate on the basis of temporary continuing resolutions.

At the same time that annual authorizations may be troublesome to the Executive in terms of efficiency, they can be of assistance to executive leadership in a number of ways. They may provide support for presidential programs that are unpopular with the appropriations committees and suffer continually at their hands, such as foreign aid.

Annual and short-term authorizations can also aid the President in shaking up the bureaucracy and getting control over ongoing programs. When the authorization of a program expires, the proposal to reauthorize it is initiated in the Executive and must be reviewed in the Executive Office of the President before it is forwarded to Congress. This procedure gives the President a greater opportunity than he might have otherwise to influence the outcome.

On balance, then, one should not dismiss annual and short-term authorizations out of hand, as did President Eisenhower and the OMB, because they adversely affect efficiency. Efficiency is not the only criterion for evaluation, nor necessarily the most important one. Recall the maxim that men who think first and foremost of efficiency are seldom democrats. And in any case the OMB has used efficiency as a pretext for other motives.

Short-term authorizations, as a means for involving the legislative committees in periodic review of agency programs, should be seen as a creative response of Congress to the increased size and complexity of government. The Executive is ever searching for new techniques—such as planning-programming-budgeting systems (*ppbs*), management by objective (*mbo*), systems analysis, evaluation, and many others—to control the bureaus and their programs. Congress should do the same or its influence in policy and administration will decline in relation to that of the Executive. In this context, Congress's liveliness in developing techniques such as short-term authorizations and the legislative veto (which we discuss in chapter 11) is to be applauded, while at the same time Congress should give attention to improving them and confining them to their most effective uses. It ill behooves the Executive to object so strenuously to Congress's efforts to improve American government.[6]

At the same time, annual authorizations should be compared with alternative techniques which might accomplish similar ends—for example, three- or five-year authorizations, investigations, legislative vetos, and combinations of these and other techniques. For several of the benefits of short-term authorizations that we have given, benefits to the Congress and to the President, annual authorizations may nonetheless not be the most effective technique. There is a risk that, as yearly exercises, they will become too automatic, too routine. Also, it is inappropriate to talk in terms of uniform time limits for all governmental programs. As a Joint Committee on Congressional Operations said in a report to Congress in 1971:

> These authorization structures are not neutral. Each type results in a different kind or level of committee and congressional control and oversight over program management and operation by the Executive. Each of these structures reflects a basic policy decision by the committee involved. . . . Federal programs and activities have differing administrative requirements. And the degree of consensus on or amount of support for their objectives and requirements also varies from program to program. Thus it is unlikely that any single procedural change or formula for scheduling authorization enactments or funding conditions can be devised and agreed upon within Congress. . . .

8

Appropriation Procedures

CONGRESS'S most effective ways and means for controlling policymaking where the Executive has been granted broad discretion and for controlling policy implementation have been those associated with appropriations.

The President's initiative, which constitutes Congress's agenda in appropriations, is *The Budget of the United States Government*. Submitted to Congress each January, it is both a program of action and a report on past activity. As such it is a good instrument for congressional oversight. For each major program there is included a justification of the President's proposal for the next fiscal year, which begins on October 1, and a comparison of this with expenditures and activities for the year underway and the previous year. (See table 8.1.)

The President's Budget is referred to the appropriations committees for review and action. The House Appropriations Committee, the chamber's largest and one of three exclusive committees, has fifty-five members and a normal ratio of 3:2 for the majority party. There the Budget is divided and assigned to thirteen subcommittees, each with jurisdiction over programs of certain departments and agencies—for example, Appropriations Subcommittee on Agriculture, Rural Development, and Related Agencies; Appropriations Subcommittee on Defense. Each appropriations subcommittee holds extensive hearings, marks up an appropriations bill, and drafts a report. The full committee meets to review and discuss the subcommittee bill and report and normally approves them with few, if any, changes. The bill is then reported to the floor of the House, and, for reasons to be explained, the House usually approves it also with few, if any, changes.

The Budget Control Act of 1974 inaugurated a range of congressional preappropriation procedures, called budget procedures, through which the

TABLE 8.1

The Budget of the United States Government, Fiscal Year 1981 [1]

NATIONAL SCIENCE FOUNDATION

Federal Funds
General and special funds:
RESEARCH AND RELATED ACTIVITIES [2]

For necessary expenses in carrying out the purposes of the National Science Foundation Act of 1950, as amended (42 U.S.C. 1861–1875), title IX of the National Defense Education Act of 1958 (42 U.S.C. 1876–1879), and the Act to establish a National Medal of Science (42 U.S.C. 1880–1881); services as authorized by 5 U.S.C. 3109; *lease of one aircraft with option to purchase;* maintenance and operation of aircraft and purchase of flight services for research support; hire of passenger motor vehicles; not to exceed [$2,500] *$5,000* for official reception and representation expenses; not to exceed [$58,100,000] *$60,700,000* for program development and management; uniforms or allowances therefor, as authorized by law (5 U.S.C. 5901–5902); rental of conference rooms in the District of Columbia; and reimbursement of the General Services Administration for security guard services; [$906,050,000] *$1,056,800,000* to remain available until expended [September 30, 1981: *Provided,* That not more than $60,-900,000 shall be available for Applied Science and Research Applications]: [3] *Provided* [*further*], That receipts for scientific support services and materials furnished by the National Research Centers and other National Science Foundation supported research facilities may be credited to this appropriation: [4] *Provided further,* That to the extent that the amount appropriated is less than the total amount authorized to be appropriated for included program activities, all amounts, including floors and ceilings, specified in the authorizing Act for those program activities or their subactivities shall be reduced proportionally [5] [: *Provided further,* That if an institution of higher education receiving funds hereunder determines after affording notice and opportunity for hearing to an individual attending, or employed by, such institution, that such individual has, after the date of enactment of this Act, willfully refused to obey a lawful regulation or order of such institution and that such refusal was of a serious nature and contributed to the disruption of the administration of such institution, then the institution shall deny any further payment to, or for the benefit of, such individual]. [6] (*Department of Housing and Urban Development—Independent Agencies Appropriation Act, 1980;* [7] *additional authorizing legislation to be proposed* [8])

Program and Financing (in thousands of dollars) [9]

Identification code 49-0100-0-1-251	1979 actual	1980 est.	1981 est.
Program by activities:			
Direct program:			
1. Mathematical and physical sciences	208,865	226,412	264,700
2. Astronomical, atmospheric, Earth, and ocean sciences	211,615	217,862	240,000
3. U.S. Antarctic program	51,091	55,840	63,400
4. Ocean drilling programs	11,625	19,475	29,600
5. Biological, behavioral, and social sciences	154,704	166,531	181,100
6. Engineering and applied science	109,860	110,334	134,500
7. Scientific, technological, and international affairs	23,562	27,103	28,100
8. Cross-Directorate Programs	16,863	26,025	54,700
9. Program development and management	54,766	60,564	60,700
Total direct program	842,951	910,146	1,056,800

Author's Explanatory Notes

1. Reprinted from The Budget of the United States Government, Fiscal Year 1981, appendix, p. 935.
2. This is the language of the previous year's appropriation statute. The President's Budget proposes that the material enclosed in brackets be deleted and that the language printed in italics be added.

(continued on next page)

President's Budget must now pass before it is referred to the appropriations committees. These procedures, which are analyzed in the next chapter, require the participation of new budget committees in both Houses as well as of legislative committees and appropriations committees, and they have, as their designers intended, affected the way Congress deals with appropriations. We shall, where appropriate, compare appropriation procedures before and after the Budget Control Act.

Norms of Appropriation Procedures

Certain norms of conduct have operated in the House Appropriations Committee, the most important of which are economy, unity, and seniority along with apprenticeship and specialization. Richard F. Fenno, Jr., was the first to specify these norms in his classic study of the committee, completed in the mid-1960s.[1]

ECONOMY

Members of the Appropriations Committee view themselves as guardians of the Treasury. They emphasize cutting requests for money. The Executive is looked upon with suspicion and distrust. Fenno showed that liberal northern Democrats who serve on Appropriations experience changes in terms of this economy norm that enable one to distinguish them from their liberal northern Democratic colleagues who are not on the Appropriations Committee.

At the same time, the committee, in practicing its economy norm, does not get far out of line from the tenor of the whole House. It is subject to two sets of expectations of the whole: one, that the committee should supply money for programs authorized by Congress, and the other, that the committee should fund these programs in as economical a manner as possible. The committee has adapted to these expectations by concentrating its budget-cutting efforts within

3–6. These are statutory provisos. The President proposed that 3 and 6 be deleted, but Congress retained them, the first with modifications.

7. At the end of the paragraph and printed in italics within parentheses is a citation of the previous year's appropriation act from which the preceding text is taken.

8. The note concerning additional authorizing legislation refers to the fact that the National Science Foundation is subject to annual authorizations. One of the provisos in the statutory language, marked 5, further spells out relations between the authorization and appropriation.

9. The Program schedule, with its three columns, is for Congress's information. The last column is the proposed budget for the fiscal year that begins October 1, 1980, and ends September 30, 1981. Its total corresponds to that in the proposed statutory language. The middle column is estimated expenditures for the fiscal year in progress, and the first column reports expenditures for the last completed fiscal year. The Budget also includes a narrative statement of objectives, performance data for each program, schedules of obligations by expenditure categories, details relating to personnel numbers and average salaries, and other information not reproduced here.

a "safe" zone, defined at the upper level by the President's Budget and at the lower, by last year's expenditures. Three-quarters of the 575 House Appropriations Committee decisions that Fenno examined were below the President's estimates; just about this same proportion was higher than the previous year's level. "On the whole the Committee supports programs and effects economies —*both at the same time.*" All the same, there were significant variations among the programs so that 27 percent of them were cut below the zone, and 26 percent were either at or above the top barrier.[2]

UNITY

Subcommittee members believe that disagreements should be ironed out within the subcommittee so that the subcommittee can present a united front to the full committee; and the full committee wants to present a united front to the floor. Unless this is done, so dictates the norm, the sacred cow of economy will be butchered on the floor.

There are several important consequences of this unity norm. The work of the Appropriations Committee and its subcommittees has been nonpartisan on all but a few issues. We should reflect on this. Congress's role is principally oversight and control of the President's proposed programs. Its most important means for oversight and control, especially where there is broad executive discretion, are those associated with appropriations. Yet these have been largely nonpartisan.

Another consequence of the norm of unity is that the recommendations of the subcommittees are infrequently changed by the full committee or by the whole House. Reciprocity prevails among the subcommittees, since this is a way of making unity effective. Members of the subcommittee on appropriations for agriculture will vote for the markup and report of the subcommittee on appropriations for defense in the expectation that the latter will in turn support them. As a result the full committee makes few changes in the subcommittees' recommendations. Also due to the norm of unity, it is infrequent that the committee is challenged and overruled on the floor. When it is, it usually requires a combination of several factors: an issue of significant policy importance that is easily understandable by the ordinary member; a split in the ranks of the Appropriations Committee; and participation, cooperation, and direction by the House leadership in the effort to overrule the committee.

SENIORITY, SPECIALIZATION, AND APPRENTICESHIP

There is a great deal of expertise on the appropriations subcommittees. Often three or four members of a subcommittee will know more about a department or agency than the political executives who are testifying before the committee in defense of the President's budget. An assistant secretary of

Interior who is explaining and defending his department's budget, for example, may have been on the job for no more than several months. Only career employees can match the appropriations subcommittee members' knowledge of the department. For this reason the subcommittees hear more testimony from career employees than from political executives, and this fact has important implications for executive–legislative relations. Also, junior members of the committee are expected to follow the lead of more experienced members while they are acquiring the necessary expertise.

DIFFERENTIATED ROLE OF SENATE APPROPRIATIONS COMMITTEE

The Senate Appropriations Committee and its subcommittees have not duplicated the work of the House committee for the most part. As a rule the Senate units do not review the budget estimates comprehensively nor in detail. Most of the subcommittees, most of the time, sit rather as appeals boards to which departments and interests that are dissatisfied with what the House has done make a case for increases above those amounts. In this situation, the agenda of a Senate subcommittee is usually the department secretary's letter and testimony in which the secretary summarizes changes in the President's budget made by the House and states which of these changes the department feels it can "live with" and which changes it requests the Senate to overrule. Some of the Senate subcommittees have considered a number of appropriations de novo, but even in this case they fail to make thorough, detailed, program-by-program reviews as do the House subcommittees. Thus the activities of the two Houses in appropriations are not a typical example of bicameralism, where each House does roughly the same thing, as is the case with the legislative committees of the two chambers. In appropriations oversight the Senate has differentiated its role from that of the House.

HAVE THE NORMS CHANGED?

Two recent studies of appropriation and budget procedures by Allen Schick and Lance T. LeLoup conclude that the appropriations committees can no longer be characterized by these norms, due principally to the congressional reforms of the 1970s that have attenuated budget cutting as the guiding objective of the House committee, led to independence of committee members which is contrary to collegiality and unity, fostered partisanship in the committees and juniority in opposition to seniority, and forced the Senate committee into a more active role than mere appeals forum.[3] These conclusions are exaggerated insofar as they relate to committee performance in appropriations.

Schick claims that House Appropriations Committee members have been converted from budget cutters and economizers into claimants for money, promoters of programs, and spenders, a claim which he supports with data showing "the paucity of real budget cuts" between 1970 and 1975. On close examination, however, the data for these years are not significantly different from those for the preceding twenty years.[4] Public statements of committee members, especially the chairman, give little support to the view that the committee has abandoned or substantially altered its concern for economy. In 1980 testimony before the House Budget Committee, chairman Jamie L. Whitten (D. MS) said, with obvious satisfaction:

> The value of the annual review by the Appropriations Committee, as an arm of Congress, is proven by the fact that—of the portion of the Budget that is handled by the Appropriations Committee—for each of the thirty-five years since World War II, appropriations have been well below the Budget requests with only one small exception. . . . In fact, I would point out that only one year—just one year—since World War II has the action of Congress, through the recommendations of the Appropriations Committee on spending items within its jurisdiction, been over the President's budget requests. . . . So the traditional authorization and appropriation process has served the Congress and the Nation well.

There is no question but that reforms in the 1970s of congressional organization and procedures, especially those for open meetings, selection of appropriations subcommittee chairmen (but not chairmen of other subcommittees) by the majority party caucus, and giving greater weight to members' preferences in subcommittee assignments, have promoted independence among committee members and simultaneously demoted collegiality. Nonetheless, the destructive impact of these reforms on the norms of unity and seniority should not be overestimated. In support of unity Fenno cited the absence of dissent in committee reports (which are in fact reports of the subcommittees) and the success of the committee in warding off floor amendments to its bills. With respect to the first of these, there has been a significant growth in recent years in the number of separate statements in committee reports, leading Schick to observe: "The triumph of individualism has been reflected in the abandonment of the tradition against public dissent in committee reports. . . . This tradition no longer prevails." He notes that whereas Fenno reported for the years prior to congressional reform that 94 percent of the bills reported by the Appropriations Committee received unanimous endorsement, in recent years three-quarters of the regular appropriation bills have carried separate expressions of opinion by one or more committee members.[5]

Here again one must look carefully at the data. For the five fiscal years 1977–1981, the average yearly number of separate statements in reports on the thirteen regular appropriation bills was 1.7 per bill. Of these, however, only 18 percent were related to the economy norm; the remainder were statements concerning the administration of programs or other expressions of individual views which had little or no impact on economy.

Example. In "Additional Views" in the committee report on the Treasury Department appropriation bill for fiscal year 1978, four Democrats, Edward I. Koch (NY), Max Baucus (MT), Norman D. Dicks (WA), and Louis Stokes (OH) objected to paying funds to former President Richard M. Nixon for office expenses, under the Former Presidents Act, while Nixon, according to them, owed back taxes to the Internal Revenue Service.

The point is that the unity norm relates principally to funding levels of programs rather than to these other views, so that growth of the latter, while it may represent some sort of a "triumph of individualism," is largely irrelevant. Of the separate statements relating to the economy norm, over 50 percent were signed by only one member, and only one statement was labeled by its author as a minority view. The others were called additional, supplemental, or separate views, and of these more than one-third were statements, mostly by Republicans, supporting more spending on national defense.

What about the committee's success on the floor? All House committees in recent years have been subject to more floor challenges as a result of greater "democratization" of the House and the determination of junior members to participate more actively in the legislative process. But the Appropriations Committee has maintained its strong position in this regard. In the period before 1970 the whole House overruled the committee in approximately 10 percent of the cases, approving the committee's recommendations in 90 percent. These proportions held in the years after 1970, as has the committee's success in defeating amendments it opposes.[6] In 1980 more than 150 amendments were offered on the floor to the twelve regular appropriation bills, of which 60 percent were approved (the Foreign Operations bill was not considered on the floor). Of those adopted 81 percent were accepted by nonrecorded votes, many of the amendments having been sponsored by the subcommittee or approved by the subcommittee chairman on the floor. In none of these cases did the chairman request a record vote. For all twelve bills only eighteen amendments were approved by record votes, eight of them dealing with funding and ten with legislative riders such as the use of funds for abortions or to enforce rules against prayer in schools. Of the funding amendments, seven were opposed by both the subcommittee chairman and a majority of his subcommittee, and of these, two increased recommended appropriations and five decreased them, four by across-the-board cuts.[7]

Given, then, the increase in number and controversiality of governmental programs in recent years, the norm of unity, when measured by committee reports and floor amendments, appears to be robust in the internal operations of the House Appropriations Committee. Furthermore, it is sufficiently robust, combined with the norm of efficiency, to continue to subdue partisanship in the committee, even though the committee, with an extraordinary party ratio favoring the majority, has been subject to strong party pressures from the Democratic caucus. Amendments to appropriation bills that are subject to record votes are likely to be the most controversial. Taking all such funding amendments in 1980, those adopted and those rejected, nineteen in all, and focusing on the votes of subcommittee members, the votes on only two amendments were partisan in the sense that a majority of one party voted against a majority of the other. In 47 percent of the cases the subcommittee members were either unanimous (five cases) or no more than one member of either or both parties voted against the majority of their colleagues (four cases). As for the full Appropriations Committee, seven cases (37 percent) were partisan. Nor was there any significant partisanship in committee reports of the same year. Among the twenty-one separate statements in reports on the thirteen regular appropriation bills, there was one "minority" view, signed by the three Republicans on the Foreign Assistance subcommittee and complaining about waste in the foreign aid program, and nineteen "additional" views, eleven of them signed by one member, five by members of both parties, and three by two or more members of a single party.

Finally, the new preappropriations procedures have put pressure on the norm that differentiates the Senate's role from that of the House. Because these procedures must be completed before appropriation bills can be reported, the time interval between House and Senate consideration of appropriation bills has in some years been shortened, so that Senate subcommittees have conducted their hearings before the House bills have been reported and passed. Nonetheless, the appeals role continues to be characteristic of the Senate committee.

The Appropriations Committee, then, has retained its operating norms and its influence in the House, although it is no longer as unilaterally dominant in the sum of budget and appropriation procedures as it was before the Budget Control Act of 1974, for reasons to be examined in the next chapter.

Control Techniques in Appropriations

There are several techniques used by Congress to oversee and control the Executive in appropriations.

PURPOSES AND FUNDS

First, Congress can specify the purposes for which money is appropriated; and second, it can set fund levels for these purposes. This is illustrated in table 8.1: "For necessary expenses in carrying out the purposes of the National Science Foundation Act, $1057 million." For both of these control techniques the President takes leadership; he proposes in the Budget the specified purposes and the funds. Congress may change the fund levels. Less frequently will it change the specified purposes.

Example. In 1972 the President's Budget for operating programs (excluding construction grants) of the Environmental Protection Agency was one lump sum of $446 million. The House Appropriations subcommittee increased the amount by $50 million (while reducing construction grants by $100 million) and broke it up into five separate appropriations—research and development ($185.2 million), abatement and control ($240.9 million), enforcement ($28.9 million), facilities (zero), agency and regional management ($42 million)—"in order to provide better congressional visibility and control." The Senate committee cut out the separate appropriations, but the conferees restored them with the addition of authorization for EPA to transfer up to 7 percent of any appropriation to any other appropriations.

But normally it is the Executive's definition of purpose with which the Congress deals.

STATUTORY PROVISOS

A third technique is to attach statutory provisos or limitations, frequently called riders, to appropriation bills to control matters of policy or administrative performance.

Example of policy control. The House added a proviso to the State Department appropriation bill for fiscal year 1953 that barred the use of any funds appropriated to the department to support a mission to the Vatican unless the Senate had previously confirmed the appointment of an ambassador to that post.

On October 20, 1951, the day the first session of the Eighty-second Congress adjourned, President Harry S Truman nominated General Mark W. Clark to be Ambassador to the Vatican. Although President Franklin D. Roosevelt had appointed a personal representative to the Holy See, as had Truman, the United States had not had formal diplomatic relations with the Vatican State (except intermittently during the period 1846–1863). Of the so-called major powers the United States and the U.S.S.R. were the only ones without diplomatic missions there, and Truman said, when he nominated Clark, that "direct diplomatic relations will assist in coordinating the effort to combat the Communist menace." Nonetheless the nomination incited strong opposition among scores of Protestant church groups, the National Council of the Churches of Christ calling it "an alarming threat to basic American principles [of

136

separation of church and state]." In January 1952, as the second session of the Eighty-second Congress was assembling and before the Senate Foreign Relations Committee had scheduled hearings on the nomination, the White House announced that Clark had requested withdrawal of his name. The House Appropriations Committee then initiated the proviso to prevent the President from establishing such a mission without an ambassador. A move to strike the proviso was defeated on the House floor by an unrecorded vote of 82 to 159. Subsequently the Senate, following the recommendation of its Appropriations Committee, dropped the proviso, and it was not included in the final act. Regardless, the United States to this day does not have a formal mission at the Vatican.

Example of both policy and administrative control. The National Science Foundation appropriation for fiscal year 1981, used as the illustration in table 8.1, has one proviso relating directly to policy—that funds are to be denied individuals who seriously disrupt institutions of higher education by refusing to obey their regulations —and a number relating to administration—for example, to the extent that the amount appropriated is less than the amount authorized, all amounts specified in the authorizing act for specific programs are to be reduced proportionally.

Most statutory provisos are written by the appropriations committees; others are adopted by floor amendments. Of approximately 225 new provisos approved by the House in 1977, 200 were attached by the Appropriations Committee and 24 were initiated in the full House. Under House rules, statutory provisos that make affirmative changes in existing law, so-called legislative riders, are out of order in an appropriation bill unless they result in a direct reduction in expenditures. Most of the provisos written by the appropriations committees fall in this category. Statutory provisos that do not make an affirmative change in existing law, but bar the use of funds in an appropriation bill for specific purposes, such as abortions, or disruptive professors, are called limitation riders. These are not prohibited by the House rules because, as we noted earlier, the right of the House not to appropriate for a purpose, even if that purpose is authorized in law, is considered a fundamental part of the appropriation power of the Congress. Virtually all of the provisos initiated on the House floor are in this category.

There has been debate in Congress in recent years over the propriety of provisos that limit the use of funds for particular purposes. Proponents of these riders hold that they are an essential part of Congress's power of the purse; opponents, that provisos are legislation which has no place in an appropriation bill, regardless of existing House rules. Also, riders in appropriation bills are considered to be less justified for programs that are reauthorized periodically than for programs with permanent authorizations. If it were to come up today, a provision to define the conditions under which the United States could establish a mission at the Vatican, such as that in the 1952 example, would in all likelihood be considered in connection with the annual authorization bill for State Department expenditures, which did not exist at the earlier date, rather than the annual appropriation bill.

There have been a number of proposals to ban or restrict such riders, but the House has reached no agreement on any of them. The most radical proposal would change House rules to prohibit both the Appropriations Committee and the House from including in any appropriation bill any provision which would impose a limitation not contained in existing law. Another would apply the above prohibition to House floor amendments only, leaving the Appropriations Committee free to offer provisos. A third proposal would prohibit provisos unless the authorizing committees in each case approved them, or, alternatively, unless these committees had been given an opportunity to consider proposed provisos and make recommendations to the House on whether or not they should be approved. Another proposal would require a two-thirds rather than majority vote to approve riders. Finally, it has been proposed that the Rules Committee, on an ad hoc basis, write rules for individual appropriation bills that protect or prohibit specific riders.

In January 1980 the chairmen of seventeen legislative committees (all except the Committee on Energy and Commerce) and the ranking minority members of five of these committees addressed a joint letter to the House Select Committee on Committees (Patterson committee) proposing that all legislative provisions in appropriation bills be referred to the appropriate legislative committees for their recommendation before the bills were considered on the House floor—a version of the third alternative. Not surprisingly, the chairman of the Appropriations Committee objected to the proposal, arguing in part that such provisos were necessary for the committee to effect its economy norm. The select committee took no action.*

NONSTATUTORY TECHNIQUES

Fourth, there are nonstatutory means of control. The Appropriations subcommittees use hearings, reports, debate on the floor, and less formal techniques to oversee the Executive, although none of these are legally binding on the agencies since they are quite apart from language included in the appropriation statutes.[8] In hearings, problems are raised and often understandings reached. Appropriation reports are used to tie down the subcommittees' most important intentions. These reports are filled with words of guidance, advice, and warning, employing an elaborately developed lexicon. A report may "direct" an agency to do something; or it may "earmark" a portion of the appropriation for that purpose; or the subcommittee may "expect" the agency

---

*At the beginning of the Ninety-eighth Congress in January 1983, the House adopted a rule prohibiting votes on legislative riders, other than those proposed by the Appropriations Committee, unless the House has previously adopted a rule that authorizes votes on specific riders.

to do it; or "urge" it; or "recommend" that it be done. Each of these words has an explicit meaning in the world of agency budget officers and appropriation committee members and staff. In testifying before the Monroney-Madden committee in 1965, I mentioned appropriation committee reports. After the hearing Jack B. Brooks (D. TX), a committee member, said: "I'll tell you, Professor, I'll let you write the statute if you let me write the committee report."

In addition to hearings and reports, debate on the floor of the House is used to establish a record of subcommittee purpose. And less formal techniques are used by subcommittee chairmen, members, and staff to state intentions and reach understandings with departmental and bureau officers.

Each stage of the legislative or administrative process in Congress can be used for nonstatutory control, and a nonstatutory instruction or suggestion can be initiated or modified at any one of them. Thus a House Appropriations subcommittee report may state one intention; the Senate Appropriations subcommittee report, another; and debate on the floor yet a different one. The administrator must wind his way among these, using his discretion.

Why do appropriations committees use nonstatutory techniques at all? Why not rely on statutory provisos? There are two principal reasons. The first is flexibility. The subcommittee may want to leave an agency the opportunity to change its proposed allocation of funds from one activity to another—to "reprogram"—without the need to obtain an amendment to the appropriation statute.

Example. Some years ago the appropriation statutes for the Corps of Engineers included allocations of funds to major water resource projects. Today these allocations are not in the statutes, which provide a single lump sum for construction of most projects. Instead they are specified in the subcommittee report. Assume that the funds allocated in a given year to Little Goose Dam on the Lower Snake River in Washington cannot be entirely spent because of unanticipated foundation conditions that require additional preparatory work, whereas more money than allocated can be spent on Libby Dam on the Kootenai River in northwest Montana, due to unusually mild weather that has extended the normal construction season. If the funds were allocated to these projects in the statute, the only way to transfer money from Little Goose to Libby would be to enact an amendatory statute, a lengthy procedure when it is recalled that the allocation may be for a single year. If, on the other hand, the allocation is in the nonstatutory report, the funds can be reprogrammed expeditiously.

The appropriations subcommittees and the executive departments have established nonstatutory reprogramming routines under which the departments provide the subcommittees with advance notice of plans to shift funds from one activity specified in a subcommittee report to another, and the subcommittees approve or veto these plans.

Example. In March 1981 President Reagan proposed, as part of an emergency aid program to El Salvador, that $5 million in military loans be reprogrammed from funds earmarked in the committee report for other countries. The Senate Appropriations subcommittee approved the proposal 6 to 2 on March 16; the House subcommittee, by 8 to 7 on March 24. The regular members of the Foreign Operations subcommittee opposed the President by 7 to 6. However, under House Appropriations Committee procedures, the chairman and ranking minority member of the full committee can vote in each subcommittee. They seldom do so, but in this case the Administration convinced both of them to vote in support of the President.

Reprogramming has in recent years become an important technique for congressional control of the Executive. For the defense budget it may amount to several billions of dollars in any given year.

There is another rationale for flexibility which leads the appropriations committees to use the nonstatutory committee report as their control technique. The committees may want to see a program intensified or reduced, but they do not know how to translate this into precise dollar amounts or precise statutory language, so they state their intent as clearly as they can in the committee report and leave it to the Executive to carry through.

Example. The House subcommittee report on the National Science Foundation appropriation for fiscal year 1981, which is used as the illustration in table 8.1, states: "From within funds available, the committee urges the foundation to initiate a study using economic models to analyze a forum for economic cooperation between Canada, Mexico, and the United States. This effort should be undertaken by an association of universities and coordinated by a lead university selected at the foundation's discretion." This instruction is nonstatutory for the sake of flexibility. At the same time, subcommittee members felt sufficiently clearly and strongly about the allocation of funds to two other programs to draft their decisions in the form of statutory provisos. Their report states: "Bill language has been included limiting funding for a new Center for Innovation Development and the Two-Year Four-Year College Instrumentation program to zero and $5,000,000, respectively. This limitation is proposed to ensure that an unacceptable level of unbudgeted items does not erode funding for basic research programs, which is, and continues to be, the raison d'être of the foundation."

In addition to flexibility, a second reason for controlling by means of committee reports is to circumvent the rules of the House and Senate. These rules, as we have seen, prohibit legislation in appropriation bills. Any member can raise a point of order against legislative language unless it is a limitation on the use of funds or a change in law that results in a direct reduction in expenditures. Many of the nonstatutory instructions in the committee reports could be stricken as legislation in appropriation bills if they were presented as statutory provisos. Occasionally the House Appropriations Committee, having included a legislative proviso in an appropriation bill, will seek to protect it by requesting the Rules Committee to grant a rule that prohibits points of order against the offending language. But the committee is loath to go this route since it invites intervention by the Rules Committee, which normally does not have jurisdiction over appropriation bills, and because the House normally is unsympathetic to rules that sanction irregular procedures. The committee prefers, where appropriate, to use the nonstatutory committee report.

Example. The Housing Act of 1965 authorized a new program of rent supplements whereby the federal government contracted to pay developers of new housing units to be occupied by low-income families the difference between the rent that tenants could afford to pay, defined initially as 25 percent of their income, and a fair market rental over a period of forty years. Also, nonprofit developers—church groups, labor unions, service clubs, and so on—could borrow up to 100 percent of the project costs at below-market interest rates.

In 1967 the Senate Appropriations subcommittee with responsibility for housing programs concluded that nonprofit developers, to heighten their sense of responsibility for projects they sponsored, should put up 5 percent of project costs. As such a requirement would change existing law and, therefore, be subject to a point of order if drafted as a proviso, the committee instead instructed the department in the committee report to require sponsors to contribute the 5 percent. Opponents of this proposal could not move to strike or delete it, as it was not in the bill. Consequently, numerous senators spoke against it on the floor, in hopes that housing officials would interpret their advice as more representative of the sense of the Senate than was that of the committee report. Committee members, on the other hand, cautioned the agency against ignoring the recommendation, indicating that to do so might endanger future appropriations for this and related housing programs.

The following year the Senate subcommittee failed to include the 5 percent language in its report. When this action was challenged on the floor, the subcommittee chairman acceded to a request that the report be withdrawn and reprinted to include the limiting language.

Evaluation of Appropriation Procedures in Terms of Executive–Legislative Relations

With the knowledge that we now have about appropriation procedures, we can evaluate them in terms of our model of executive–legislative relations.

WHOLE OR PARTS

First, have the procedures led to legislative oversight and control by the whole Congress or to oversight by one of its parts, the appropriations committees and their subcommittees? The House Appropriations Committee's norm of unity and its consequence of reciprocity among the subcommittees would appear to transfer Congress's most powerful oversight technique to small groups of representatives on the subcommittees whose policy views, emphasizing as they do the norm of economy, are likely to be distinct from those of a majority of Congress. As a consequence of the norm of unity the full committee approves the markups and reports of its subcommittees with few changes and the whole House finds it difficult to overrule the committee on the floor.

At the same time, the Congress has sanctions that it can use against the appropriations committees if it is strongly dissatisfied with their performance. Congress can limit the committees' discretion by enacting detailed and short-term authorizations. For certain types of programs Congress can take jurisdiction away from the appropriations committees by authorizing that the programs be financed through the back door, that is, by direct borrowing from the Treasury or by dedicated funds. Congress can enact entitlements that leave the appropriations committees no alternative but to provide the money. Congress can, as it did in 1974, provide for preappropriation procedures that limit the discretion remaining to those who direct appropriations.

Furthermore, the House Appropriations Committee is sensitive to the mood of the whole and moves with it. There are years in which all of the appropriations subcommittees have changed their previous years' attitude on economy, all acting in unison to cut more severely, or in unison to be more liberal with money. In each such year, change in committee performance has corresponded with a perceptible change in the temper of the whole House. The committee, in other words, seeks out the temper of the whole. Committee members know that there are limits to their capacity to impose their operating norm of economy on the whole. They are careful to determine these limits, for they fear most of all being overruled. In extraordinary circumstances, this sensitivity to the will of the House has turned the Appropriations Committee into what Schick has called subdued guardians of funds for authorized programs. The large Democratic majority in the House was adamantly opposed to President Richard M. Nixon's efforts to drastically cut back or eliminate some of Lyndon B. Johnson's Great Society programs. In these circumstances the Democrats on the Appropriations Committee felt a special attachment to the House expectation that they should provide funds for authorized programs.[9]

Example. The Clean Waters Restoration Act of 1966, approved by President Johnson, authorized $1 billion in grants for construction of sewage treatment plants in fiscal year 1970. President Nixon recommended only $214 million in his budget.

There was wide support in the House for appropriating the full $1 billion that had been authorized three years previously, from Republicans such as William E. Minshall (OH) and Frank T. Bow (NY) as well as Democrats. Sensing the mood of the House, the Appropriations Committee proposed $600 million, the minimum amount that they believed the House would accept. An amendment to increase this to $1 billion lost on the floor by a nonrecord vote of 146 to 148, and a motion that would have permitted a record vote was defeated 215 to 187. The committee's antennae were well adjusted.

Apart from this question of subcommittee-committee-floor relations, the extent to which appropriation procedures lead to oversight and control by the whole, rather than by its parts, depends on the techniques used by the appropriations committees. Of these the nonstatutory techniques—for example, the committee report and reprogramming procedures—raise the most difficult questions. The whole House cannot normally revise the wording of a committee report, nor does it approve subcommittee decisions on reprogramming. From the Executive's point of view there are mitigating factors. The nonstatutory controls are not legally binding, and the administrator can, therefore, disregard them if he is strongly enough opposed to be willing to incur the displeasure of the appropriations subcommittee. Indeed, he has a responsibility to disregard a nonstatutory instruction if, in his view, it would result in a narrow, minority control over his agency. Furthermore, the Office of Management and Budget, the Treasury, and the General Accounting Office do not help Congress enforce nonstatutory controls by disallowing agency expenditures, as they do in enforcement of statutory provisos. Also, where there are differences between the records made at the several stages of appropriations—for example, the House subcommittee report says one thing and the Senate report another—the administrator will have some freedom. Skillful administrators sometimes promote this freedom by asking friends of their agencies in Congress to establish records of congressional intent on the floor that are contrary to those stated in appropriations committee reports.

BROAD AND GENERAL OR NARROW AND PARTICULAR

A second question for evaluating appropriation procedures in terms of our model of executive–legislative relations is whether they encourage the Executive and Congress to focus on broad issues of policy and on general characteristics of administrative performance, or lead them into considering narrow policy and details of administrative performance. A key factor here is the form in which the Budget is prepared and presented by the OMB—is it in terms of appropriation accounts that are narrow in scope and classified by object of expenditure and unit of organization, or in terms of broad accounts, classified by function and program? Before World War II the Budget was of the first type, narrow accounts. Since then there has been a steady trend toward the second type. In the early 1950s the move to broader accounts was called performance budgeting. The number of separate budget accounts was reduced from 2000 in the early 1940s to 375 in 1955, and the justification and analysis for each of these was stated in program terms. The number of appropriation accounts is now about 1200, but the increase over 1955 is due principally to new governmental programs. Modern versions of performance budgeting, called planning-programming-budgeting-systems, management by objective, and other names, benefit from analytical techniques of operations research and systems analysis that were not available in the 1940s and early 1950s.

Despite these important changes in the form of the President's Budget, some critics have not been satisfied that appropriation procedures have emphasized sufficiently broad policy. Thus more than twenty-five years ago Arthur Smithies argued that the defect of appropriation procedures lay in their attempt to determine future programs and to review and control past performance in the same operation; that the details required for a review of the past complicate and obscure consideration of programs for the future.[10] He would have divided appropriation procedures into two separate categories, one relating to appropriations for the future, emphasizing broader policy, and the other relating to review of past performance, with more details. Though superficially appealing, this argument has, it seems to me, serious defects. Appropriations control is so effective as a technique for oversight in part because it combines a review of past performance and the relation of past performance to proposed expenditures. If the two were to be separated, Congress's most important technique for exercising its role in policy and administration, where the Executive has wide discretion, might well be blunted.

Other critics have pointed to a need for coordinated review of the whole Budget. The President's Budget is fragmented into thirteen separate appropriation bills, thereby denying Congress the opportunity to make an overall decision on expenditures or on priorities among major categories of expenditures. In response to this type of criticism, there were efforts to achieve greater coordination in 1946 and 1950 but they failed. The first of these was the Legislative Reorganization Act of 1946. It provided for a Joint Committee on the Budget, consisting of all members of the two tax committees—House Ways and Means and Senate Finance—and of the two appropriations committees sitting together. This joint committee was to convene at the beginning of each session and within sixty days to report a resolution establishing a ceiling on expenditures. Once approved by Congress, this resolution was to serve as the guideline for the appropriations subcommittees. In 1947 the House and

Senate could not agree on a figure, so no resolution was adopted. In 1948 a resolution was passed but it was subsequently ignored by the appropriations subcommittees. After 1948 no effort was made to comply with this law. It lay on the statute books unenforced until 1970 when it was repealed.

There are several reasons for the failure of this effort. With over 100 members, the joint committee was too unwieldy to undertake any penetrating analysis of the President's Budget. The time limit within which the committee was required to report, sixty days, was too short. The committee was poorly staffed. The House Appropriations Committee was unenthusiastic about this joint procedure because it undermined the preeminence of the House in matters relating to appropriations.

A second effort at greater coordination in appropriations was the Omnibus Appropriations Bill of 1950, a concept proposed by the then chairman of the House Appropriations Committee, Clarence A. Cannon (D. MO.). As usual, the Budget that year was divided among the subcommittees for analysis and recommendation. However, a central subcommittee was established to examine the recommendations of the subgroups before they were submitted to the full committee. The central subcommittee served as a coordinating agency, which could suggest changes to the respective subcommittees but could not itself make such changes. In practice, the central group proposed alterations to almost all of the chapters it reviewed. The separate subgroup reports were then compiled into one 427-page bill, and the Appropriations Committee, after reviewing it for one week, sent it to the floor. For six weeks the House debated the bill and amended it chapter by chapter.

In January 1951 the House Appropriations Committee, with strong support of party leaders, voted overwhelmingly to abandon this second reform experiment, for several reasons. The bill was large and complex so that little time was spent on each major section in full committee review, and few members had an opportunity to familiarize themselves with even the major issues. As a result the single bill did not provide an effective vehicle to strengthen Congress's capacity to review overall fiscal policy. Nor did the procedure facilitate congressional oversight of administrative performance. For six weeks Appropriations Committee members monopolized the House floor. Patience grew short and members, unaccustomed to debating a single item for such a great length of time, wanted to move on to other business. In this context, the Omnibus Bill was particularly vulnerable to legislative riders. Finally, the comprehensive bill failed to achieve substantial cuts in expenditures; the procedure failed to implement the wishes of many members to "trim the waste out of government."

The most recent effort to achieve coordinated review of the whole Budget is the Budget Control Act of 1974, to be discussed in the next chapter.

More on the Roles of Legislative Committees and Appropriations Committees

At the beginning of chapter 7 I said that the relative roles of legislative committees and appropriations committees are defined by the rules of the House and Senate which, with exceptions, provide on the one hand that no appropriation can be made for a program that has not previously been authorized, and no legislation can be included in an appropriation bill; and on the other hand, that no appropriation can be made in an authorization bill.

Developments in recent years have, however, blurred this differentiation of roles based on the rules. The appropriations committees have encroached on the discretion of the legislative committees with their increasing use of non-statutory controls. By means of the committee report they have circumvented the House rules. The rules allow points of order against legislation in appropriation bills, but there is no point of order against a nonstatutory instruction in a committee report. Analogously the legislative committees have encroached on the discretion of the appropriations committees by increasing use of annual and short-term authorizations and of entitlements.

In light of these developments, one can ask again, what are the relative roles of the two types of committees? Congress is not presently transmitting a clear signal, but through the static I hear the following response. Most members have two major interests: economy in government—a government-wide interest and probably the most commonly shared view of members as a group; and enthusiasm for certain programs, frequently those of the legislative committees on which they serve. Individual members are themselves incapable of reconciling these conflicting interests—of forming a single preference function—or they simply do not want to have to do so. Instead they support an institutional arrangement that will accomplish the reconciliation for them. They feed their enthusiasm for certain programs by reporting authorizations from their legislative committees and guiding them through the House. They feed their belief in economy by supporting the Appropriations Committee when it cuts appropriations for various programs, including some of the very same ones they have previously supported. As John J. Rooney (D. NY), chairman of the appropriations subcommittee on Justice Department funds, said in July 1969 to a department official who was urging the subcommittee to appropriate the full authorization for law assistance block grants: "Mr. Velde, have you not ever heard that the Appropriations Committee is the saucer that cools the legislative tea? That is the theory on which I have operated all these years."

This use of congressional institutions and procedures makes good sense, but it can get out of hand. If the gap between authorizations and appropriations is too wide, questions will be raised about the integrity of a government that promises more than it delivers.

An Alternative Interpretation of Appropriation Procedures

There is on this subject a different view than that presented here, a view represented by the writings of Aaron Wildavsky.[11] Wildavsky claims that appropriation procedures are fragmented and nonprogrammatic and that this is desirable.

According to Wildavsky, the important characteristics of appropriation procedures, both preparation of the Budget in the Executive and review and approval of proposed appropriations in the Congress, are these. They are *incremental*, that is, the base for decision making is how much money was voted in the previous year, and attention is focused on changes from the base. They are *fragmented*, that is, incremental adjustments of the budgets proposed by executive bureaus take place at many points—in the department secretary's office, in OMB, in the House and Senate appropriations subcommittees. They are the *result of bargaining* in an environment of reciprocal expectations. The parties to the bargains are the bureaus, the divisions of OMB, the appropriations subcommittees. Thus there are budget whirlpools, one for each major purpose of appropriations, in which the several actors bargain for influence. Finally, appropriation procedures are *nonprogrammatic*. They don't focus on programs but on bureaucratic organizations, each bureau seeking to protect and enhance its funds.

In defense of such procedures Wildavsky says that there are no objective ways of determining which programs are better than others. And in any case, to try to compare programs on their merits would involve an impossible burden of calculation. This being the case, we need procedures based on incrementalism, bargaining, and conflict resolution that will substitute for rational program analysis. It is important to deflect attention away from programs, for "the practice of focusing attention on programs has meant that policy implications can hardly be avoided. The gains and losses for the interests involved become far more evident to all concerned. Conflict is heightened by the stress on policy differences." Because the present procedures are so incremental, fragmented, and nonprogrammatic in his view, they provide a basis for bargaining and conflict resolution in which all interests are represented at one point or another. If, on the other hand, the procedures were to focus on programs, "logrolling and bargaining [would be] hindered because it is much easier to trade increments conceived in monetary terms than it is to give in on basic policy differences."[12]

Wildavsky, however, overemphasizes the lack of concern for broad policy and general administrative performance in appropriation procedures both in the Executive and in Congress. There is in the OMB a serious effort to equate marginal expenditures on major programs. We have progressed long since from project budgeting to program budgeting. His analysis misses entirely the potency of appropriations committee norms. The norms of economy and unity give considerable coherence to Congress's appropriation procedures. Also, Wildavsky used organization as his unit of analysis rather than program. In other words, he concluded that appropriation procedures are nonprogrammatic, without using program as the key variable in his analysis.[13]

Wildavsky assumes that because the focus in appropriation procedures is incremental, it is therefore nonprogrammatic. But this does not necessarily follow. Perhaps the best way to focus on programs is to focus on incremental changes. Wildavsky himself talks about the need to simplify many calculations. By focusing on increments, the actors in appropriations have used a very subtle method for simplifying calculations and thereby for focusing on programs. Any student of economics knows that to examine the worth or value of one good in relation to other goods one examines the two at the margins. Marginal or incremental analysis is the great analytical technique that makes possible program comparisons.

Wildavsky's conclusion—that fragmented, nonprogrammatic, whirlpool appropriation procedures are desirable—leads him to be against all efforts, such as *ppbs*, to improve procedures, and to predict that all such efforts will fail. He says that both the executive agencies and Congress will defeat efforts to further rationalize appropriations in terms of comparing programs, because such efforts would reduce interest group bargaining. To the contrary, both the President and Congress have realized that they will have greater control over the programs of government if they have available as the instrument of control a well-planned and programmed Budget, certainly greater than if the instrument is fragmented and nonprogrammatic. We shall return to this point in chapter 13.

Finally, and not surprisingly, Wildavsky's view of the public interest is at odds with the view on which this book is based. He says:

I am prepared to argue that the partial-view-of-the-public-interest approach is preferable to the total-view-of-the-public-interest approach, which is so often urged as being superior. First, it is much simpler for each participant to calculate his own preferences than for each to try to calculate the preferences of all. It is difficult enough for a participant to calculate how the interests he is protecting might best be served without requiring that he perform the same calculation for many others who might also be affected. . . . The partial approach is more efficient for resolving conflicts, a process that lies at the heart of democratic politics. . . . It permits each participant to go his own way until he discovers that the activities of others interfere. Effort can then be devoted to overcoming the difficulties that do exist. The formation of alliances in a political system that requires them is facilitated by the expression and pursuit of demands by those in closest touch with the social reality from which they issue forth. Then it is not a matter of a kind of *noblesse oblige* that assures that rival demands are considered. It is, rather, that the articulators of these demands insist on being heard and have the political resources to compel a hearing. A partial adversary system in which the various interests compete for control of policy (under agreed-upon rules) seems more likely to result in reasonable decisions—that is, decisions that take account of the multiplicity of values involved—than one in which the best policy is assumed to be discoverable by a well-intentioned search for the public interest for all by everyone.[14]

All of these points have been argued, with different results, in the first chapter of this book.

9

The Congressional Budget:

Preappropriation Procedures

THE Congressional Budget and Impoundment Control Act of 1974 sanctions a new set of preappropriation procedures, for which there are new institutions and new techniques of congressional control over governmental programs. The act was initiated by Congress, not the Executive, and is, therefore, an example of the secondary mode of executive–legislative relations in the legislative process. However, President Richard M. Nixon and the Office of Management and Budget, while forfeiting leadership to Congress, gave strong support to the legislative effort.

In 1972 Congress established a Joint Study Committee on Budget Control for the purpose of proposing procedures for "improving congressional control over budgetary outlay and receipt totals." The joint committee consisted of seven members from each of the appropriations and tax committees —House and Senate Appropriations, House Ways and Means, Senate Finance—and two members at large from each House. The joint committee was chaired jointly by the chairmen of the two House committees in recognition of the House's responsibility to act first on money bills (with few exceptions). The delegations from each House included nine Democrats and seven Republicans. The joint study committee had no authority to report legislation, so that its recommendations, which were made known in April 1973, were subsequently considered in the House by the Committee on Rules and in the Senate by the Committees on Government Operations and on Rules and Administration. Although the subject matter was potentially very controversial, the joint study committee and the legislative committees in both Houses worked hard and successfully to achieve a broad consensus. The recommendations of the study committee were unanimous; the House bill was reported unanimously by the Rules Committee and passed with only twenty-three negative votes; a bill was adopted in the Senate unanimously. After a conference to settle differences between the House and Senate bills, the House voted for final passage with six dissents; the Senate, without dissent. In signing the bill on July 12, 1974, President Nixon said:

I take special pleasure today in signing the Congressional Budget Control Act of 1974. I commend the Congress for this landmark legislation and I pledge the full support of the executive branch in helping fulfill the great promise of this bill. In each of my five Budget Messages I have urged the Congress to review and reform its procedures for considering the Federal budget and pledge the support and cooperation of this Administration in achieving this vital national goal.

Budget Machinery

The act of 1974 created new budget committees in each House. The House Budget Committee has thirty members, with an extraordinary 3:2 party ratio (in 1981, eighteen Democrats and twelve Republicans). Five members are chosen from the Appropriations Committee, five from Ways and Means, eighteen from other standing committees, and two are selected by House leaders, one from each party. Members are limited to six-year terms and are appointed without regard to seniority. They are selected by procedures similar to those for the other elite committees, meaning that party leaders play an important role.

The Senate Committee had twenty-two members in 1981, twelve Republicans and ten Democrats. Unlike the House Committee, there are no fixed terms and there is no specification of other committee assignments. Members are, however, also appointed without regard to seniority.

The committees have large professional staffs to assist them. The Congressional Budget Office (CBO), which serves both committees, has a well-financed staff of over 200. In addition to CBO, each budget committee has its own staff of more than 75 persons. Overall the staffs for the new preappropriation procedures are several times larger than those for appropriations.

Budget Procedures

The act's new procedures include congressional budget resolutions, a first one to be adopted by May 15, and a second one by September 15; changes in the scheduling of appropriation bills and bills that authorize spending; legislation to enforce the budget resolutions by "reconciling" their funding ceilings with amounts previously voted in authorizations and appropriations; and control over the President's impounding of appropriated funds.

FIRST CONGRESSIONAL BUDGET RESOLUTION

The budget committees recommend, and Congress is to adopt by May 15, a congressional budget resolution, which includes for the budget as a whole target ceilings in each of the following categories for the next fiscal year: revenues; expenditures (both authority to obligate funds and estimated expenditures); credit commitments that do not involve direct expenditures, with separate targets for loan obligations and loan guarantees; the surplus or deficit; the public debt, and the amount the statutory debt limit should be increased or decreased. The resolution also includes target ceilings on expenditures and on credit commitments for nineteen major categories of programs, such as national defense, agriculture, and income security. These spending ceilings relate not only to funds over which the appropriations committees have discretion, but also to direct spending from the Treasury, spending under entitlements, and the granting of credit. Thus the resolutions provide targets not only for the appropriations and tax committees, but also for legislative committees. For example, the target for income security may be based in part on the assumption that entitlement criteria for food stamps will be tightened, which can be accomplished only if the agriculture committees report legislation that is then adopted by Congress, amending the food stamp act.

In addition to the next fiscal year, the resolutions include targets for the two subsequent years. These are not binding, however, since Congress enacts budget resolutions annually and will amend previously approved future targets as they become more current.

The assumptions on which the nineteen categorical targets are based are not stated in the text of the resolutions, but in the budget committee reports, and are, therefore, less binding than the targets themselves. The House Budget Committee has been more explicit than the Senate committee in stating its assumptions, to the point of setting forth targets for specific programs, a practice to be discussed later in this chapter.

To aid them in drafting resolutions for consideration by the whole House, the budget committees receive a great quantity of data from a variety of sources. The House and Senate legislative committees submit to their respective budget committees by March 15 their comments on the President's budget proposals and their views and estimates of appropriate levels of spending for all programs within their jurisdictions. The House and Senate appropriations committees report to their respective budget committees their preliminary views and estimates of appropriations required in each category, based on the President's Budget. The Ways and Means Committee in the House and the Finance Committee in the Senate present their views and estimates of appropriate levels of aggregate revenues, outlays, public debts, and deficits and surpluses, comparing these to the President's proposals. And the Joint Economic Committee submits to the budget committees its recommendations on fiscal policy. Finally, the CBO prepares reports on fiscal policy and national priorities.

With all of this information, the budget committees draft resolutions which are debated and adopted in each House and finally reconciled by a conference committee. Since these resolutions guide or control the subsequent behavior of Congress with regard to expenditures and taxes, and do not directly obligate or constrain the other branches of government, they do not require the President's signature.

The House Budget Committee has not developed integrative norms for this preappropriation procedure like those that dominate the conduct of the Appropriations Committee.[1] The Budget Committee has been partisan and fractious. The budget resolution has been a Democratic resolution, normally supported by all Democrats on the committee and opposed by all Republicans. Many of the outcomes have been determined in caucuses of the committee's Democratic members, who have made little effort to write a resolution that would draw support from, or soften the opposition of, their Republican colleagues. Except for 1980 Republicans have had virtually no input into the process. Committee members, while united with their party colleagues in committee votes, most especially in votes on amendments offered by Republicans, have not suppressed their individual views, however, which they state frequently in supplemental and additional statements in the committee reports. Between 1976 and 1981 reports on the first resolutions included, in addition to majority and minority reports, an average of ten separate statements, seven of them signed by one or more majority members and three by minority members.

The principal reasons for the absence of integrative norms and the high degree of partisanship are the newness of the committee and its procedures and the committee's composition. Republicans on the committee have been more conservative than the average Republican in the House, and committee Democrats more liberal than the average House Democrat, creating a liberal–conservative schism between the party delegations that has been too great to be bridged by any marginal adjustments in total or categorical targets. Since the party leaders have had a heavy hand in determining membership of the Budget Committee—it is one of the four senior committees—these leaders have to a degree willed the partisan result. Republican leaders were initially concerned that if each party filled its seats with a balanced or representative membership, the committee would be disposed toward high government spending and big budget deficits, while Democratic leaders, fearing conservative results from a committee with representative Democrats and conservative Republicans, loaded the committee with liberal spenders. Using the scores compiled by Americans for Democratic Action (ADA) to represent liberal orientation and those compiled by Americans for Constitutional Action (ACA) to represent a conservative one, table 9.1 compares the whole House and the Budget Committee in 1980. But this doesn't tell the whole story, for whereas 33 percent of the House Democrats scored between 75 and 100 on the ADA score, 50 percent of the committee members had such high liberal scores; and whereas 53 percent of the House Republicans scored between 75 and 100 on the ACA score, 75 percent of committee members were in this category. There were similar cleavages in prior years.

TABLE 9.1

Comparison of Political Ideology Ratings, Whole House and Budget Committee Members, House and Senate, 1980 (Ninety-sixth Congress)

	ADA		ACA	
	Full Body	Budget Committee	Full Body	Budget Committee
All House Members	44	50	46	44
Democrats	57	67	30	16
Republicans	21	24	75	82
All Senators	46	46	45	46
Democrats	58	57	26	25
Republicans	29	28	73	76

I have said that a high level of partisanship in House floor votes, or alternatively a dominance of ad hoc majorities, depends on how committees do their work; and this can be seen in voting on budget resolutions where alignment in the House has resembled that in the committee. The Democrats have carried the resolution on the floor. Republicans have been united in opposition —on average between 1975 and 1980 only ten Republicans supported the first resolution. Thus the Democrats have needed to hold the support of a preponderant majority of their own members for resolutions that have been crafted by a group markedly more liberal than that majority. To achieve this result the Democratic leaders have had to play a more active role than on the average bill, which seems fair enough, since they are largely responsible for the liberal tilt of the committee. The leaders have relied on exhortations to support the budget procedures rather than on reductions in spending targets. " 'Vote the process, not the numbers' has been the argument used time and again to whip lukewarm Democrats into line. The message to Democrats is that they will be held culpable for the failure of budget reform and that they therefore must vote for the resolutions even if they are unhappy with the budget's priorities."[2]

In 1979 moderate and conservative Democrats began to kick up their heels over the unrepresentative character of their party delegation on the Budget Committee and of the resulting resolution. To fill eight vacancies on the committee, the Democratic Steering and Policy Committee (DSPC) had recommended members with an average 1979 ADA score of 77, while the average for all Democrats in that year was 58. They included one conservative, Bill Nelson (FL), and without him the average ADA score of the remaining seven was 87. James R. Jones (OK), a moderate to conservative member of the Ways and Means Committee, decided to challenge in the Democratic caucus the members nominated by DSPC to represent his committee, and he defeated the liberal Joseph L. Fisher (VA). After his victory Jones said: "The leadership learned that the so-called liberal Democrats can't carry the show."[3] In the next Congress, after Reagan's election and a switch of thirty-three seats in the House from Democratic to Republican, the Democratic leadership nominated for vacancies on the Budget Committee seven members with an average 1980 ADA score of 48, compared to 57 for all Democrats. One member, Phil Gramm (TX), had an ADA score of zero; the average score of the remaining six was 56, the average for all Democrats.[4] Also, Jones challenged a liberal Democrat, David R. Obey (WI), for committee chairman and he won in a close caucus vote, 121 to 116. Jones then pledged that the committee would try to fashion budget proposals acceptable to "the vast majority of Democrats," and said that he hoped the committee's resolutions would also be supported by the Republicans. "However, if confrontation politics is demanded by the other side, we'll put together a Democratic budget."[5]

Jones tried to write a bipartisan first resolution for fiscal year 1982, but the Republicans wanted substantially greater reductions than the committee Democrats were willing to accept. Republicans dissented from the resolution, offering their own alternative which for the first time was accepted on the House floor. Seventy-four percent of the Democrats supported their leaders in opposing the substitute, not unlike previous percentages, but the remaining sixty-three Democrats were sufficient, with an enlarged and unified Republican delegation, to adopt a Republican budget resolution, 253 (63D., 190R.) to 176 (176D.).

The Senate Budget Committee has been much less partisan. Republican senators have played an important role in fashioning the resolutions. The committee has been able to put together a broad coalition for its decisions. Committee members have filed fewer dissenting or separate statements in committee reports than in the House. And as a result voting on the floor has been less partisan than in the House. An overwhelming majority of Democrats were supported by approximately 50 percent of the Republicans on average in passing the first budget resolutions in the years 1975 to 1980, and when the Republicans gained control of the Senate and the committee in 1981, 61 percent of the Democrats joined an overwhelming majority of the Republicans to pass a resolution that was supported by President Ronald Reagan.

Institutional differences between the House and Senate account in part for the dissimilar conduct of the two committees. With smaller committees and fewer than one-fourth as many colleagues to deal with in the full body, resulting in greater intimacy; accustomed to operating under parliamentary procedures that depend on unanimous consent; and representing larger, more heterogeneous constituencies for longer terms, senators are frequently more harmonious in committee than members of the lower House. In this context the first chairman and ranking minority member, Edmund S. Muskie (D. ME) and Henry Bellmon (R. OK) respectively, worked closely together.

More important, committee members have been more broadly representative of their parties in the Senate than in the House, as shown in table 9.1. This is not fortuitous, but the result of decisions by party leaders: whereas Republican and Democratic leaders in the House tilted their committee delegations to the conservative and liberal ends respectively, Senate leaders have sought greater balance. Majority leader Mike Mansfield (D. MT) said when the committee was organized: ". . . there is an imperative need for balance as among geographic areas and ideological nuances. . . . The Democrats who sit on the Budget Committee should . . . reflect an accurate cross-section of the Democratic members of the Senate."[6] As a consequence of these several factors, the Senate committee has been more strongly influenced than its House counterpart by the integrative norm of making the new budget procedures work.

APPROPRIATION BILLS

After the first budget resolution has been adopted, and with guidance that it provides, appropriation bills are marked up by the appropriations committees and considered and passed by Congress. The Budget Control Act imposes certain duties and constraints on the appropriations committees, not all of which have been observed. By March 15 the committees are to report to the budget committees their preliminary views and estimates of the appropriations required in each budget category. Because the appropriations committees have not completed their hearings by this early date, they have tended to ask for more in their March 15 reports than they will subsequently propose in the appropriation bills, and frequently more than the President has proposed in his Budget. They err on the high side to protect their own discretion. This response to the new budget procedures has led certain observers to conclude that the appropriations committees have been converted from fiscal "guardians" to "reluctant claimants" and "budget busters," but it is questionable that such characterizations are pertinent beyond these preliminary March reports.[7]

Before any regular appropriation bill is considered on the floor the House Appropriations Committee is to mark up and report all such bills and to inform the Congress on how all of these actions compare with the targets in the first budget resolution. To comply with this requirement it was anticipated that the committee would have to accelerate and coordinate more closely the deliberations of its subcommittees. Although the committee accomplished much in this regard in the early years of the new law, it subsequently relaxed discipline to the point that the requirements of the act are no longer met today (see table 9.2). In 1977 the Committee reported all of the bills (except that for the District of Columbia) within a one-month period (May 26–June 21); seven bills were reported on a single day. By 1981 the time spread had grown to three months.

Congress is to complete action on all appropriation bills by one week after Labor Day, but this requirement, too, has been ignored. In 1977 (fiscal year 1978), for example, three large appropriation bills—Defense, Housing–NASA–Veterans, and Foreign Aid—had not cleared by the deadline, and in 1979 (fiscal year 1980) only two of them had passed, both on the Monday after Labor Day.

As a matter of fact, decision making by the appropriations committees has not been altered significantly by the new budget procedures. The committees continue to use the President's Budget rather than the Congressional Budget Resolution as the yardstick for their actions. As Schick has noted:

Far greater than any possible change, a shift from a presidential to a congressional perspective would have wrenched the appropriations committees from their traditions and disoriented them. No such shift has occurred. From the moment the executive budget is released through the end of the appropriations process, these committees

TABLE 9.2

Timing of House Appropriations Committee Reports on Twelve Regular
Appropriations Bills (excluding District of Columbia Bill)

	Number of bills reported within two weeks	Number of bills reported within four weeks	Bills reported after four weeks		Elapsed time between first and last report in days
			number	names	
1977 (fiscal year 1978)	9	12	0		26
1979 (fiscal year 1980)	9	10	2	Energy Defense	112
1980 (fiscal year 1981)	5	9	3	Foreign Aid Labor–HHS Defense	83
1981 (fiscal year 1982)	6	7	5	Legislative Transportation Foreign Aid Labor–HHS Defense	90

direct their attention to the President's figures. . . . One can read thousands of pages of appropriations hearings without encountering a single mention of the congressional budget process or of the amount allocated in budget resolutions.[8]

As we shall presently see, this conclusion needs to be modified in small degree for 1981 when the first budget resolution included massive reconciliation instructions.

There is more talk about the congressional budget when appropriation bills are debated in the whole House than in committee. In floor debates appropriations committee members sometimes refer to the congressional budget for the purposes of providing additional justification for committee actions and of helping the committee ward off unwanted floor amendments that would also exceed the budget targets. Also, when appropriation bills are debated, the chairman of the Budget Committee usually takes the floor briefly to announce whether or not they are consistent with congressional budget targets.

Despite the apparent indifference of the appropriations committees to the dictates and norms of the new preappropriation procedures, there are more grounds for cooperation than for friction between the two sets of committees and their procedures. From the beginning the appropriations committees have welcomed the discipline of the new budget procedures because they have provided a means for subjecting to fiscal constraint that large percentage of the annual budget which had escaped from appropriation control, being funded through the back door by means of Treasury borrowing, entitlements, contract authority, credit guarantees, and the like. While questioning "whether Congress needs its own general budget plan independent of the President's Budget for guidance in passing upon many detailed recommendations and requests," George H. Mahon (D. TX), chairman of the Appropriations Committee in 1974, nonetheless supported the Budget Control bill because it would control backdoor spending.

More important, perhaps, a convergence of appropriation and budget interests has come to dominate relations between the two sets of committees. Even with partisan conflict in the House Budget Committee between liberal Democratic spenders and fiscal conservative Republicans, the mutual preoccupation of both committees with funding and spending targets and ceilings and with limits on authority to obligate and commit and lend money has led to a significant degree of empathy and cooperation. As a result, in Schick's words: "Both parties [meaning committees] try to accommodate to each other's interests and usually find themselves on the same side of an issue. They can operate in this manner because their substantive interests (as opposed to jurisdictional ones) do not greatly diverge."[9]

The major source of friction has been the tendency of the House Budget Committee to state in their reports targets for specific programs as well as the broader budget categories. The House Appropriations Committee has warned against this repeatedly, through testimony of its chairman and statements in committee reports. Thus the Appropriations Committee's March 15, 1976, report to the Budget Committee stated:

> The Committee notes with concern the tendency to identify and make recommendations for specific line items. While these line item recommendations have no actual effect, they do tend to obscure the overall macroeconomic responsibilities of the Budget Committee and to needlessly duplicate much of the hearings and deliberations that are the responsibility of the authorizing committees. The Committee urges that the content of the reports on the concurrent resolutions to the Budget be confined to the purposes set forth in the act.

In 1980 chairman Jamie L. Whitten (D. MS) was testifying in much the same vein before the Budget Committee when he said:

> I think it is obvious to most everyone who has followed the course of budget resolutions through the Congress, that their progress has become entangled by the consideration of individual budget line items. Part of the problem in the House has been the floor amendments but to a great extent this stems from the detail of the Budget Committee procedures and the recommendations made.... This level of detail

should be avoided since it will only serve to focus the overall debate on the 'means' and mechanics of federal programs, not the broad-based macroeconomic objectives of the federal budget.

Budget Committee members have defended the practice by saying that they have an obligation to inform the House as accurately as they can on their assumptions in arriving at the numbers in the nineteen categories.

SECOND BUDGET RESOLUTION

The first budget resolution's targets are advisory, not binding, on the appropriations and authorizing committees, and for this reason points of order cannot be raised successfully against spending and revenue bills that breach the targets. After the spending bills have been enacted, however, Congress is to adopt, by September 15, a second congressional budget resolution which, according to provisions of the Budget Control Act, is to be enforced by two means. First, any legislation exceeding its ceilings that is brought to the floor after Congress adopts the second resolution is out of order, unless Congress amends the second resolution or adopts an additional one to accommodate the proposed spending. In practice, Congress has avoided enforcement by using the bypass procedures frequently—the second resolutions for fiscal years 1979 and 1981 were amended to accommodate greater spending, and a third resolution was adopted for the same purpose for fiscal years 1977, 1978, and 1980.

Second, there is a reconciliation procedure. If the ceilings on expenditures in the second resolution are lower than the expenditures that have already been voted by Congress, or if the target for revenues in the second resolution is higher than the tax laws will yield, the resolution is to include instructions to the relevant committees to propose changes in existing laws that will rescind appropriations, reduce entitlements, or increase taxes in order to bring expenditures and revenues into line. Nor has Congress been willing to use this enforcement procedure in connection with the second budget resolution. The Senate Budget Committee in 1977 proposed a provision requiring the agriculture committees to report legislation trimming $700 million from crop support entitlements which had been approved by the Senate in a farm bill only several months previously. The Senate rejected the proposal and voted instead to accommodate the farm spending by increasing the budget allocation for agriculture. In 1979 the Senate Budget Committee again included reconciliation instructions in the second resolution. The committees of Congress had already voted approximately $4 billion more than the budget committees agreed to in the second resolution, and the Senate committee proposed; therefore, that six legislative committees and the appropriations committees be required to cut this amount from authorized spending for fiscal year 1980. This time the Senate supported its Budget Committee. But Democratic majorities in the House Budget Committee and the whole House refused to go along, although the Republicans strongly favored reconciliation. The Senate was forced to retreat. The final budget resolution stated only that it was "the sense of Congress" that the overspending committees report legislation cutting back funds.

The second resolution, then, has not become an instrument for enforcing budget procedures, as was originally envisioned in the act.[10] Congress has used the procedure simply to ratify or accommodate the spending decisions that it has made in the interim since the first resolution was approved. One reason for this is timing. The second resolution comes late in the congressional session, in recent years, long after the September 15 statutory deadline for its adoption, and after the beginning of the fiscal year on October 1—for example, the resolution for fiscal year 1980 was adopted on November 28, 1979, that for 1981 on November 20, 1980, and for 1982 on December 10, 1981. By this time there is little legislative energy left for rewriting the laws. A second reason relates to the partisan performance of the House Budget Committee and the resulting close votes on budget resolutions on the House floor. In rejecting the Senate's reconciliation proposals in 1979, Robert N. Giaimo (D. CT), chairman of the House committee, said: "I can't take on seven committees in the House." The Republican leader, John J. Rhodes (AZ), offered to help him do so, promising that Republicans, even though they disagreed with the spending ceilings, would vote for the resolution if it contained reconciliation instructions. The Democrats spurned this offer.

Until 1980 enforcement of the new budget procedures depended largely on the success of the budget committees in convincing their colleagues to respect the targets of the budget resolutions—informing members of the prospective impact on these targets of bills being debated on the floor; urging members to reject spending proposals that would exceed the targets, although this was done more frequently in the Senate than in the House; and trying to involve legislative committees in the budget procedures themselves, as in the March 15 reports.

RECONCILIATION AND THE FIRST BUDGET RESOLUTION

In 1980 for the first time Congress attached reconciliation provisions to the first budget resolution, a procedure neither contemplated nor specifically authorized in the act of 1974, "due to the necessity of acting quickly and effectively to balance the budget and realizing that there may not be time to act on reconciliation instructions [after the second budget resolution has been adopted]," according to the House Budget Committee in its report on the resolution. There was bipartisan agreement in committee on this extraordinary innovation, and for the first time in its history the House Committee reported a resolution with bipartisan support, 19 (11D., 8R.) to 6 (all liberal Democrats). The reconciliation procedure encountered strong opposition from the chairmen of the legislative committees, however. Fifteen out of eighteen chairmen signed a joint letter to the Speaker opposing the Budget Committee's proposal, arguing that reconciliation "undermines the committee system, reposing in the Budget Committee authority to legislate substantively with respect to the nature and scope of federal activities." They offered an amendment to discard reconciliation which failed by a surprisingly large bipartisan vote, 127 (107D., 20R.) to 289 (158D., 131R.).

The concurrent resolution, as enacted on June 12, directed eight House and Senate legislative committees to report within three weeks legislation saving $6.4 billion in outlays for fiscal year 1981 from entitlements and direct spending. The resolution specified the total savings to be made by each committee, and the House Budget Committee's report on the resolution—but not the Senate's—named the specific programs that should be trimmed, while leaving the legislative committees "free to determine what provisions of law will be changed and how these changes will be made." In addition to spending savings, the resolution included reconciliation instructions relating to revenues. The House Ways and Means and Senate Finance Committees were to report legislation increasing revenues $4.2 billion through a variety of tax reforms.

The resulting recommendations of the legislative committees, which to a remarkable degree complied with the reconciliation instructions, were directed to the budget committees, to be assembled into an omnibus reconciliation bill. The budget committees lack authority to revise the legislative committees' recommendations, but committee members can propose amendments to the omnibus bill once it reaches the floor. In the House, therefore, a key factor in determining the outcome of reconciliation is the rule under which an omnibus bill is debated—whether it is open to the offering of amendments, closed, or restricted, and if restricted, how many and which amendments are in order. In this case, the Democratic majority offered a restricted rule that allowed consideration and, as it turned out, adoption of several amendments which reduced somewhat the savings recommended by the committees. A reconciliation bill, unlike a budget resolution, makes new law and, therefore, requires the President's signature. Jimmy Carter signed the bill on December 4, 1981.

RECONCILIATION AND THE REAGAN BUDGET

This brand-new procedure, developed by Congress for its own use, had just been put in place when the Reagan Administration assumed office and decided to use it as the principal means for effecting a radical executive initiative for reducing the scope and intensity of the U.S. government's intervention in the economic and social life of the nation—cutting spending, narrowing the authorizations for many programs, and terminating others. The Administration proposed reducing spending outlays for fiscal year 1982 by about $48 billion, approximately 70 percent of this to be achieved by reconciliation, and greater amounts in fiscal years 1983 and 1984.

The House Budget Committee, in a partisan vote by seventeen Democratic members, reported a resolution requiring fourteen authorizing committees to prepare reconciliation legislation that would reduce spending for entitlements and other uncontrollable programs by about $16 billion in fiscal year 1982 and somewhat larger sums in the following two fiscal years. An additional $20 billion was to be trimmed from discretionary or controllable programs by appropriation procedures, in response to spending targets proposed in the budget resolution, and similar amounts were to be saved in the next two fiscal years. This proposal was unsatisfactory to the Administration and committee Republicans for reasons it is important to understand. They wanted large reductions in expenditures for the next fiscal year for the purpose of reducing the deficit, "bringing the budget under control," and reducing the double-digit inflation that they had inherited from the previous Administration. But the Reagan Administration wanted much more than this; they wanted to make the reductions as long-lasting as they could for the purpose of permanently reducing the federal government's participation in the nation's life. Thus they proposed to use the reconciliation procedure to curtail the basic authorization of many programs and terminate the authorization of others, including programs whose expenditures were discretionary and controllable by means of appropriation procedures. The reconciliation instructions to legislative committees proposed by the Administration would not only require them to put tighter caps on entitlements and direct spending for the next three fiscal years, but also to reduce or eliminate the amounts authorized to be appropriated for many other programs, and in some cases, where previously there had been no monetary limits in authorizing legislation, to impose these for the next three fiscal years at least.

The use of reconciliation with the first budget resolution to control the uncontrollables was an important innovation in 1980; the Administration's proposal to use this procedure in 1981 as a general alternative to regular authorization procedures was more radical. Also, the Republicans had broad support among moderate and conservative Democrats for the first purpose of reconciliation—relating to the deficit and inflation—and narrower support for the second one relating to the ubiquitousness of the federal government.

Budget Committee Republicans offered an alternative budget resolution that, in addition to lower budget targets, instructed fifteen legislative committees to reduce program spending by a total of approximately $35 billion in

1982, $46 billion in 1983, and $56 billion in 1984, one-third of this on average to come from reductions in direct spending and two-thirds from lowering authorizations for appropriations. The exact proportions were specified for each committee and each year. Responding to this proposal, the chairmen of all of the legislative committees sent a joint letter to all members complaining that the Reagan proposal "wipes out traditional flexibility afforded under the Budget Act for legislative committees to act cooperatively with the Appropriations Committee to comply with the overall spending ceiling established in the budget resolution . . . [and would] destroy the integrity of the legislative process as well as the budget process." Nonetheless the Republican alternative carried by a vote of 253 (63D., 190R.) to 176 (176D.). A similar resolution passed the Senate, 78 to 20.

The final version of the first budget resolution for fiscal year 1982, which was enacted on May 21, 1981, allowed the legislative committees in the House and Senate only twenty-two days in which to draft, debate, and approve amendments, many of them highly complex, to laws governing 250 programs. Surprisingly, they met the deadline, with the exception of one House committee, and for the most part they fulfilled, however grudgingly in some cases, the letter and purpose of their instructions, although the Administration was not satisfied with some decisions of the House committees and won approval on the floor for additional reductions. The legislative committees' recommendations, when combined into an omnibus reconciliation bill by the budget committees, covered 933 pages, the longest single piece of legislation ever considered by Congress and possibly the most complex. The laws relating to trade adjustment assistance (financial aid for those who lose their jobs as a result of competition from imports), extended unemployment benefits, retirement of railroad workers, housing subsidies, public television, regulation of commercial broadcasters, consumer product safety, dairy subsidies, farm loans, railroad subsidies to Amtrak and Conrail, maritime subsidies, distribution of food stamps, community services, aid to families with dependent children, social services, student loans, compensatory education for disadvantaged students, health care for the elderly (Medicare and Medicaid), other health programs, small business loans, and many others were rewritten in part; spending ceilings were set for many more programs; and some were terminated. President Reagan signed the Omnibus Budget Reconciliation Act of 1981 on August 13, scarcely six months after he had first proposed using reconciliation to carry out his election promises to trim federal spending and federal activities.

As of this writing (January 1982), it is difficult to know or predict how reconciliation, used with the first budget resolution, will effect in the long run relations between the Executive and Congress and the relative significance of budget, appropriation, and authorization procedures as means for conducting these relations. Reconciliation with the first resolution was devised by Congress in 1980, and used in extraordinary circumstances and with extraordinary results by the Executive in 1981. The 1981 scenario is unlikely to be replayed without modifications, however, if only because of broad congressional concern for the violence that was done to fundamental legislative norms. Many of the nation's laws were rewritten in a period of three weeks by a truncated legislative process which generally excluded the public and interest groups. There were no hearings, no detailed committee reports, little debate, and little opportunity for members to offer amendments. "Hardly anyone in Congress believes that reconciliation [as practiced in 1981] is a sensible or responsible way to handle legislation."[11] Even fiscal conservatives who applauded the overall results were concerned about the process.

Examples. Representative Barber B. Conable, Jr. (R. NY): "This has been a terrible way to legislate but we have no alternatives."

Senator William Proxmire (D. WI): "Congressional procedures were greatly abused, in spite of the innovative nature of the original reconciliation idea . . . Unless we stop short, take stock, and revise some of the procedures, the budget reform act . . . may destroy the Senate as a deliberative body."

Representative James R. Jones (D. OK), chairman, House Budget Committee: "Reconciliation ought to allow the authorizing committees to work in a much more orderly fashion in the future."[12]

We can assume that Congress will soon modify reconciliation procedures to mitigate serious infringements of democratic legislative norms.*

We can assume also that the 1981 experience was unique in the sense that the new Administration used reconciliation in a dramatic effort to turn the country around with regard to federal involvement in its life. This effort will continue, but probably without the same intense dramatics and not necessarily by means of reconciliation.

Given these assumptions, what are the possible consequences of the continued use of chastened reconciliation procedures associated with the first resolution? Until 1980–1981, the new budget procedures had not had a major

---

*In 1982 the first budget resolution (for fiscal year 1983) directed that nine House committees and eight in the Senate report legislation to cut expenditures. Instead of consolidating the consequent legislative proposals into an omnibus reconciliation bill as was done in 1981, the House debated and passed each committee's recommendations as a separate bill, combining only those relating to a uniform cap on cost-of-living allowances for civil service, foreign service, and military personnel. Also, Congress did not pass a second budget resolution in 1982. Instead it instructed that the targets of the first resolution, along with the reconciliation instructions that accompanied it, be binding, unless the targets were specifically waived, as was done subsequently to accommodate President Reagan's multibillion-dollar program for the construction and repair of highways and mass transit systems.

impact on authorization procedures and the conduct of the legislative committees. To be sure, the budget resolutions applied to legislative committees as well as to appropriations, and as a result the authorizing committees developed a greater awareness of the budgetary implications of their legislative proposals. Also, in adopting categorical targets in the first resolution, Congress could reject in advance major new legislative programs that involved large expenditures, such as national health insurance. But the first resolution was not binding, so that legislative committees could nonetheless propose the new programs, and, if Congress adopted them, the spending would in all likelihood be accommodated in the second resolution. The legislative committees were also able to insure that spending for entitlement programs under existing laws would continue as prescribed, by simply not reporting amendatory legislation that would reduce the basis for payments.

Thus the legislative committees had not been much inhibited in their program advocacy role. The March 15 reports to the budget committees, to the contrary, encouraged them to play this role. In these reports the committees are asked to estimate next year's costs of current legislation and also to identify and promote the legislative initiatives that they might propose during the year. "The March 15 process forces committees to behave as program advocates, not merely presenting their estimates, but marshalling arguments and support in behalf of legislation they favor."[13]

For the purpose of reconciliation as practiced in 1981, however, the traditional advocacy role of the authorizing committees was hobbled to the extent that the committees were required to report legislation reducing authorization of appropriations for controllable programs, not only closing large gaps between authorizations and existing levels of expenditures, but frequently reducing the authorizations below these levels, and reducing expenditures on uncontrollable programs by revising the entitlement criteria that do control them. Reconciliation forced legislative committees to conform existing law to current budget decisions. There are conflicting views in Congress about the wisdom of compelling this change in the traditional role of legislative committees. All House legislative committee chairmen have opposed it. On the other hand, some members have championed the use of reconciliation as a means for co-opting the legislative committees into the setting of budget priorities and requiring them to integrate and coordinate their legislative activities more closely with each other and with the activities of budgeting and appropriating. Pete V. Domenici (R. NM), who became chairman of the Senate Budget Committee in 1981, has said: "The authorizing committees now feel like they're very much a part of budget restraint and have a great deal more to say about what gets included in various alternatives. . . . Reconciliation . . . has strengthened the legislative process [as well as the budget process]."[14]

I have discussed the impact of budget resolutions on appropriation procedures and the conduct of the appropriations committees. What about reconciliation in this context? The appropriations committees have rejoiced at the
use of reconciliation to control entitlements and direct spending, which was
the only use to which it was put in 1980. They were less enthusiastic about
the use of reconciliation in 1981 to force legislative committees to cut drastically the authorization of expenditures on programs that could be controlled
through appropriations. The reconciliation instructions in many cases mandated a reduction of authorizations below existing levels of appropriations,
which meant that there was little room for additional trimming by the appropriations committees, whose actions were preordained. But it is important not
to exaggerate, as some observers have, the opposition of the appropriations
committees to reconciliation because it reduces the committees' discretion.[15]
The committees have from the beginning welcomed the discipline of the new
preappropriation procedures not only as a matter of strategy to control backdoor spending, but also as a matter of principle, namely the economy norm.
House Appropriations Committee chairman Whitten, commenting after the
1981 reconciliation bill was enacted and with regard to possible encroach-
ments on his committee's discretionary powers, said: "We have by and large
agreed with the objectives, and so we rocked along."[16] Protection of turf is
not everything.

The most striking aspect of the 1981 reconciliation experience was that the
Congressional Budget Control Act, which was designed to give Congress
greater control over the executive budget, was, by this means, put to use by
the Executive to control the legislature. The Congress was forced to consider
the President's package whole and on his terms, and in this type of decision
structure the President was at a considerable advantage, as the votes demonstrated. In the short run this can be attributed in good part to the President's
skill and popularity. But there are likely to be long-term consequences of this
reversal of roles, as discussed at the conclusion of this chapter.

IMPOUNDMENT CONTROL

The Budget Control Act also provides procedures for congressional control
over executive impoundments of appropriated funds. At the time the act was
being written Congress was angry and frustrated by President Richard M.
Nixon's frequent and broad use of impoundment, and they were determined
to place restrictions on the Executive in this regard. Typically, Nixon would
propose reduced appropriations for activities that had been part of his predecessor's Great Society program, and the Democratically controlled Congress
would respond by increasing the President's budget when it passed the appropriation bills. Nixon would sign the bills and then by executive action he would

impound the increased funds, thereby restoring his original budget and in effect excluding Congress from decision making for appropriations. Many in Congress from both parties challenged the legality and constitutionality of the President's actions, which he based largely on a broad and loose interpretation of the President's "constitutional duties," including an implied executive power known as "executive privilege." If Nixon didn't like Congress's spending decisions, they said, he should veto the appropriation bills and give Congress the opportunity to override the veto. Instead, he signed the bills and then overruled them by executive action.

Both House and Senate agreed that the President should be required to report any proposed impoundments to the Congress, but they disagreed on the specifics of an enforcement procedure. The House bill provided that the proposed impoundments would be sanctioned unless either House of Congress disapproved them within sixty days; the Senate bill, that the impoundments would be sanctioned only if both Houses approved them within sixty days. These are two versions of the so-called legislative veto, which is the subject of chapter 11. In the end the Budget Control Act included both procedures. Impoundments were divided into two categories, rescissions and deferrals. In the first category, the President proposes that appropriated funds not be spent, that they be rescinded, but they must be spent unless Congress passes a rescission bill within forty-five days following notification by the President. In the second category, the President defers the obligation of appropriated funds, and his action remains in effect unless or until either House vetoes it by passing a simple resolution.

The first year after enactment of the act, President Gerald R. Ford used the impoundment provisions liberally in an effort to rescind billions of dollars added by the Democratic Congress to his budget for social programs. But Congress refused to approve the rescission of approximately 90 percent of these funds which then had to be spent. This was a very different result from that achieved before the act. By impoundment control, Congress has been able to prevent the President from unilaterally ignoring Congress's budget priorities by withholding funds.

Objectives and Evaluation

Supporters of the act of 1974, like proponents of all of the major congressional reforms of the period, had multiple and sometimes inconsistent objectives. One objective, to impose effective limits on governmental spending—"to get the budget under control"—was shared by fiscal conservatives in Congress, particularly members of the appropriations committees, and by the President and the Office of Management and Budget. To this end the act included expenditure targets and ceilings, and provisions to relate the expenditure and tax sides of the budget, to control the uncontrollables, to combine consideration of the spending impacts of all thirteen appropriation bills, to sensitize the legislative committees to the spending implications of their actions, to encourage more timely decisions, and to reconcile budgetary decisions with those relating to authorizations and appropriations.

Contrary to this objective, some supporters of the act saw it as an opportunity to free expenditure decisions from the restrictive influence of the economy norm. Fiscal liberals in Congress believed that the new procedures could be used to break up the existing pattern of executive–legislative relations in fiscal matters, which involved principally the President's Budget and the OMB, on the one hand, and Congress's appropriation procedures and the appropriations committees, on the other. They were intent on involving the legislative committees in the new budget procedures, for, contrary to the fiscal conservatives, they saw this as a means for influencing decisions in the direction of greater program support. They also sought successfully to prevent the budget committees from being dominated by members who served also on the appropriations and tax committees.

Another objective was to enable Congress to develop and pass alternatives to the President's Budget. The new preappropriation procedures were to increase participation by Congress vis-à-vis the President in determining program priorities. As we observed in chapter 3, providing means for Congress to develop both legislative and budgetary alternatives to the President's programs was a major objective of the reformers of the 1970s. For this purpose the Budget Control Act provided for *congressional* budget resolutions to guide Congress in appropriations and other spending legislation, the preparation of alternatives to the President's estimates by legislative and appropriations committees and by budget committee staffs, the control of executive impoundments of appropriated funds, and other provisions.

Contrary to this objective, some supporters of the act saw it as an opportunity for the Executive to obtain from Congress a more positive response to the President's Budget. These members believed that the President's Budget should be the dominant influence in the new preappropriation procedures as it was in appropriation procedures, and during initial hearings on the act they sought a commitment from OMB that the agency would provide Congress with basic data to make this possible. With alacrity OMB made the commitment. Indeed, OMB and the President supported the legislation because they wanted this very result.[17]

We have, then, two sets of opposing objectives—fiscal conservatism versus fiscal liberalism, and increasing the influence of Congress versus increasing that of the President in budgetary policy. How has it turned out? The procedures are inherently conservative, as was observed earlier in discussing relations between the budget and appropriations committees. "The congressional budget process is making liberals sound like conservatives," said the *New York Times* in 1977.[18] Nonetheless, liberal Democrats in the House made a remarkably successful run to dominate the new procedures. Between 1975 and 1980 they brought to pass generous budget targets for social programs and restrictive ones for national defense. They were successful so long as the Democratic majority in the House was large, Democratic leaders were able to get moderate and conservative Democrats to support liberal budget resolutions by convincing them of their responsibility for the success of the new reform procedures, and moderate and conservative Democrats failed to challenge the liberals and the leadership in the Democratic caucus on appointments to the Budget Committee. Once these three factors began to change, so did the liberal spending consequences of the budget procedures.

As for the relative influence of the Executive and Congress, the Executive continues to dominate appropriation procedures and has come to dominate the new preappropriation procedures. The President's Budget is the most important factor in congressional budgeting. The President and OMB called the tune for Congress's actions on reconciliation in 1981, so much so that budget committees and congressional leaders hesitated to begin drafting the second *congressional* budget resolution until they received directions from the White House.

Examples. James R. Jones (D. OK), chairman, House Budget Committee: "I don't have any intention of providing a committee alternative. Basically it's the President's program."

Pete V. Domenici (R. NM), chairman, Senate Budget Committee: "We need some real official iteration from the White House on where the Budget is going and what they expect us to do."

Leon E. Panetta (D. CA), chairman, Task Force on Reconciliation, House Budget Committee: "The White House is going to have to play a role."[19]

To be sure, 1981 may turn out to have been unusual, but it is highly unlikely that the reform objective of congressional independence from the Executive in determining program priorities will be realized in the long run. The principal adversary of the budget committees is less likely to be the President's Budget and the appropriations committees than the legislative committees with their interests in authorizing new and bigger programs. The efforts to co-opt legislative committees into support for budgeting procedures are fragile. On the other hand, the large professional staffs of the Congressional Budget Office and the House and Senate budget committees have developed sympathies and alliances with the similarly trained and similarly oriented staffs of OMB and of the appropriations committees. And budget committees themselves may develop symbiotic relations with the appropriations committees and the OMB, just as the agriculture committees of Congress have such relations with the Department of Agriculture. If this turns out to be the long-run case, then we will have an informal alliance among the budget committees, CBO, appropriations committees, OMB, and, to a certain extent, the President, on the one side, representing fiscal conservatism; and the legislative committees and the departments and agencies they supervise, on the other, representing a demand for greater spending.

In terms of our model of executive–legislative relations, the preappropriation procedures have contributed to whole House control over its parts. The budget committees are less autonomous than the appropriations committees. Despite the fragility and adversarial nature of relations between authorizing and budget committees, the legislative committees have participated in budgetary policy. The debate on budget resolutions, although limited by restricted rules, has been more fulsome and vigorous than that on appropriation bills. And it has been more partisan. A number of the 1970s reforms discussed in chapter 3 sought to strengthen party. In this their proponents assumed a greater degree of party homogeneity and partisanship than existed in the House, and they underplayed the strength of ad hoc majorities. Budget reform was based less on party partisanship than were these other reforms, and more on congressional partisanship contra the President. Otherwise it made little sense to charge Congress with enacting annually congressional budget resolutions as alternatives to the President's Budget when, in at least half of the years, both branches were likely to be controlled by the same party. Perversely, however, partisanship came to dominate budget procedures in the House, not in the Senate, from 1975 to 1980.

The preappropriation procedures have also contributed to an emphasis on broad rather than narrow issues of policy. The fiscal coordination sought unsuccessfully in 1946 and 1950 has been achieved in some significant degree. In this regard the disagreement between the House Appropriations and Budget committees over the amount of detail in the reports on budget resolutions is important.

10

Congressional Controls over

Executive Personnel

DURING most of this century Congress's involvement in personnel matters has focused on two interests:

1. To assure that the President is not able to set up a personnel patronage system disguised under Civil Service rules and regulations.

2. To assure that the President does not dominate national policy and national administration by virtue of having complete command over the experts, administrators, and policymakers in the bureaucracy. A certain degree of independence of the bureaucracy from presidential discretionary power is necessary, Congress believes, to permit Congress to exercise its duties of oversight and control.

To the extent that Congress succeeds in its second interest, both the President and, to a lesser degree, the Congress will rely on the bureaucracy to help them carry out their respective roles in the legislative and administrative processes. Because such an arrangement is untidy in terms of organization charts and command hierarchies, some scholars of the Executive have been critical of it and unsympathetic to Congress's purpose. Also, supporters of "whirlpools" and "iron triangles" have relied heavily on the consequences of this arrangement to justify their model of executive–legislative relations which, it will be recalled, deemphasizes any uniquely defined roles for the two branches of government. However, the consequences of Congress's objective of avoiding executive dominion over the bureaucracy can be understood just as well, indeed better, in terms of our model of executive–legislative relations.

They are inconsistent with this model only in the abnormal case where the relations between executive bureaus and congressional committees become so intimate and so ubiquitous that the President and Congress as a whole are excluded from effective participation in policy and administration.

Congress has developed a number of ways and means to pursue its two principal interests in personnel administration, some of them directed at the permanent civil service—the career executives—and others at political, noncareer executives.

Control over the Civil Service

In regard to the civil service, Congress has resorted chiefly to the following mechanisms: detailed legislation, concentrating responsibility for personnel administration in a partially independent agency, requiring civil service experts to testify before congressional committees, and investigations.

DETAILED LEGISLATION

Congress's first means for following its interests in the civil service has been to limit the President's discretion by enacting detailed statutes that regulate all aspects of the civil service system and, at the same time, by opposing any actions by the President that do this by executive orders. Thus details frequently not proposed by the Executive have been written into the laws on pay scales, retirement systems, reductions in force, hours of work, merit awards, training programs, numbers of top level personnel, and other matters. The title of the U.S. Code that deals with the civil service is a lengthy one.

SINGLE, INDEPENDENT PERSONNEL AGENCY

Secondly, Congress has limited the President's discretion by centralizing control over civil service personnel in a single agency—until 1979 the Civil Service Commission (CSC)—and then controlling this agency carefully, making it more dependent on Congress than other bureaus of the Executive. In the legislation of 1883 establishing the civil service system and the CSC, steps were taken to make the commission partially independent of the President: only two of the three commissioners could be of the same political party; and the commissioners were given fixed and staggered terms so that they were not entirely subject to the President's pleasure to continue in office.

As the federal service became larger and more complex, Congress realized that if it was to have some control over the bureaucracy, it needed a large, central executive-type agency to help it—to provide data about the civil service; to provide a single source to which Congress could express its dissatisfaction and views on the public service with an expectation that remedial action would be taken. The Civil Service Commission was then, in large measure, the instrumentality that made a significant degree of congressional control possible, and for this reason Congress jealously and zealously guarded the commission against intervention by the President and the executive departments.

Several examples will illustrate detailed legislation and independent personnel agency as two means of congressional control.

Example. The President's Committee on Administrative Management (Brownlow committee) in 1937 and the Commission on Organization of Executive Branch (first Hoover commission) in 1948 recommended a new and powerful White House personnel office on the theory that control over personnel is an important executive management function. Legislation to effect these proposals made no progress in the Congress although other recommendations of both groups were enacted in 1939 and 1948.

Example. President Dwight D. Eisenhower appointed Philip Young, chairman of the CSC, to also be presidential advisor on personnel management in the Executive Office of the President (EOP). Members of Congress objected to this arrangement of allowing Young to wear two hats. As chairman of the CSC he had a special duty to keep Congress informed, but as an advisor to the President he would have no such obligation. As a consequence of Young's being able to claim a privilege not to report on personnel matters being considered by the EOP, Congress might in the end lose information on which it had previously relied. Responding to these objections, Eisenhower terminated the arrangement in 1957 when Young was succeeded as CSC chairman by Harris Ellsworth.

Subsequently under President Lyndon B. Johnson, CSC chairman John W. Macy, Jr., apparently did the same thing. He served in the White House as talent scout and advisor to the President in filling top-level political positions while he was chairman of the commission. But Macy claimed that there was a real difference between his assignment and Young's, as seen in the following excerpt from hearings before the House Committee on Post Office and Civil Service in 1967:

H. R. GROSS (R. IA): "I might ask you, Mr. Macy, which hat do you wear when you evaluate abilities of a political nominee to one of these top jobs?"

MACY: "I have only one hat. I am Chairman of the Civil Service Commission."

GROSS: "When did you lose the other hat?"

MACY: "I have never had more than one hat. I have been exclusively the Chairman of the Civil Service Commission. I have done some additional work in that capacity with respect to advising the President on some of his appointments, but I have only one job, as Chairman of the Civil Service Commission, and only one salary. All of my concern is with providing leadership for the Civil Service Commission in the evaluation of those appointments on the basis of merit in selection for positions in the Federal Government. Where I occasionally assist the President, it is also in terms of evaluating candidates he is considering in terms of merit, not on any other terms."[1]

Example. In 1955 the Commission on Organization of the Executive Branch (second Hoover commission) recommended that there be established a senior civil service corps to be comprised of top-level career executives with significant management experience who then could be assigned to management jobs in any government agency as needed. In March 1958 President Dwight D. Eisenhower, following this recommendation, established by executive order a career executive program to be directed by a board appointed by the President and independent of the CSC. Congress reacted by attaching to the Federal Employees Salary Act of 1958 a provision that appointments to the senior civil service grades may be made only on approval of the qualifications of the proposed appointees by the CSC. It also attached to the relevant appropriation bill a provision prohibiting expenditure of any funds to carry out the President's order. It was not that Congress disapproved, necessarily, of a new career executive service. It disapproved of the President's initiating this major reform by executive order, thereby providing no opportunity for Congress to consider it, and his charging a presidentially appointed board with sole responsibility for implementation.

Some eight years later, in November 1966, President Lyndon B. Johnson also issued an executive order to establish a career executive program. This time Congress allowed the plan to go into effect. But there were significant differences from Eisenhower's plan: (1) The Johnson order was much more tightly drawn than the earlier one; (2) the congressional committees had had more time to study the problem; (3) most important, responsibility for the Johnson program was centered in the CSC, and it was in the form of an amendment to the civil service rules administered by the commission; (4) finally, CSC chairman John W. Macy, Jr., said at House hearings that he would have no strong objection if Congress wanted to legislate the plan. The committee turned down the opportunity, and the executive order went into effect.

In February 1971 President Richard M. Nixon proposed legislation to Congress to broaden this program and give it greater status—to establish a federal executive service that would absorb the career executive program (which had been established by Johnson) and also various supergrade positions in the federal service, which were filled by both career employees and political appointees. The federal executive service would include approximately 7000 persons in the executive branch, 75 percent of them career employees and 25 percent political appointments. The CSC would each year decide how many of these 7000 positions should be allocated to each department and major agency and how many of the positions allotted to each department and agency should be filled by career employees or by political and noncareer officers.

President Nixon's proposal was very carefully drawn to be responsive to Congress's special concerns on personnel. Thus it was a legislative proposal that Congress could amend. It called for an annual "stewardship" report to Congress. It vested important authority in the CSC. It provided that the CSC's annual plan for distributing the 7000 jobs among agencies and bureaus should lie before Congress for ninety days before going into effect.

The Nixon bill passed the Senate in 1972, but not the House. Before reporting the bill, however, the Senate Committee on Post Office and Civil Service amended it to give more authority to the CSC. It said in its report: "The Committee believes that if the Federal Executive Service is to succeed, it must be administered by the Government's central personnel agency—the Civil Service Commission. The bill as introduced made provision for collaboration between the Commission and the Office of Management and Budget on such matters as the ratio of career to noncareer executives. The chairman of the Civil Service Commission or his representatives are, of course, free at any time to consult with the director of the Office of Management and Budget, but the Committee views with some concern the intrusion of that Office into substantive business, unrelated to budgetary matters, of departments and agencies; and rejects the proposal that Civil Service Commission–Office of Management and Budget collaboration be required by law."

Legislation to establish a senior executive service, with many features of the Nixon proposal, was finally enacted in 1978 as Title 4 of the Civil Service Reform Act.

In 1978 Congress accepted, with amendments, President Jimmy Carter's radical personnel proposals which, among other things, abolished the CSC, transferred its functions to two new agencies, and allowed the Executive greater flexibility in personnel administration. In doing so, however, Congress continued to promote its long-term interests in personnel matters—avoiding executive spoils and avoiding monopolistic control by the Executive over the experts, managers, and top-level decision makers in government.

Under the new law an Office of Personnel Management (OPM) is responsible for the personnel management functions of the former CSC, that is, for developing personnel policies governing all aspects of civilian employment in executive agencies and for assisting the agencies in implementing these policies. It is headed by a director and deputy director who are appointed by the President and confirmed by the Senate for four-year terms.

A Merit Systems Protection Board (MSPB) is responsible for insuring that the OPM and the departments adhere to merit system principles. It investigates and acts on alleged abuses of the merit system and adjudicates employee appeals against their agencies. The Board is composed of three members, only two of whom may be of the same political party. They are nominated by the President and confirmed by the Senate for seven-year terms, and can be removed only for specified reasons. The President selects the chairman from among the three members, but this choice, too, must be confirmed by the Senate. Also, the principal lawyer for the MSPB, called the Special Counsel, is nominated by the President and confirmed by the Senate. He serves a five-year term and can be removed by the President only for specified reasons.

The act states the merit system principles that are to be followed and protected. Appointment and promotion are to be based on ability, knowledge, and skills, and are to be free from political interference, political patronage, and nepotism. There is a newly stated right—in a sense an obligation—of civil servants to disclose to Congress or the public instances where they believe their bosses or agencies are guilty of violating laws or regulations, or of mismanagement or waste of funds. In addition, they are to report agency policies that they believe to be substantial dangers to public health and safety. "Whistle-blowers" who exercise this right cannot be fired, transferred, demoted, or otherwise disciplined. And the special counsel in MSPB is charged with enforcing this.

The principal objective of the President and Congress in the civil service reforms of 1978 was to improve productivity in the bureaucracy, by encouraging greater efficiency in the delivery of governmental services. The existing personnel system was seen as containing disincentives to greater productivity. The rewards granted to those responsible for running public services were largely unrelated to efficiency. Also, the vast accumulation of statutory provisions and rules and regulations relating to the civil service was seen as inhibiting initiative, flexibility, and productivity.

Congress, then, supported civil service reform because it was convinced that this was needed to improve productivity in the bureaucracy. Given the general character of the reforms, it had to seek different means for protecting its enduring interests in executive personnel, since the old means were one source of the inefficiency that was to be exorcised. It is unlikely that Congress will have as much influence over OPM as it did over CSC. The new agency, led by a single director rather than by a three-member bipartisan commission, is more clearly under the President's control. At the same time, provisions of the new law relating to the MSPB give significant protection against the President's politicizing the civil service. The board, which is relatively independent of the President, has authority to review all OPM rules and regulations and to veto those that in its opinion constitute prohibited personnel practices.

As for guaranteeing congressional access to the experts, provisions relating to whistle-blowing were taken very seriously by those in Congress who were most involved in passing the reform law. Civil servants have been notified that blowing the whistle on their bosses and agencies in testimony before congressional committees or other groups is de rigueur in contemporary public service, that they are to suffer no adverse consequences as civil servants from doing this, and that the independent MSPB is to insure that this is so. Furthermore, the board's special counsel may require an agency to investigate and file a written report on a whistle-blower's allegations of agency wrongdoing if the counsel finds substantial likelihood that the allegations are true, and this report is sent to Congress.

REQUIRING TESTIMONY FROM EXPERTS

A third means used by Congress to prevent the President from having full dominion over national policy and administration by virtue of having exclusive control over the career experts in the bureaucracy is to demand that these employees be available to testify before congressional committees. The regular testimony of career officers before appropriations subcommittees was mentioned in chapter 8. Frequently it is only they who can match the knowledge of senior subcommittee members on departmental operations. Career officers also testify regularly before the legislative committees, especially on annual and short-term authorizations.

It is rare that career personnel refuse to testify, although these rare occasions receive such exposure in the media that one might believe that they are a common occurrence. When they decline to give testimony, civil servants usually claim executive privilege on behalf of the President or their more immediate political superiors. Executive privilege will be discussed in the last chapter, on Congress's "right to know." Also, the whistle-blowing provisions of the new civil service law are designed, in part, to insure that Congress will receive information it needs from the bureaucracy.

INVESTIGATING ADMINISTRATION OF THE CIVIL SERVICE SYSTEM

Finally, to protect its interests in the federal personnel system, Congress has guarded the sanctity of the civil service by means of investigations which are initiated typically by members of the party that does not hold the presidency.

Example. Charles F. Willis, Jr., was a White House assistant to President Dwight D. Eisenhower. He developed the Willis plan, under which a new position of "special assistant" to the head of each department and major agency was established, with responsibility to report to the Republican National Committee (through Charles Willis's White House office) all job vacancies at Grade GS-14 and above. The Republican National Committee would then publicize these vacancies among deserving party members and solicit their applications for jobs. All candidates for these vacancies were then to be cleared by the Republican National Committee through Republican members of Congress or Republican state officials.

Initially the Willis plan was addressed to vacancies. It was soon expanded to include a "qualifications review" of all federal employees at Grade GS-14 and above, to see if they were fit to continue office under a Republican administration (made covertly on a special White House form). The acknowledged purpose of this review of qualifications was to liberate a large number of key career jobs for deserving Republicans.

Any patronage activity on this scale was bound to arouse career personnel officers, other career executives, Washington journalists, and the Congress. And indeed it did. A secret White House briefing document describing the workings of the Willis plan came into the hands of the Senate Post Office and Civil Service Committee. The chairman ordered a full-scale investigation which sounded the deathknell of the Willis plan, embarrassed the White House, established the Democratic majority in the Senate as the stalwart defenders of the merit system, and turned considerable employee opinion against the Eisenhower Administration. Out of this investigation came personal pledges by the President that the merit system would be protected against political infiltration and renewed vigilance by Congress against any resurrection of the Willis plan.

Subsequently during the Johnson Administration, the Republicans on the House Post Office and Civil Service Committee, being in the minority, established a task force on the civil service merit system "to protect federal government workers from arm-twisting pressures applied for political purposes." Any federal employee subjected to pressure was invited "to bring his problem to our attention." During the Nixon Administration the House Committee exposed several violations of the merit system, and in these cases, it is interesting to note, the reports documenting the violations were prepared by the Civil Service Commission and released by the House Committee on Post Office and Civil Service.

Thus, contrary to popular lore that pictures Congress as a supplicant for patronage, ever willing to violate merit system principles, the legislature is in reality a defender of the system.

Control over Political Executives

To fulfill its personnel interests in regard to top level policymaking positions that are not under civil service, Congress has used primarily two means: participation first in establishing positions and subsequently in selecting those who are to fill them.

ESTABLISHING POSITIONS

Laws that authorize major programs typically establish offices and define their duties—for example, the number of assistant secretaries of Defense and their respective jurisdictions; set the tenure of office—for example, there is no fixed tenure for assistant secretaries of Defense, but members of the Securities and Exchange Commission (SEC) are appointed for terms of five years; decide which offices shall be subject to Senate confirmation and which not—for example, deputy and assistant secretaries of Defense are subject to confirmation, deputy assistant secretaries are not; define the qualifications of office; prescribe the procedures that the Executive must follow in making appointments—for example, for the Railroad Retirement Board the President must solicit recommendations from representatives of the employees and of the carriers and select one from each list; and other provisions. In most of these matters, since they are legislation, the President takes the initiative. If Congress votes a five-year term for members of the SEC, this is probably what the

President recommended. At the same time, Congress amends the Executive's recommendations in many cases and in others it proposes additional requirements for these top-level positions.

We can take a closer look at the decision to require that the President's appointments to certain offices be subject to confirmation by the Senate. The Constitution provides for Senate confirmation of ambassadors, judges of the Supreme Court, and all other officers whose positions are established by law, except that laws can vest appointment of these other officers in the President alone, in the courts, or in the heads of departments.[2] Thus except for ambassadors and Supreme Court judges, the decision on whether top executive and judicial officials should be subject to Senate confirmation is made by the President and Congress, normally in the legislation that authorizes the programs and activities that they administer. These statutes determine which officials are to be career executives under civil service, which are to be political executives, and among the political executives which are to be confirmed by the Senate.

To a degree this decision has been routinized for the departments and major agencies in that it is now customary that all department secretaries, deputy and assistant secretaries, and general counsels be subject to confirmation, as are the directors and deputy and assistant directors of major independent agencies. The crucial decision that determines the extent of the Senate's formal participation in appointments to each department and agency is, therefore, the number of positions of deputy and assistant secretary or director that is approved in the authorizing legislation. It is also well established and provided in law that all federal judges (in addition to those on the Supreme Court), members of independent regulatory commissions and boards, and U.S. attorneys and marshals be confirmed by the Senate. Beyond these uniform categories, some bureau chiefs—for example, Chief of the Children's Bureau in the Department of Health and Human Services—and other miscellaneous officers are required by law to be confirmed.

In some of these cases the requirement has been proposed by either the President or Congress because they want to establish high rank for the positions; in others, the requirement has been initiated by Congress because it wants by this means to have greater influence or control over the Executive. Thus during and immediately after Watergate there were congressional efforts to rein in the President by subjecting to Senate confirmation some of his most important personal advisors in the White House and executive office—directors of the Office of Management and Budget, National Security Council, Domestic Council, Council on International Economic Policy, and Office of Science and Technology, all of whom were also assistants or personal advisors to the President. Of these proposals, the only ones to be enacted required that the director and deputy director of OMB be confirmed as well as the director of the Office of Science and Technology.

In all about 1000 major positions in the executive branch, including approximately 150 ambassadors and 190 U.S. attorneys, and marshals, and 550 positions in the judicial branch, mostly judges, require the Senate's consent.[3]

CONFIRMATION PROCEDURES

While the decision to require confirmation in any particular case involves the House as much as the Senate, the confirmation itself is largely a Senate affair. Under the Constitution, as interpreted by the Supreme Court, Congress cannot enact legislation that allows the House to participate in confirmation of executive and judicial appointments.[4] Thus the Senate, in performing this function, is acting for Congress as a whole.

Table 10.1 shows the numerical results of the Senate's confirmation activity for the seventeen-year period, 1961 to 1977. Only four of the President's nominations were rejected by floor vote; nine were rejected by committee; and twenty-seven nominations were withdrawn by the President due to Senate opposition.[5] A nomination that is likely to be defeated on the floor rarely gets there. If there is a case to be made against a nominee, it is usually made in committee, and if the case is strong enough, the nomination usually terminates with a negative committee vote or it is withdrawn by the President.

TABLE 10.1

Major Nominations Confirmed and Rejected by the Senate, 1961–77[a]

Years	Confirmed	Rejected			
		Rejected by floor vote	Rejected by committee vote	Withdrawn by President	Total rejected
1961–72	1897	3	0	5	8
1973–77	954	1	9	22	32
Total	2851	4	9	27	40

SOURCE: Gordon Calvin Mackenzie, *The Politics of Presidential Appointments* (New York: The Free Press, 1981), pp. xiv, 177.
[a]Does not include U.S. attorneys and marshals.

It will be observed that the total of rejected nominees in the five-year period, 1973–1977, is four times as large as that in the previous twelve years and that the number rejected by committee votes or withdrawn by the President during the same five-year period is six times greater than in the previous twelve years. This appreciable change in the Senate's recent conduct is due to a number of factors. Increased staff and other resources were made available to congressional committees in the 1970s, and as a result most Senate committees were able for the first time to give one or two staff members principal responsibility for making detailed inquiries and investigations of presidential nominees. Under the congressional reforms of the 1970s the committee decision-making process became more open to public view. This meant that senators were not only forced individually to face the consequences of their confirmation votes, but they were also encouraged to put on a good show before the media and television audiences by aggressively questioning at-times hapless nominees. Consumer, environmental, and minority groups became very active in monitoring the appointment process. Also, there was the growing media obsession with so-called investigative reporting, which led to endless and sometimes mindless delving into a nominee's life, associates, and opinions. Finally, greater Senate attention to confirmation was consistent with one of the broader objectives of the congressional reforms of the 1970s, namely to increase Congress's influence in public policy and administration.

The spurt of attention to confirmation in the 1970s notwithstanding, one might conclude from the numbers in table 10.1 that the President nearly always has his way with the Senate. But this would be "the wrong conclusion drawn from the wrong evidence," as the Scots-American scholar, Gordon Calvin Mackenzie, has shown so well. "Confirmation is a process, not simply a vote. And . . . the confirmation process provides ample opportunity for the Senate to influence the President, his nominees, and their subsequent policy decisions without rejecting any substantial number of nominations."[6]

The Senate's confirmation power, as provided in the Constitution, was intended primarily to enable Congress to check on the character and qualifications of those whom the President selects for major policy positions. It continues to be used for this purpose, but the Senate has also come to use the power much more broadly as a technique for congressional control over the policy and administrative processes and for helping to insure that Congress will have the data that are needed for this purpose. The likely impact of nominees on public policy and their willingness to cooperate with congressional committees are now the Senate's dominant concern in confirmation proceedings. Thus committee hearings are used to instruct, to warn, and even to humiliate nominees whom the Senate ultimately plans to confirm. By these means the Senate can achieve a considerable degree of influence over candidates, for it is likely that they will give careful thought to subsequent actions that violate the views expressed by any important groups of senators in their confirmation hearings and to actions that violate promises or strong expressions of opinion that they themselves have offered in these hearings. "Because," as Mackenzie concludes, "the confirmation process is more complex and more deliberate than is commonly believed, the opportunities for using the process to influence appointment decisions and to shape the direction of public policy are more abundant and more sophisticated than the mere calling of the role on a nomination."[7]

CONFIRMATION AND PERSONAL QUALIFICATIONS

As for personal qualifications, the Senate uses confirmation to examine nominees and pass judgment on the likelihood that they will be fair and objective and that they will take a broad, rather than a narrow, view of the public interest. In this context there are two potential conflicts of interest that Congress seeks to guard against, one resulting from nominees' financial holdings, the other, from their intellectual or attitudinal predispositions. Since most political executives subject to confirmation are in-and-outers—that is, they come to the federal service from private occupations or from universities and state and local governments, and return to the same or similar jobs—the potential for such conflicts is considerable. Anything approximating purity in this regard is impossible to achieve, or possible only by standards that would discourage candidates with the necessary experience from accepting appointments.

Presidents are as eager to avoid the fact or appearance of financial conflicts of interest as is the Congress. As a result they rarely nominate individuals whose potential conflicts cannot be resolved to Congress's satisfaction, by requiring nominees to dispose of certain stocks, to put them in a blind trust over which they have no control or from which they cannot profit while in public service, or some other means.

Predispositional conflicts are most likely to arise when nominees have worked in industries that fall within the jurisdiction of the agencies to which they have been nominated; have represented the special interests of cities, states, or regions either as elected or appointed officials; or have been consistent and vigorous supporters of a major political party. In such cases the Congress has used confirmation hearings "to sensitize nominees to the problem, to make them cognizant of the aspects of their own backgrounds that may well conflict with their government responsibilities, to emphasize the importance of objectivity, and, in some cases, to ask nominees to state their commitment to impartiality for the public record."[8]

Example. In January 1969 President Richard M. Nixon nominated Walter J. Hickel, Governor of Alaska, to be his Secretary of the Interior. As Governor, Hickel had strongly objected to several actions of the Interior Department, under Democratic Secretary Stewart Udall, which threatened to restrict the economic development of Alaska where over 90 percent of the land area was controlled by the U.S. government. In Senate hearings, there was the following exchange:

SENATOR HENRY M. JACKSON (D. WA), CHAIRMAN: "Governor, concern has been expressed in the press and in many letters to the committee that you may have conflicts of interest which would preclude your making objective decisions in the national interest in many areas which are within the jurisdiction of the Secretary of the Interior. . . . As Governor of Alaska you have taken positions on a number of issues of national concern. You understandably took positions which I assumed you believed were in the best interests of your state. In your new position as Secretary, you may be called upon to deal with some of these same issues. . . . The American people, of course, have a right to expect your decisions as Secretary to reflect your best judgment of the interests of the Nation as a whole in these matters. One point of concern is a reported remark that you 'could do more for Alaska' as Secretary than as Governor. Do you think that you will be able to take an unbiased national view of your duties as Secretary even where Alaskan interests are involved?"

GOVERNOR HICKEL: "Thank you, Senator Jackson. I believe sincerely that interests that Alaska might be involved in, whatever they may be, as Secretary of the Interior I will take the broad national interest because if it were for the betterment of the Nation as a whole, then it would be betterment for my country of Alaska. So I see no conflict in my mind and philosophy and I would without a doubt, Mr. Chairman, take the broad national interest."

(It would be an understatement to say that Hickel did not excel in the use of the English language, but it appears that he was not given the opportunity, as are most witnesses, to "clean up" the stenographic record of his testimony before it was published.)

Another technique used by the Senate to counter predispositional conflicts is to insist on balance where there are several top-level political appointments in an agency.

Example. Congress also used this technique in confirmation of Hickel. Moved by the views of conservation groups which opposed Hickel's nomination, several senators pressed him and the White House to appoint Russell E. Train, president of the private, nonprofit Conservation Foundation, as undersecretary. Although Hickel had not met Train previously and undoubtedly would have preferred someone else for the position, he endorsed the proposal, and the White House announced its intention to nominate Train before the Senate Committee on the Interior voted to approve Hickel. The following exchange took place before the White House announcement:

HICKEL: "I have selected in my mind my undersecretary. I have sent that name to the President. I selected him for the reason that after talking with him, our views were compatible. I think that he is a very competent man. I think the President will name him."

JACKSON: "Do you wish to indicate who you have recommended as undersecretary of the Interior? There's been a lot of speculation in the press."

HICKEL: "Mr. Chairman, I think that it is the prerogative of the President. It is a presidential appointment and I think it would not be right for me to do that, and I think speculation could somewhat be pretty close."

JACKSON: "Is it appropriate to say that what you have in mind is an individual who has been professionally associated with the conservation movement and long active in that field?"
HICKEL: "Yes, I think that would be a fair statement."
JACKSON: "That is your plan at this time, and you have recommended to the President a man with that background?"
HICKEL: "Yes, Mr. Chairman."

In addition to possible conflicts of interest, the Senate judges the character and integrity of nominees. As Mackenzie shows, however, Senate committees spend relatively little time on these questions because candidates will have been thoroughly investigated in these terms by the Executive before their names are submitted to Congress. If, nonetheless, such questions are raised in Senate hearings, they will be investigated scrupulously.

Finally, among personal qualifications there is the question of competence. But here the Senate committees are unsure how to evaluate the knowledge and accomplishments that nominees have acquired in the private sector. As a consequence they are likely to devote significant attention to competence only if there are charges that the nominees do not satisfy the statutory and technical qualifications of the positions for which they have been chosen, or if significant criticism of their past performance is raised in the hearings.

On all of these matters there are few specific and uniform criteria used by all or most of the Senate committees. The great variety of agencies that make up the federal government, the broad range of backgrounds of the people recruited by different administrations to fill political positions in them, and the variations in patterns of executive–legislative relations that pertain to different programs make uniformity unachievable and probably undesirable.

CONFIRMATION AND INFLUENCING PUBLIC POLICY

Mackenzie finds that the confirmation process is "a versatile tool for the Senate in its efforts to enlarge its influence on public policy decisions."[9] The Senate can reject nominees because of dissatisfaction with their policy views, but it seldom does this. Occasionally it withholds final action on confirmation until nominees or the Administration agree to pursue policies about which Senate committee members feel strongly. More commonly the committees require nominees, as a condition of confirmation, to make policy-related promises during confirmation hearings.

Example. In November 1971 President Richard M. Nixon nominated Earl F. Butz, professor of agricultural economics and dean of agriculture at Purdue University, to be Secretary of Agriculture. Butz's previously stated views on farm price supports, agribusiness, the family farm, and food stamps were unpopular with many farm-state senators of both parties. He was questioned about these at his confirmation hearings and asked to make certain commitments on policy that would satisfy Agriculture Committee members. Initially he refused, saying that he could not make any commitments before taking office. As opposition to him became more manifest, however, and threatened his confirmation, Butz relented. Before the committee voted 8 to 6 to recommend his appointment, he had pledged to support existing price support policies and take action to strengthen grain prices. And before the Senate voted 51 (14D., 37R.) to 44 (40D., 4R.) to confirm him, Butz had committed himself in writing to support the food stamp and school lunch programs, to take further action to raise corn prices, and to win release of Agriculture Department program funds which had been impounded by the Office of Management and Budget.

CONFIRMATION AND ADMINISTRATIVE OVERSIGHT

The confirmation process provides an opportunity for Senate committees to explore the administrative practices of particular governmental agencies and the implementation of programs. Questions are raised frequently about the recruitment and development of agency personnel and about the decision-making process, most especially who makes which decisions. In both of these matters the Senate's special concern is to keep policy direction in the hands of those to whom Congress has the greatest access, who are likely to be those whom it has the power to confirm.

Occasionally the confirmation process is used to tie down how an activity for which the nominee is responsible will be carried out. The nomination of Eliot L. Richardson to be Attorney General in 1973 is an extraordinary example of this.

Example. While Congress was investigating the Watergate scandals, President Richard M. Nixon nominated Richardson to be Attorney General, replacing Richard Kleindienst, who had resigned under fire. At the same time Nixon suggested that a special prosecutor be appointed for the sole purpose of investigating the scandals.

Richardson initially appeared before the Senate Judiciary Committee on May 9. Committee members soon made it clear that they would not confirm him until he had selected and announced the name of a special prosecutor who was acceptable to the committee, and had committed to writing the procedures that would govern the prosecutor's work, which must guarantee independence of the prosecutor from supervision or interference by the President, the White House, and the Attorney General. These procedures were to be reviewed by the prosecutor and by the Senate committee. Richardson, after a period of initial reluctance, acceded to the committee's demands. He named Professor Archibald Cox of Harvard Law School as the special prosecutor on May 21 and submitted to the committee a detailed statement of Cox's duties and responsibilities. He was confirmed as Attorney General two days later.

The statement included a provision that "the Special Prosecutor will not be removed from his duties except for extraordinary improprieties on his part." Nonetheless, in October the President, after an acrimonious conflict with the special prosecutor over the release of White House tape recordings, directed the Attorney General to discharge Cox. Richardson resigned rather than do so, stating to the President that he could not, in the light of the "firm and repeated commitments" given to the Senate Judiciary Committee in his confirmation hearings, carry out the President's directive. The President accepted Richardson's resignation "with an understanding of the circumstances which brought you to your decision," and said at a subsequent press conference that "Mr. Richardson felt that because of the nature of [his] confirmation [his] commitment to Mr. Cox had to take precedence over any commitment that [he] might have to carry out an order from the President."

CONFIRMATION AND CONGRESS'S INSTITUTIONAL NEEDS

The Senate also uses the confirmation process to insure as best it can that nominees will cooperate willingly with congressional committees by providing information that Congress believes it needs for oversight of legislation and administration. Committees frequently require nominees, as a condition of their confirmation, to promise to testify and to provide information freely during their terms of office. This became a primary concern of Senate committees in the mid-1960s, especially the Committees on Armed Services, Foreign Relations, and Atomic Energy, which depended so heavily on the executive branch as a source of information.[10] And in 1973 Democrats in the Senate added their party's support to committee demands that nominees promise to provide information and testimony, when they approved the following resolution:

Resolved by the Democratic Majority of the Senate:
1. That a prerequisite to confirmation is the commitment of presidential appointees to appear and testify before duly constituted committees of the Senate in response to committee requests;

2. That all Senate committees bear a responsibility to determine, prior to confirmation, the commitment of presidential appointees to comply with committee requests to appear and testify before committees of the Senate;

3. That committee reports to the Senate on all cabinet designees and such other appointees as deemed appropriate should contain an evaluation of their commitment to respond to committee requests to appear and testify before duly constituted Senate committees.

If committees are convinced that nominees will be uncooperative, they are unlikely to confirm them.

Example. On June 19, 1959, the Senate rejected President Dwight D. Eisenhower's nomination of Lewis Strauss, then chairman of the Atomic Energy Commission, to be Secretary of Commerce, by a roll-call vote of 49 to 46. His was the eighth cabinet appointment ever to be rejected by the Senate and the first since the Senate in 1925 refused to confirm President Calvin Coolidge's nomination of Charles B.

Warren as Attorney General. The following excerpt from the report of the Senate Commerce Committee, which had conducted lengthy hearings on the nomination, explains the Senate's action in good part.

"We do not believe that a man can be adjudged competent for a Cabinet post unless there exists a sound basis for mutual confidence between him and the Congress, despite a showing of the capabilities for competence. As we have already indicated this does not depend upon political agreement. Now and in recent years Congress has enjoyed satisfactory relations with many executive officials who frequently held sharply opposed views on fundamental policy. This has been true because there existed mutual respect and esteem between them and because the Congress felt assurance that these officials were dealing openly and fairly with it and that the information imparted to the committees of Congress was reliable and sufficiently complete to serve as the basis for congressional action. The country gained by this relationship. We are forced reluctantly to conclude that there is no likelihood that this vital mutual respect and its resulting relationship can exist between Mr. Strauss and the Congress. . . .

"Based in part upon the past record of his relations with different committees of the Congress, and even more strongly upon his conduct before our committee, we have come to the conviction that Mr. Strauss does not understand the proper relationship between the legislative and executive branches. The record indicates he claims for himself the right to withhold certain information from Congress. The record also indicates such withholding is without basis in law, and that the nominee has no concern for the law in this respect. From the record it is clear that the nominee time after time has resisted furnishing the appropriate committees of Congress with information needed in order for Congress to properly perform its legislative functions. . . . .

"In our opinion, he sought to mislead our committee either by means of what we consider direct misinterpretations of fact or by resort to half-truths intended to divert the committee from full discovery of the relevant facts. This course of conduct was repeated so often that it must be judged to have been deliberate. He has so impaired our confidence that we cannot recommend his confirmation."

CONFIRMATION AND CONSTITUENCY SERVICE

Senators may use confirmation hearings to pursue specific interests of their constituencies. They tell the President's nominees the problems of their districts and explore with them possible solutions to these problems, seeking thereby to sensitize the presumptive policymakers to constituency concerns. In this activity Senate committees rarely act as a unit since the constituency interests of individual committee members are not necessarily shared, and not infrequently they are diametrically opposed. "Instead, individual Senators or groups of Senators use the public hearing as a forum for expressing their own concerns . . . hoping in whatever way possible to keep their concerns in the public eye and in the nominee's purview."[11]

Informal Participation in the Appointment of Senior Executives

To this point our analysis has been confined to the formal confirmation process. But the influence of members of Congress in the appointment of senior executives is not limited to the Senate's exercise of the confirmation power. Members of both houses recommend candidates to the White House and to cabinet secretaries for senior executive jobs, both those that require confirmation and those that do not. When we focus on those recommendations for appointment which members make seriously, and ignore the vast majority in which they simply forward to the Executive the applications of constituents who are job seekers, we find that the principal incentive of members is to influence the formulation and implementation of public policy.

For positions that require confirmation, the Executive regularly seeks to determine, prior to nomination, what Congress's response is likely to be. It may drop a potential nominee if key members of Congress register strong objections. "This institutionalized form of conflict-avoidance," as Mackenzie calls it, "provides members of Congress with substantial opportunities to influence selection decisions."[12]

Example. The programs administered by the Interior Department affect particularly the western states. In 1971, Rogers C.B. Morton, a former representative from Maryland, was nominated by President Richard M. Nixon and confirmed by the Senate as Secretary of the Interior, one of very few non-westerners to hold that post in this century. Later that year Morton selected James R. Schlesinger, an eastern economist with experience in national security and defense, who was then assistant director of OMB, to be undersecretary. Gordon Allott of Colorado, ranking Republican on the Senate Interior Committee, made it clear to the White House that he and other committee members did not think that Schlesinger was sufficiently familiar with the political, social, and economic problems of the West and that they would not support the nomination. Morton and the White House congressional liaison staff tried to talk Allott and other senators out of their opposition, but they were unsuccessful and, as a result, the formal nomination was never made.

Morton then chose for the position William T. Pecora, a long-time career civil servant who was director of the Geological Survey. After the White House cleared his name with Allott, committee chairman Henry M. Jackson (D. WA) and others, President Nixon nominated Pecora who was confirmed.

The effectiveness of informal congressional participation in appointment decisions depends principally on the nature of the positions. The view is widely shared in Congress that the President should be given the broadest latitude in selecting his cabinet and assistants in the Executive Office of the President. Thus he is generally free to disregard congressional advice in filling these positions. The President's control remains strong for positions at the subcabinet level in the departments and positions in the independent executive agencies, but here Congress's influence may be significant, as was seen in the example of the undersecretary of the Interior. Members of Congress are likely to have their greatest influence in selection procedures for the independent regulatory commissions, since Congress does not consider these agencies to be clearly within the President's hierarchical chain of command, as are the departments and executive agencies.

This concludes the analysis of Congress's role in the appointment of senior executive personnel. Congress also plays a role, albeit a more limited one, in the removal of these officials. It has the seldom-used constitutional power of impeachment; the legislative power to prescribe in law limitations on the Executive's authority to remove personnel, such as whistle-blowers; and informal influence. But these are less significant sources of legislative power than the means used to influence appointments.

11

The Legislative Veto

IN RECENT YEARS Congress has developed a new technique, the legislative veto, for controlling public policy. By this means Congress enacts authorizing legislation that gives discretion to the President to take certain actions —greater discretion in many cases than it would be willing to approve otherwise—and reserves the right to subsequently approve or veto these actions. Congress, that is, subjects the President's use of the discretion granted to a further legislative check. A familiar example is the law that authorizes the President to prepare plans to reorganize the executive bureaus—to consolidate agencies and shift bureaus from one department to another. These reorganization plans are submitted to Congress, and they go into effect unless either the House or the Senate votes to veto them within a short period of time that is specified in the law—sixty days, for example. Congress can either accept the President's plans by failing to act on them within the prescribed period or reject them if either House adopts a veto resolution. It cannot amend them, however, and there is good reason for this. If Congress could amend the President's plans, it could, in effect, legislate without the President having an opportunity to use his constitutionally provided right of veto. Also, the reorganization law, like all laws that use the legislative veto, amends normal parliamentary procedure, providing that if a resolution of disapproval is introduced in either House, that House will have the opportunity to vote on it before the fixed time expires. If this were not the case, friends of the President would be able to filibuster and use other tactics to delay congressional action until the plans had gone into effect.

The reorganization law, adopted initially in 1939, was an early use of the legislative veto. Beginning in the 1950s, Congress began to elaborate and perfect the technique for several purposes, and since then it has provided for use of the veto in legislation authorizing a number of major programs—for example, disposal of government-owned synthetic rubber-producing plants (1953), atomic energy (1954), space (1958), railroad reorganization (1973), war powers of the President (1973), sale of arms to foreign nations (1974), impoundment of appropriated funds (1974), rules and regulations of certain agencies, including but not limited to those of the Department of Education (1974), Federal Elections Commission (1975), Department of Energy concerning oil allocations, allotments, and other matters (1970s), Federal Trade Commission (1980). A survey by Joseph Cooper and Patricia A. Hurley has identified 273 veto provisions enacted between 1932 and 1976. Fifty-eight percent of these were passed between 1970 and 1976, eighty-three of them in the two-year period 1974–1975, which was in part a legislative response to Watergate. These provisions for congressional review of executive actions covered a broad range of policy areas. Of those enacted between 1970 and 1976, approximately 23 percent related to energy and natural resources programs, 17 percent to national defense and military construction, 15 percent to foreign affairs, 11 percent to education and research, 11 percent to public works and transportation, and the remainder to several other areas of public policy.[1]

Forms of the Legislative Veto

The veto has several forms. In the *negative form* Congress authorizes the President to prepare and submit plans. The President initiates. The plans go into effect in x days, depending on the specific law, unless Congress vetoes them. The law can provide that the veto be in the form of a concurrent resolution of disapproval to be voted on by both Houses—a two-House veto; a House or Senate resolution to be approved by a simple majority (or in a few cases a constitutional majority) of either House—a one-House veto; a House or Senate resolution to be approved by a simple majority of one House, unless the other House votes to approve the President's plan—a modified one-House veto; or committee resolutions of disapproval to be voted by committees that have jurisdiction over the subject matter in both the House and Senate—a two-committee veto—or by the committee in either House—a one-committee veto.

In the *affirmative form* Congress authorizes the President to prepare and submit plans. The President initiates. The plans go into effect when they are approved by Congress, either by a concurrent resolution of both Houses or by committee resolutions in either or both Houses, depending on the specific law.

There is also a special type of the affirmative form, which is designed to terminate a presidential action rather than, as in the other cases, to authorize one to begin. The impoundment control provisions of the 1974 Budget Act illustrate this unusual form of legislative veto. The President impounds funds that have been appropriated and reports to Congress that he has done so. To make the President's actions stick, both Houses of Congress must within forty-five days pass a concurrent resolution approving the President's action and rescinding the funds. If Congress fails to pass such a resolution, the President's impoundment ceases and the money must be spent.

Another example of the special affirmative form is the War Powers Resolution of 1973. The President's action in committing U.S. troops to combat is to cease within sixty days unless within that period Congress has passed and the President has signed a joint resolution declaring war or specifically authorizing the President's action. But Congress can by concurrent resolution, which does not need the President's signature, require that armed forces be withdrawn before the sixty-day period.

Finally in the *waiting period form*, Congress authorizes the President to prepare and submit plans. The President initiates. The plans go into effect after they have lain before Congress x days. Formally, the only way Congress can prevent a plan from going into effect at the conclusion of the waiting period is to pass a law prohibiting it. Informally, by developing a record of objections in hearings and on the floor, Congress can frequently get the Executive to withdraw a plan to which a significant number of members take exception and possibly resubmit it with modifications.

Among these many alternative forms, Congress selects in each case the one that corresponds to the degree of control over the Executive that it believes to be desirable. Between 1970 and 1976 the three most frequently used forms were waiting period, which is also the least restrictive on the Executive (45 percent of all cases), one-House veto, the most restrictive of the non-committee forms (21 percent); and two-House veto (11 percent). The dominant form in each of the policy areas for which the veto was used most frequently during this period was the one-House negative form for energy and natural resources (35 percent of cases in this area), waiting period for national defense and military construction (59 percent), two-House negative for foreign affairs (32 percent), waiting period for education and research (59 percent), and committee veto for public works and transportation (36 percent).

Executive and Judicial Objections to the Legislative Veto

All presidents since Harry S Truman, except John F. Kennedy, have been in conflict with the Congress over use of the veto, holding the veto procedure to be unconstitutional. In essence they argue that if Congress delegates authority to the President, it cannot subject the exercise of this authority to a subsequent veto or control by Congress, except by the enactment of another law which the President can then veto. This argument has not impressed many members of Congress as valid for several reasons, principally because Congress, all the time and in many ways, subjects authority that it has by legislation given to the Executive to subsequent legislative control.

Despite the claims by several Presidents that the legislative veto is unconstitutional, the Supreme Court as of January 1983 has not ruled on the matter. In December 1980, the Ninth Circuit Court of Appeals in San Francisco ruled unconstitutional the legislative veto as used in the Immigration Act of 1952, which grants the Attorney General discretion on whether or not to deport certain aliens who have violated immigration laws. The statute allows either House by legislative veto to overturn Department of Justice orders to suspend the deportation of individual aliens, and the court ruled that this violated the constitutional separation of powers. The statute in this case is an unusual use of the veto for it relates to quasi-judicial administrative proceedings involving individuals, whereas normally the legislative veto is used in connection with broader questions of legislative policy. The immigration case has been appealed to the Supreme Court. If the Court upholds the Ninth Circuit, it is possible that its decision will be based on the special circumstances of the statute, rather than on the broader question of the veto as a technique for congressional control over public policy.

In January 1982, a three-judge panel of the Circuit Court of Appeals for the District of Columbia ruled that the legislative veto provision of the Natural Gas Policy Act of 1978, which provided for deregulation of natural gas, was unconstitutional. The law authorized either House to veto proposed rules of the Federal Energy Regulatory Commission. The court held that this violated the separation of powers and also the constitutional requirement that all laws be passed by both Houses of Congress and then presented to the President for his signature or veto. The Circuit Court held that the legislative veto "contravenes the constitutional procedures for making law," but congres-

sional supporters of the technique do not consider veto actions to be legislation. In October 1982, the same circuit court held that the legislative veto
provision of the Federal Trade Commission (FTC) Improvements Act of
1980, which required that FTC rules be subject to a two-House veto, was
unconstitutional on the same grounds. These opinions, too, have been appealed to the U.S. Supreme Court. Although it would be unwise to predict
how the Court will decide these two cases, one can agree with Joseph Cooper
that it is highly probable that the legislative veto will survive in some form.
Certainly Congress could make the appropriation of funds for a program or
agency contingent upon compliance with the veto procedures.[2]

Let us, then, put aside the question of constitutionality as unresolved and,
instead, analyze the legislative veto as a technique for congressional oversight
of policy and administration and evaluate it in terms of our model of executive–legislative relations.

Evaluation of the Legislative Veto: Its Special Advantages

The legislative veto has proved to be a powerful technique in a number of
situations where the more usual means of congressional control over executive
conduct—appropriation, authorization, and investigation procedures—fall
short of insuring what Congress believes to be an adequate degree of oversight
or control. In this context, Congress has used the veto to control executive
discretion, protect the internal integrity of complex programs, and, occasionally, to break stalemates in the legislative process.

CONTROL DISCRETION

The legislative veto is used most frequently where guidelines for the administrator cannot be defined clearly in the authorizing statute and where, at the
same time, appropriation procedures are unlikely to be effective in controlling
the administrator because money is not significant; that is, it costs as much
to carry out one policy as to carry out a very different one. Where these
conditions prevail, the administrator could have wide discretion unchecked by
the legislature were it not for a device like the legislative veto. There may be
several reasons why guidelines cannot be defined clearly in the legislation,
among them insufficiency of data and uncertainty regarding future events.

Example. The Eisenhower Administration decided in 1953 that the government should dispose of the synthetic rubber-producing plants that the government had built in World War II and still owned. The President sent a legislative proposal to Congress to authorize the Executive to put the plants up for sale. In considering that proposal, members of Congress expressed two objectives. One objective was that the government should get as much for these plants as it could since the government had paid for them in the first place. A second objective was to avoid greater concentration of rubber production in a small number of industries, that is, to dispose of the plants in a way that did not frustrate the government's antitrust policies. Congress could not at the time decide what relative weight to give to each objective because to do so depended on which companies would bid for the plants. However, the companies would not bid until there was legislation authorizing the Executive to dispose of them.

In these circumstances, Congress passed a bill stating the two objectives, directing the President to put the plants up for bid and, having received bids, to prepare a single plan for disposing of all of the plants, with these two objectives in mind. This plan would then go into effect unless either House of Congress vetoed it within thirty days.

Having called for and received bids for the plants, President Eisenhower prepared a single plan on how to dispose of them and submitted it to Congress. Both Houses of Congress held hearings, a Senate subcommittee under Paul Douglas (D. IL) extensive hearings. The committees decided that the President had established an equitable balance between the two objectives and they recommended that his plan not be vetoed.

Example. In 1974 Congress decided that it should have a voice in decisions to sell large amounts of arms to foreign governments, which until then was largely a matter of executive discretion. But it was difficult to write meaningful standards in an authorizing bill for several reasons, principally the sudden and radical changes that can occur in unstable foreign governments. The legislative veto was adopted in lieu of standards. The President initiates a sale plan and, in this case, it requires a concurrent resolution of both Houses to veto a sale proposed by the President. The legislative veto provisions of the 1974 act were refined and expanded in the Arms Export Control Act of 1976.

Certain critics of the legislative veto have argued that Congress will fall into a habit of opting for future control through the veto in place of present control through the definition of clear statutory goals. Presumably this could happen, but the facts are clear that it hasn't happened, and there are no reasons to believe that Congress is likely to use the veto as a device for avoiding its duty to define goals in lawmaking.[3]

PROTECTING INTEGRITY OF PLANS

A second type of situation in which the legislative veto has unique advantages occurs when there is a perceived need to protect the internal integrity of a plan or program. Recall that the plans prepared by the Executive may not be amended by Congress. Congress can only veto an entire plan; it is all or nothing. Two examples will illustrate this use of the veto.

Example. The Regional Rail Reorganization Act of 1973 provided for federal support in reorganizing the bankrupt freight rail systems in the Northeast and Midwest, which included the Penn Central, Lehigh, Central of New Jersey, and others. A slimmed-down system would be operated by a new government-sponsored entity, Conrail, but planning for the system, including specifying the routes to be retained and routes to be abandoned, was to be done by another organization called the United States Railway Association (USRA). USRA's final system plan was to be submitted to Congress and to become effective sixty days thereafter unless it was vetoed by either House in that period. If vetoed, then USRA was to submit a revised plan which would also be subject to a legislative veto.

A principal reason for using the legislative veto in this case was to control the inevitable objections that would be made in Congress to abandonment of specific routes. The Massachusetts congressional delegation, for example, would likely object to abandoning trackage that served Gardner, Massachusetts, and the Pennsylvania delegation to abandoning routes that served Hershey, Pennsylvania. Without some constraints on amendments to retain routes that USRA considered to be uneconomical and irrational, the internal integrity and economic viability of the new system might be in jeopardy. With a legislative veto, however, no members could succeed in amending the plan for the purpose of preventing abandonment of routes in their districts. They could only vote against the full plan.

When USRA presented its plan to Congress in 1975, there was grumbling by a number of members about routes that were to be abandoned, and several bills were introduced that would have directed USRA to continue certain routes, but the plan was not vetoed and the bills were not adopted.

Example. The Carter Administration's 1978 arms sale package of $4.8 billion in war planes to Egypt, Saudi Arabia, and Israel, submitted under authority of the previously mentioned 1976 act, is another example of the use of the legislative veto to protect the internal integrity of plans. Israel's supporters in the United States objected strongly to tying the three together. They wanted to deny arms to Egypt and Saudi Arabia but to approve them for Israel. The President presented the three-in-one plan and insisted that tying the three together was a linchpin of U.S. foreign policy in the Middle East. A resolution of disapproval was introduced, but it was defeated in the Senate. The House did not then need to vote since under the Arms Export Control Act it requires a concurrent resolution of both Houses to kill the President's plan.

BREAKING STALEMATES IN THE LEGISLATIVE PROCESS

Where there is agreement among major parties that legislation is needed, but where there is a temporary stalemate, either within the Congress or between Congress and the Executive, that makes it impossible to reach agreement on the specific provisions of a program, the legislation can be enacted in general terms, and the detailed provisions can be considered subsequently when the President has initiated his plans. Use of the veto for this purpose is rare.

Example. In 1977 legislation to extend authorization of the Export-Import Bank for two years, the House included a ban on the export of Alaskan oil to Japan. The Senate refused to go along with a total ban. The compromise, struck in a conference of the two Houses and enacted, authorizes the President to allow exports if he finds this to be "in the national interest," but his decision is subject to a veto by either House of Congress within sixty days.

RESOLVING CONFLICTS INVOLVING CONGRESSIONAL DISTRUST OF EXECUTIVE AGENCIES

In infrequent cases congressional distrust of an executive agency is so profound that the legislature is hesitant to grant to administrators the type of discretion that would normally be granted and that is necessary to carry out the agency's program. In such cases the legislative veto is a conflict resolving measure that enables a program to move forward, while Congress keeps its administrators on short rein.

Evaluation of the Legislative Veto: Its Several Forms

With this understanding of the unique qualities of the legislative veto as a technique for congressional oversight of policy and administration, its several forms can be evaluated.

First, the negative form of the legislative veto, in which the President's plan goes into effect unless vetoed by either or both Houses, is almost always preferable to the affirmative form, in which the President's plan goes into effect only if both Houses of Congress approve it by concurrent resolution. The reasons for this are illustrated in the following example.

Example. In chapter 9 I described the circumstances that led to enactment of the impoundment control provisions of the Budget Control Act of 1974. To control the President's impounding of appropriated funds, Congress could have passed legislation prohibiting the practice but this they did not want to do, because there would always be many cases where most members would agree that appropriated funds should not be spent. Nor was Congress able to draft meaningful standards specifying the conditions under which the President should be allowed to impound because these conditions varied so much from program to program. Thus they adopted the legislative veto.

The bill approved by the House used the negative form—a President's order to rescind appropriations would be effective unless either House vetoed it within sixty days. The Senate bill used the affirmative form—a rescission order would expire after sixty days and the money must be spent unless both Houses approved it by concurrent resolution. The Senate refused to yield on rescissions and its form was accepted reluctantly by the House. But from the point of view of congressional control of the Executive, it was the weaker, less effective form.

The point is this: the President may submit dozens of rescission orders in any fiscal year. Under the affirmative form, Congress must consider all of them, especially the least controversial ones, for without congressional action in both Houses, the President must spend the money. Under the negative form, Congress can focus only on the controversial orders. It can devote its time and attention to salient, important programs and ignore the others since the President's proposals to rescind funds for the latter will be effective unless vetoed.

In other words, the Senate bill was the stronger of the two only in a formalistic sense, only in terms of abstract categories of statutory instruments. In a realistic sense the House bill was more powerful, for it retained legislative power in the Congress and at the same time enabled the Congress to focus on important issues and priorities, by selecting the impoundments that should, in their view, be debated in terms of possible veto.[4]

Second, the one-House or two-House forms of the legislative veto are almost always preferable to the committee form—that is, the form in which the President's plan goes into effect unless vetoed by committee resolutions or goes into effect when approved by committee resolutions. The problem with the committee form is that by using it, Congress could be delegating too much authority to its committees. Committees play an important role in legislative veto actions in any case. Proposals to veto the President's plans are referred to committees which hold hearings on the plans and recommend to the whole House whether or not they should be vetoed. The issue is authority to make final decisions for Congress. Clearly Congress would not vest in its committees powers of final decision over legislation. On the other hand, Congress is willing to grant to its committees final powers with respect to selecting the witnesses for their hearings. Legislative veto actions lie between these two extremes. But if the legislative veto is used for the reasons that I have suggested, it will normally concern matters of such importance that the whole House should have an opportunity to review the work of its committees if it wishes to do so.

Third, a straightforward form of the legislative veto procedure is preferable to a convoluted form. In 1979 the Carter Administration, having opposed the legislative veto with vigor, said it would not object to a new proposed form which was adopted in the Gasoline Rationing Act of that year. According to this form, the President's plan can be vetoed by a joint resolution of both Houses of Congress. The President can then veto the joint resolution, and the Congress can by a two-thirds majority in both Houses override the President's veto of the joint resolution which vetoed the President's plan.

Such a convoluted parliamentary procedure can only reduce the confidence of citizens in their system of government. Imagine, if you will, a voter trying to make sense out of daily newspaper reports on the extended parliamentary moves involved in such a procedure. The one-House and the two-House legislative vetoes are, on the other hand, straightforward enough.

Fourth, the form of the legislative veto authorizing the President to submit to Congress the plans that are subject to veto is almost always preferable to the form which authorizes the executive departments and agencies to submit plans directly to Congress or to congressional committees. The point is that the agency form can encourage a type of agency–committee relations in which the President, the only elected member of the Executive, is cut out of the decision process.

The Legislative Veto and Administrative Rules and Regulations

Between 1972 and 1981 Congress initiated statutory provisions for legislative veto of the rules and regulations of several agencies, and since 1975 it has been considering legislation to apply the procedure to the rules and regulations of most departments and agencies. Use of the veto to oversee and control agency rulemaking fits squarely into the first category for which the veto is so well adapted—where administrators have been given broad discretion because guidelines cannot be defined clearly in authorizing statutes and where appropriation and other procedures are ineffective in controlling this discretion. For agencies with broad discretion, their rules and regulations are important policy instruments. As such the rules should be subject to congressional oversight to determine if they are consistent with the intent of the legislation that they purport to implement. In recommending use of the legislative veto for agency rules and regulations under the Education Amendments Act of 1974 the House Committee on Education and Labor said: "The problem which this amendment seeks to meet is the steady escalation of agency quasi-legislative power, and the corresponding attrition in the ability of the Congress to make the law."

The late Judge Harold Leventhal of the Circuit Court of Appeals for the District of Columbia testified before the House Rules Committee in October 1979, opposing legislation to subject administrative rules and regulations to congressional veto. He said in effect that the examination of rules and regulations to determine if they are in accord with legislative intent is more properly a function of the courts than of the legislature. But how can this be? Is the Congress not likely to have a more accurate and policy-relevant view of legislative intent than a random judge? In opposing the legislative veto, Judge

Leventhal argued that the veto would, by its nature, tend to reduce judicial scrutiny of arguments that agencies' actions exceed legislative "contemplation." Perhaps it is not unwise to supplement a judge's opinion of what the legislature contemplated with the legislature's opinion of its own contemplation. The legislative veto is a means for doing this in cases where other techniques, such as appropriations, do not provide adequate oversight of agency rulemaking.

At these same hearings, Richard Bolling (D. MO), chairman of the Rules Committee, expressed his concern that legislative veto of agency rules and regulations would lead to excessive influence by special interests and that the agencies would become too sensitive to the current preferences of certain legislators, especially those on the committees that review executive proposals that are subject to veto. Bolling's concern is similar to that of certain academic critics who have argued that the legislative veto encourages a pathological form of bureau–committee relations. Iron triangles and whirlpools involving bureaus, committees, and interest groups derive advantages from broad legislative standards coupled with a legislative veto.[5] These criticisms and apprehensions are misplaced or exaggerated for several reasons. First, use of the preferred forms, which enable the whole House to review committee actions and the President to review agency proposals, reduces opportunities for excessive influence by special interests. Joseph Cooper of Rice University said in the excellent paper that he submitted for the record when he testified before the Rules Committee:

> The overall result of veto usage is therefore not unresponsive and unaccountable control by committees, but rather extension of the political processes that lie at the heart of representative government into areas of administrative policy-making where they are weak and attenuated. If reliance on committees in the veto process impairs representative government, this constitutes an unanswerable indictment of the regular legislative process as well.

Second, in response to Congressman Bolling's concern, special interests work wherever authority lies. If Congress elects to review agency rules and regulations for certain major programs, the lobbyists will work in the agencies to get them to draft agreeable rules and then in Congress to get the rules approved or vetoed. If Congress elects not to review agency rules and regulations, then the lobbyists will simply increase their efforts in the agencies. The corridors of the departments are as crowded with lobbyists as are those of the Capitol.

Some critics of the legislative veto complain that it introduces unnecessary political considerations into administrative rulemaking, reducing the fairness and objectivity of the process as it is conducted in the agencies under "notice and comment" provisions of the Administrative Procedure Act. But these critics' views of agency rulemaking are a fiction; the record is clear that interest groups, frequently those with the greatest financial resources, have a tremendous influence on the process. As West and Cooper have said: "It is simplistic to assume that intense, well-organized interests gain a special advantage in the veto-based legislative oversight process which they lack in administrative rulemaking."[6] Furthermore, only some of the agency rules for which legislative vetoes have been adopted or are being considered are covered by the Administrative Procedure Act.

A procedure for legislative veto of proposed rules and regulations, if it is structured to require that the President transmit the rules to Congress, has the additional advantage of firming up the President's control over the bureaucracy in rulemaking. Some members believe, however, that the President should not have supervision over rules and regulations of the so-called independent regulatory commissions. In that case, the President could be required to submit the proposed rules as drafted by the commissions, but with his own comments attached to them. These could include, if he believes it desirable, a recommendation that they be vetoed.

In conclusion, if used with restraint in the types of cases I have indicated, this new technique of legislative control, the veto, has great significance as a device for improving congressional oversight and, at the same time, improving presidential leadership. A State Department official responsible for arms sales has said of the veto: "It focuses executive branch decision-making in a way no other thing can. It makes the executive branch think about the real purpose of selling weapons in the first place—rather than just giving in to a good friend —because you know you're going to be confronted with those questions when you get to the Hill."[7] If on the other hand Congress uses the veto widely and without discrimination, then it will serve neither purpose well.

As government programs have become more numerous and complex, both the Executive and Congress have sought new techniques to implement and control them. For the Executive there have been legislative clearance, program budgeting, systems analysis, and the like. For the Congress, new budgetary techniques, short-term authorizations, and the legislative veto. As Cooper said in his statement before the House Rules Committee:

> Opponents of the veto should perhaps be reminded that the role of parties in our system, the use of the President's veto for policy purposes, presidential bill-drafting and bargaining in the lawmaking process, the attachment of provisos to appropriations bills, continuing oversight by congressional committees—all at one time or another violated conventional conceptions of sound or good practice and were bitterly attacked. Yet, all represented adaptations to institutional needs, survived, and have subsequently been regarded as quite tolerable and even essential.

12

Investigations

BEFORE we can analyze investigations as a technique for congressional oversight and control, we must answer the question: What is an investigation? There is, unfortunately, no satisfactory response in the vast literature on American government.[1] For our purposes one needs to be able to distinguish investigations from other congressional procedures and techniques such as those that are associated closely with appropriations, authorizations, control of personnel, and the legislative veto. Using as a framework our model of executive–legislative relations, we can derive a typology of investigations that does this. In these terms there are three broad categories of investigations. First, there are investigations concerned with congressional oversight of the administrative process. The second category relates to congressional initiation in the legislative process, in which the investigations are largely for the purpose of developing information for congressional committees. Third, there are investigations related to Congress's informing role, where the purpose is public exposure of particular subjects.

Investigations for Administrative Oversight

The administrative oversight category includes three subclasses. The first and most common relates to continuous oversight by Congress, which is carried out initially and principally by committees. Each legislative committee has the responsibility to investigate the conduct of programs and agencies under its jurisdiction. The Legislative Reorganization Act of 1970 and the Committee

Reform Amendments of 1974 include provisions that are designed to encourage the legislative committees to give more attention to investigations for continuous administrative oversight. Consequently, an increasing number of committees have established regular oversight subcommittees, so that by 1981 eleven of the fifteen House legislative committees had such units, the remaining four leaving continuous oversight to subcommittees whose principal responsibility was legislation.

A second subclass relating to Congress's role of overseeing the administrative process is investigations for punitive action—for example, investigations of charges of executive malfeasance in which Congress plays the role of investigative judge. This subclass includes the great and dramatic investigations that have involved the President himself—the Pinchot-Ballinger investigation involving William Howard Taft, the Teapot Dome investigation involving Warren G. Harding, the Watergate investigation involving Richard M. Nixon.

The third subclass includes investigations in which Congress serves as an appeal forum for those who believe that they have been wronged by executive action. In its investigations of military procurement, for example, the House Armed Services Committee sometimes acts as an appeal forum for unsuccessful bidders who believe that the military departments have failed to follow prescribed procedures in awarding contracts.

UTILITY OF INVESTIGATIONS AS A MEANS FOR OVERSEEING
ADMINISTRATION

The efficacy of investigations as a means for oversight of administration depends in part on how committees use investigations in combination with other techniques. Where, for example, a legislative committee is involved in annual authorizations for a program, it may in the process oversee administration adequately and not need to investigate.

Example. The Atomic Energy Act of 1954 required the Joint Committee on Atomic Energy to hold annual hearings, in the nature of an investigation, on the development, growth, and the state of the atomic energy industry. The Atomic Energy Act of 1964 provided for an annual authorization of all AEC expenditures, and, at the same time, it eliminated the requirement for annual investigative hearings, stating simply that the joint committee may conduct such hearings. The point is that the committee's annual authorization hearings would normally serve the purpose of the previously mandated investigative hearings.

The use of investigations for oversight of administration depends also on the prevailing relations between committees and agencies, and these vary considerably from one committee to another.

Example. Prior to 1958 the House Ways and Means Committee used investigations regularly to oversee administration. The main purpose of Ways and Means subcommittees on Internal Revenue Taxation, Administration of the Social Security Law, Administration of Foreign Trade Laws and Policy, and Administration of Excise Taxes was investigation. When Wilbur D. Mills (D. AR) became chairman of the committee in 1958, continuing until 1974, its structure and operating procedures were greatly changed, resulting in the abandonment of investigations as an important oversight technique. The committee's work was done in full session; subcommittees were abolished. The committee relied heavily on its own professional staff and on the experienced professional staff of the Joint Committee on Internal Revenue Taxation for information and studies related to administration as well as legislation. Furthermore, the committee, as well as these two staffs, established a special rapport with the executive agencies that resulted in a free flow of information between them. The committee's professional staffs would carefully draft requests to the agencies for data, and the agencies would respond fully and promptly. In this environment investigations were eschewed. By nature they tended to be adversarial, and as such they would spoil the carefully nurtured committee–agency relations that resulted in the committee's getting all of the data that it wanted.

The Committee Reform Amendments of 1974 required Ways and Means to reestablish subcommittees—at least four of them—and in the same year Mills was succeeded by Al Ullman (D. OR) as chairman. The special relationship with the executive agencies, on which the committee had relied for information, was broken in part, and the committee began to use investigations again. Requiring the committee to establish subcommittees was a response to the reform objective of decentralizing power to junior members, but reforms in the operating procedures of Ways and Means were also motivated in part by a belief among some members that the committee's special relationship with the executive agencies was akin to the type of pathological committee–bureau nexis that we have found to be inconsistent with our model of executive–legislative relations.

Committees are unlikely to use investigations effectively where, in extraordinary cases, the bonds between them and the agencies over which they have jurisdiction are so intimate that they result in a pathological type of executive–legislative relations. Even in these cases, however, pressures from noncommittee members, House leaders, and the press can insure influential investigations.

Example. In its second term the Eisenhower Administration was confronted with considerable criticism of the independent regulatory commissions. Some of those who practiced before the commissions, professors of administrative law, and others raised questions about how these agencies enforced the statutes under which they operated, how they defined the public interest in exercising the discretion available to them, the fairness of their administrative procedures, and the objectivity of commission members.

These commissions were subject to the jurisdiction of the House Committee on Interstate and Foreign Commerce, but that committee had never exercised systematic oversight of the regulatory agencies and failed to respond to the growing criticism.

Finally, on February 5, 1957, Speaker Sam Rayburn (D. TX) compelled the committee to open an investigation. He spoke on the floor of the House, which as Speaker he seldom did, saying "I trust that the gentleman [Oren Harris (D. AR), chairman of the committee] will set up a subcommittee . . . to go into the administration of each and every one of these laws to see whether or not the law as we intended is being carried out." Such a request was equivalent to a command, and the investigation that followed turned out to be a humdinger. Before it concluded, a member of the Federal Communications Commission had resigned, as had Sherman Adams, the President's personal assistant and chief of the White House staff. In addition, Senator Frederick C. Payne (R. ME) had been defeated for reelection largely, it was believed, because of his association with matters investigated by the committee.

The committee made numerous recommendations to improve the administrative procedures of the regulatory commissions. For example, it recommended that *ex parte* communications with commission members and staff be prohibited with respect to matters designated for hearings and that any communications not authorized by law be disclosed in the public record.

The House and Senate Committees on Government Operations (the name of the Senate committee has been changed recently to Governmental Affairs) are relevant in this context. Their jurisdiction for the purpose of investigations, but not for legislation, extends to all executive agencies, so that they can step in where legislative committees elect not to tread. Congress cannot rely on these committees, however, for continuous administrative oversight of any significant number of governmental programs and agencies. The committees are more likely to conduct investigations of charges of executive malfeasance, the second subcategory of oversight investigations in our typology, where legislative committees have failed to do so.

The utility of investigations for administrative oversight depends also on the structure of committees, the size and composition of their staffs, and committee partisanship. Recent studies of variables related to committee structure are inconclusive, however.[2] Joel D. Aberbach hypothesized that the intensity of committee investigations for oversight, measured by the number of such hearings, would increase with greater decentralization of committees, measured by their numbers of subcommittees, but the correlation turned out to be not significant. Also, Aberbach appears to say that committees with oversight subcommittees are likely to be more aggressive in investigations than those that leave oversight to their legislative subcommittees (although he did not assemble his data to give a clear answer on this). A three-member task force of the Patterson committee, on the other hand, was skeptical of such a conclusion: "Theoretically, the creation of oversight subcommittees should focus a committee's attention on the need to conduct systematic program review. However, the possibility exists that . . . oversight units only fragment the process. Indeed, it may be preferable not to divorce oversight responsibilities from the subcommittees to which substantive jurisdiction is assigned."

As for partisanship in investigations, there is considerable variation among committees. A study of the House Committee on Education and Labor in the early 1970s is informative.[3] The committee had no oversight subcommittee; investigative hearings were conducted by legislative subcommittees. On some partisanship was low and on others it was high. The level of partisanship correlated with the breadth of the investigation—the narrower the coverage, the higher the partisanship; and with the results achieved by the investigation —the higher the partisanship, the lower the achievement.

The utility of investigations for administrative oversight depends, finally, on the degree to which individual committees are prepared to rely on the investigative reports and activities of certain outside agents, specifically those of the departments' inspectors general and of Congress's General Accounting Office (GAO). We know less about this than we should. There have been no scholarly studies of the inspectors general and those of the GAO have not evaluated the utility of that agency for congressional committee investigations.[4] Frederick C. Mosher, in his large 1979 study of GAO, says: "Given the multivarious forces that operate on Congress, it would be speculative to assess the impact of GAO inputs on congressional outputs."[5] But such an assessment is needed and probably could be made in the manner of Mackenzie's assessment of the impact of the confirmation process on congressional performance. Regardless, the close relations between congressional investigations and these two groups merit our attention. (The GAO will be discussed in the succeeding chapter on information systems for Congress.)

THE INSPECTORS GENERAL

In recent years Congress has initiated legislation that requires departments and major agencies to establish offices of inspector general to investigate fraud, inefficiency, and abuse of authority. These offices are to have considerable independence from hierarchical control of their departments and are to be, to a significant degree, dependent on Congress. The executive agencies have, in almost all cases, opposed such legislation. Nonetheless inspectors general were mandated by law for the Department of Health and Human Services in 1976, for six other departments and six major independent agencies in 1978, and by 1982 there were such officers in twelve departments and seven major agencies.[6]

Inspectors general are nominated by the President, "without regard to political affiliation and solely on the basis of integrity and demonstrated ability," and must be confirmed by the Senate. If the President removes an inspector general, he must communicate his reasons for doing so to the

Congress. The departments and agencies are directed to accord inspectors general virtually unlimited access to information within their departments; the inspectors general are given power of subpoena to obtain information they need; and they are to report directly to Congress if they find that the funds made available to them by their departments seriously constrain the performance of their duties. Also, at the request of any congressional committee, the President is required to provide information on the amount of appropriations originally requested by any office of inspector general where this is more than the amount provided in the President's Budget. Inspectors general are to submit annual, and in some cases semiannual and quarterly, reports to the heads of their agencies on problems and abuses found, recommendations made to correct them, the agencies' progress in ending abuses, and any corrective steps recommended by inspectors general that are not taken by the agencies. These reports are also to be submitted directly to Congress without any review by agency heads. Inspectors general are to report serious problems and flagrant abuses immediately to their agency heads and then to Congress within seven days.

In Congress the inspector general reports are read initially by staffs of the relevant committees. They have been used by appropriations subcommittees as a basis for questioning executive officers in hearings on the annual money bills and by legislative committees in hearings on annual authorization bills. They have also been used as a basis for oversight investigations where committees were not satisfied by responses given in the annual hearings, where the reports cited failure of the agencies to implement the inspectors' recommendations, or where the committees were not satisfied by performance of the inspectors general.

On the day that he was inaugurated, President Ronald Reagan fired all of the inspectors general, saying that he would replace them with persons who would be more aggressive in rooting out fraud and mismanagement. In accordance with the law, he informed Congress that he was doing so, saying that the discovery of fraud, waste, and mismanagement was an important priority of his Administration and that it was essential for him to have the fullest confidence in the ability and integrity of each inspector general. Those who were dismissed could reapply for their jobs in competition with other applicants.

The reaction in Congress among those members of both parties who were most familiar with the legislation that established the offices was highly critical of the President's action. Reagan had, they said, violated the spirit of the law; he had, in the words of L. H. Fountain (D. NC), "inevitably given the appearance of an attempt to politicize these vitally important offices." Any inspector general who wanted to keep his job would be likely to suppress findings that could embarrass his department or his President. Also, some members felt that the extraordinary powers granted to the inspectors general, on Congress's initiative, would now be used by the Administration to politicize the departments and agencies.

The President's response to this criticism was: "No, no, no, that was not intended at all." Committees in both Houses are keeping a close eye on how the Administration carries out its reform of inspector general offices and its commitment to appoint inspectors general who are "meaner than a junkyard dog when it comes to ferreting out waste and mismanagement," in the words of James S. Brady, the White House Press Secretary.[7]

WHOLE HOUSE CONTROL OVER INVESTIGATIONS FOR ADMINISTRATIVE OVERSIGHT

Apart from the utility of investigations of the Executive, there is a question, in terms of our model, of whether the investigating techniques used by Congress lead to oversight of administration by the whole House or by one of its parts—by the investigating subcommittees. Having delegated a great deal of discretion to the Executive, Congress, presumably, does not want to leave final effective control over how the bureaus exercise the discretion to committees and subcommittees. But there are problems here, for Congress as a whole has no systematic procedure for reviewing the results of investigations. The investigating committees file reports and that may be the end of legislative consideration; there is no legislative instrument like a bill that requires further legislative action.

Lacking a regular procedure for committees to report to the whole House on the findings of their investigations and regular opportunities for debating reports of investigation on the floor, the House has tried to develop other means of control, without notable success.

The House has traditionally exercised a small influence over the initiation of committee investigations by means of control over committee budgets. Legislative committees are funded from two sources, both provided annually in the Legislative Branch Appropriations Act. Each legislative committee receives sufficient funds to employ a basic, so-called statutory staff of thirty. The salaries and related expenses of these staffs constitute approximately 46 percent of committee expenditures. The appropriations act also includes a single lump-sum for House investigations, which is then divided among the legislative committees, but not according to a fixed formula as in the case of the statutory staff. Committees' requests for investigative funds are reviewed by the Committee on House Administration and, based on its recommendations, voted by the whole House. Prior to 1975 committee investigations had to be authorized by the House before funds could be voted for them. The House Rules Committee had the authority to review committee proposals and recommend authorizing resolutions to the House. This control procedure was abandoned when the House, as part of the 1970s' congressional reforms, adopted four measures relating to administrative oversight investigations by legislative committees. The purpose of these reforms was more to encourage committees to initiate and conduct such activities, however, than to encourage the House to review the results.

The Legislative Reorganization Act of 1970 required each legislative committee to report at the end of each Congress on its investigative oversight activities. The act also required the committees to report on their legislative activities, and today the committees combine the two subjects in biennial "activity reports." The intent of the requirement was "to provide the House with an additional means of appraising the results of legislation which it has approved and to emphasize the importance of the [oversight] function of the House standing committees."[8] Testimony before the Bolling committee three years later indicated that the reporting requirement had not achieved these purposes. The committee recommended, therefore, three additional reforms that were adopted, with amendments, in 1974. First, all committees were directed to either establish oversight subcommittees or require their legislative subcommittees to conduct oversight investigations. Second, at the beginning of each Congress, each legislative committee was to consider an administrative oversight agenda for the next two years. (The agenda might include hearings on reauthorization of programs as well as investigations, as defined in our typology.) The Committee on Government Operations (CGO) was to coordinate agenda-setting by the legislative committees and, within sixty days after a new Congress convenes, to report to the House the results of its meetings with the other committees and its recommendations. This report, it was believed, would both focus the attention of the legislative committees on programs that should be investigated and reviewed, and "assure that the House, for the first time in its history, would be able to conduct a coordinated review of federal agencies instead of the intermittent oversight which they had previously received." But these objectives have not been realized in any significant degree.

The CGO has performed its duties in a perfunctory way. It has exercised virtually no influence to coordinate the agenda-setting of legislative committees. CGO simply receives the committees' plans and publishes them in a single document without revision and with only a slight and cursory cover report. It has not issued standards to guide the committees in their agenda-setting, and it has made no effort to evaluate any of the proposed plans. As the committee said in its first report: "It is the belief of the Committee on Government Operations that the presentation of each committee's plan in its own words gives the House the clearest picture of what the committees see as their major oversight activities, free from any distortions or inadvertent misrepresentation that might result from efforts to interpret or evaluate the plans." Nor has CGO established any mechanism to monitor the legislative committees to determine if they follow their agendas, to say nothing of evaluating the oversight reports themselves. As CGO said, again in its first report, the committee had "neither the authority nor the desire to police the other committees of the House in the performance of their legitimate oversight duties." As a consequence, in part, of CGO's timidity, the legislative committees came to be themselves perfunctory in preparing administrative oversight agendas, which were frequently written by staff assistants with minimal member involvement.

Failure of the reform can be attributed to the following factors: (1) reluctance of the legislative committees to be monitored by another standing committee that has no special relationship to the leadership as does, for example, the Rules Committee (assigning responsibility to CGO was in fact a weak alternative to a proposal, considered and rejected by the Bolling committee, that would have made the House leadership responsible for the administrative oversight agenda); (2) the attitude of CGO which, even given the legislative committees' reluctance, could do much more in guiding the preparation of oversight agendas, analyzing them, and making recommendations to the full House; (3) timing of the CGO report—it is due sixty days after a new Congress convenes, when committees are organizing and have other scheduled duties, such as their March 15 reports to the Budget Committee; and (4) structural changes in the House that were taking place at the time that the reform was adopted—for example, decentralization of authority within legislative committees and proliferation of subcommittees.

The third reform relating to investigations that was adopted by the House in 1974 granted eight legislative committees authority to conduct administrative oversight investigations on subjects for which they did not have authority to report legislation. This was called "special oversight" and was designed for two purposes. The first was to encourage comprehensive reviews of broad program areas, as in the case of the Committee on Science and Technology, which was given special oversight over all nonmilitary research and development. The second was more specific: to bridge jurisdictional problems among committees, as in the case of the Committee on Armed Services, which was given special oversight with respect to international arms control and disarmament and military dependents' education, both of which were under the legislative jurisdiction of other committees. There have been no studies of how this reform has worked in practice.

Whole House controls relating to oversight subcommittees and to the preparation and coordination of committee oversight agendas, however deficient, have never been applied in any form to the Senate. And the requirement for biennial reporting of oversight investigations no longer applies to the upper chamber, which opted out in 1979. Yet it is the Senate that presents the greater challenge to whole House control over investigations. Frequently an investigative hearing will be held by a single senator, with the aid of staff assistants who are loyal to him and share his biases. Although the investigation is nominally conducted by a subcommittee, it is a subcommittee of one; no other senators attend. The hearing may be at the seat of government or in the senator's home state. The senator and his staff will then write a report which is issued and publicized as if it were a report of a true subcommittee, or of a Senate committee, or even of the Senate itself. It would appear that each senator has his own investigative subcommittee—many, more than one—and issues his own reports under the subcommittee's name. Some senators have been more active and talented in this regard than others, perhaps none more so in recent years than the senior senator from Massachusetts, Edward M. Kennedy.

Investigations for Initiation of Legislation

The investigation is a very useful technique for eliciting data from the executive agencies and from outside experts where Congress performs the early stages of initiation in the legislative process.[9] Where the President initiates, this investigative function is performed in the Executive, as we have seen. Congressional initiation requires one or two key legislators who serve as movers and are prepared to devote considerable time and attention to a subject. Frequently these members are chairmen of legislative subcommittees and not infrequently of investigating subcommittees. Estes Kefauver (D. TN), for example, who initiated the legislative process that ended in passage of the Drug Amendments Act of 1962, was chairman of the Anti-Trust and Monopoly Subcommittee of the Senate Judiciary Committee. He directed committee staff studies of the drug industry in 1958 and 1959 that were followed by extensive investigative hearings in 1959–1961. Kefauver said on the Senate floor in October 1962:

> In conclusion, Mr. President, this bill constitutes something of a tribute to the Founding Fathers for their wisdom in creating the legislative branch as a separate branch of government. The separation of the legislative from the executive branch has long been criticized by proponents of the parliamentary form of government. But I

doubt whether under a parliamentary system the investigation of the drug industry would ever have been made or new and original remedies conceived. I cannot stress too greatly that most of the provisions of this omnibus bill are not only the outgrowth of an investigation by the legislative branch, but the solutions embodied in the bill were conceived by the legislative branch.

This was not one of the all too frequent situations in which the role of Congress was merely that of passing on proposals developed by the executive branch, nor did it involve merely taking an old bill which had been rejected, updating it, and inserting some new touches to make it current. The bill involved new thinking, new ideas. They came from a legislative committee. At the outset of the investigation, we were actually discouraged by top officials of the Food and Drug Administration. Not only had they no remedies for most of the problems with which we were beginning to be concerned; they did not even recognize them as problems.

If the Executive does not want legislation, investigations of this type can result in highly antagonistic executive–legislative relations, especially where congressional committees deal directly with the bureaus over the President's dislike or disapproval. As we shall see in the next chapter, the committees usually get the data they want if it is available in the bureaus. The President can, of course, end any such confrontation any time he wants by seizing the issue, displacing the congressional committee as initiator.

Investigations for Public Disclosure

With regard to the third category, investigations to inform the public, Woodrow Wilson went so far as to say that the informing function of Congress should be preferred to its legislative function, in order that all national concerns be "suffused with a broad daylight of discussion."[10] Nonetheless, conflicts have developed between the right of Congress to obtain and expose information by investigations and the rights of witnesses to privacy and to protection against self-incrimination. This issue was highlighted in the flamboyant investigations of Communist activities in the United States by the House Un-American Activities Committee and the Permanent Investigations Subcommittee of the Senate Committee on Government Operations, chaired by Joseph R. McCarthy (R. WI), after World War II. In response to public outcry against procedures used by these committees, the House in 1955 adopted certain rules of fair play, a standard of conduct for all committees. According to one of these rules, a committee, if it finds that evidence "may tend to defame, degrade, or incriminate any person," must hear the evidence in secret session, and the evidence can be released thereafter only by a decision of the committee. Concurrently, a subcommittee of the Senate Rules Committee was unanimous in recommending rules to protect witnesses and insure greater control of investigations by committee majorities in the upper chamber. Although the rules were not adopted by the Senate, they came to be followed by a number of its committees.

The Supreme Court has been hesitant to rule on Congress's authority to investigate. As Justice Robert Jackson wrote in 1949: "It would be an unwarranted act of judicial usurpation . . . to assume for the courts the function of supervising congressional committees. I should . . . leave the responsibility for the behavior of its committees squarely on the shoulders of Congress."[11] But the practices of the House Un-American Activities Committee in the 1950s —for example, charging with contempt witnesses who refused to reveal their knowledge of individuals who had in the past been members of the Communist Party—brought the Warren Court to the witnesses' defense. In *Watkins v. United States* (354 U.S. 178, 1957) the court, in a majority opinion written by the Chief Justice, held that:

> The power of the Congress to conduct investigations is inherent in the legislative process. That power is broad. It encompasses inquiries concerning the administration of existing laws as well as proposed or possibly needed statutes. It includes surveys of defects in our social, economic, or political system for the purpose of enabling the Congress to remedy them. It comprehends probes into departments of the Federal Government to expose corruption, inefficiency, or waste. But, broad as is this power of inquiry, it is not unlimited. . . . We have no doubt that there is no congressional power to expose for the sake of exposure.

Thus witnesses cannot be cited for contempt of Congress for refusing to answer the questions of an investigating committee unless the investigation has a legitimate legislative purpose. And exposure or public disclosure per se is not considered to be such a purpose.

In an important respect this is an unfortunate opinion. The use of congressional investigations for public disclosure is one of three uses identified in our typology of investigations. Committees expose misconduct and wrongdoing for the sake of exposure, and their intent to do so is made abundantly clear from the manner in which they hold public hearings. Frequently there is little legislative reason for the public questioning of witnesses in courtroom style since such hearings bring forth little material that is not already available to the committee in extensive files and documents received from the bureaus and other sources. The hearings are primarily for public information and exposure.

Of course, the Court did not say that congressional committees cannot hold investigative hearings for this purpose, only that witnesses before such hearings cannot be cited for contempt if they refuse to testify. Balky witnesses, however, can be cited for contempt if the committee is working on legislation or ordinary administrative oversight. But even this limited purpose for which the rule was stated raises questions. The Court, it is believed, could have found another, less sweeping rationale for prohibiting an abusive practice that had become abhorrent to a great many Americans. And, indeed, since 1957 the Court has retreated from the opinion in *Watkins* by finding that the purposes of all investigations it has been called upon to judge, including those of the House Un-American Activities Committee, have been legitimate (for example, *Barenblatt* v. *United States*, 360 U.S. 109, 1959). As Professor Martin Shapiro has said, the courts now tend to "impregnate investigating committees with the power of legislation by strictly artificial insemination."[12]

13

Information Systems

for Congress

THE INFORMATION NEEDS of Congress are immense and immensely varied. Individual members of Congress need information for their service on committees, for voting on the floor on bills reported by other committees, for constituency services, for their election campaigns. Information for congressional decision making is a large subject that has scarcely been studied systematically. We are concerned in this chapter with only a part of the subject, focusing on the needs of congressional committees, not of individual members, and on information from the executive branch, not from other sources.[1]

For all of its procedures to control the Executive—authorization, appropriation, personnel, legislative veto, investigation—Congress needs broad access to information available in the executive branch. Does it have such access? And can Congress exploit, or put to good use, the information that it receives? The answer to the first question is yes. With only rare exceptions, congressional committees receive from the Executive all of the information that they request. The answer to the second question is more complex but by and large affirmative also, as shown at the end of this chapter.

Soliciting Data from the Executive

The techniques used most frequently by congressional committees to solicit data from the Executive are, first, hearings held in connection with annual appropriations, periodic reauthorizations, and continuous administrative oversight of programs; second, instructions to executive agencies to prepare reports for Congress; and, third, reliance on the General Accounting Office (GAO) to obtain information from the executive branch. A fourth potential source of information, case work done by individual members as constituency service, is not very useful, as it turns out.

HEARINGS

Hearings provide opportunities for the committees to interrogate the Executive and for the Executive to brief the committees. In some hearings, notably those concerned with foreign policy and intelligence, the latter mode is more common than in others, but both modes are found in most hearings, and it is hard to draw a clear line separating them. Huge quantities of information are produced in connection with hearings, but it is difficult to determine how much of it is used. In advance of hearings, agencies typically prepare large volumes of supporting data, only part of which will be printed in committee hearings. Furthermore, in these hearings one has to distinguish between questions asked to obtain new information and questions that are intended to make information that a committee has already received by other means a part of the public record.

Committee members receive answers to almost all questions they ask of executive department witnesses. The questions to which they do not get answers fall into two categories, neither of which has anything to do with executive reluctance to inform the legislature. In the first category are requests for information concerning which the Executive lacks accurate data; in the second, requests that executives believe to be outside of their jurisdictions or beyond their technical qualifications.

In addition to House and Senate hearings for the purposes of appropriations, authorizations, and administrative oversight, Senate committees use confirmation hearings to obtain information from the Executive (see chapter 10), and legislative committees in both Houses use investigative hearings for the same purpose in connection with initiation of legislation and scrutiny of alleged executive misconduct (see chapter 12). Only in the last category is there likely to be any disagreement between the branches on the availability of data.

The purpose of congressional instructions to the Executive to prepare reports for Congress may be to obtain information for legislation, for administrative oversight, for public education, or for some combination of these. Such instructions can be included in statutes that authorize programs or appropriate funds for them, or they can be nonstatutory, in which case they are included normally in committee reports that accompany legislation.[2]

As for legislation, Congress may require executive agencies to investigate and assess specific issues or general policy areas and to submit reports of their findings, frequently with recommendations for legislation. Committees may judge that they need such reports in order to help them initiate legislation where the President has failed to do so; or to put pressure on the Executive to initiate legislation; or, where the President has proposed legislation, to provide additional data to evaluate the Executive's recommendations as well as those of nongovernmental groups.

Example. The Clean Air Amendments Act of 1970 required the administrator of the Environmental Protection Agency (EPA) to establish an Office of Noise Abatement and Control "to carry out a full and complete investigation and study of noise and its effects on the public health and welfare in order to (1) identify and classify causes and sources of noise, and (2) determine (A) effects at various levels; (B) projected growth of noise levels in urban areas through the year 2000; (C) the psychological and physiological effect on humans; . . . and (G) such other matters as may be of interest in the public welfare. . . . The administrator shall report the results of such investigations and study, together with his recommendations for legislation or other action, to the President and the Congress not later than December 31, 1971."

Based in good part on this study, and on President Richard M. Nixon's proposals for legislation, which were in turn influenced by the required report, Congress enacted the Noise Control Act of 1972. In reporting the bill to the House, the Committee on Interstate and Foreign Commerce (now Energy and Commerce) said: "In the opinion of your committee the required EPA report substantiates the urgent need for a coordinated federal, state, and local effort to control and abate noise in order to protect the public health and welfare and demonstrates the need for legislation such as that recommended in the reported bill."

Occasionally the report is a substitute for legislation where there is a lack of consensus within Congress on provisions of an enforceable law.

Example. In hearings on the Solid Waste Disposal Act of 1976, conservation groups worked intensively to get Congress to adopt a ban or restrictions on the use of nonreturnable beverage cans and bottles. Congress was not prepared to endorse this proposal and instead directed the Executive to study the problem and report to Congress. The administrator of the Environmental Protection Agency was to serve as chairman of a Resource Conservation Committee, composed of the secretaries of Commerce, Energy, Interior, Labor, and Treasury; the chairmen of the Council on Environmental Quality and the Council of Economic Advisors; and a representative of the Office of Management and Budget, to conduct a full and complete investigation and study of the appropriateness and feasibility of restricting the manufacture or use of categories of consumer products or of imposing solid waste management charges on consumer products as resource conservation strategies. The study, including recommendations, was to be made to the President and the Congress not later than two years after enactment of the act. No later than six months after enactment, the President and Congress were to be provided with a preliminary report setting forth a study design with time tables.

Statutory instructions may require that a department or agency submit a report to the President for transmittal to Congress, or that the report be sent directly to Congress. In either case the report, if it is important, will be reviewed by the Executive Office of the President before it is sent to the Hill, as are other departmental reports and proposed testimonies on legislation. If the President must sign the transmittal letter, however, the report is likely to receive more attention at the higher level, and this is normally Congress's purpose when it writes the report requirement in this way. By compelling the White House to give attention to a problem, Congress may hope to convince the Executive to initiate the legislative process.

To oversee the administration of programs, Congress has required the agencies to prepare reports that evaluate their policies and programs, that recommend legislation to improve program implementation, or that simply furnish information on program operations. Two examples will illustrate these purposes.

Example. The Foreign Assistance Act of 1971 required an annual report to Congress, showing in total and for each country or international organization: (1) the value of all foreign assistance provided; (2) the amount and reason for all payments of foreign currency to the United States; (3) the value of all military equipment exported under license; and other matters pertaining to U.S. foreign aid programs. "All the information is to be unclassified except on an extraordinary finding of clear detriment to U.S. security."

Example. The Air Quality Act of 1967 included a reporting requirement relating to two aspects of administrative oversight and to new legislation as well: "In order to provide the basis for evaluating programs authorized by this act and the development of new programs and to furnish the Congress with the information necessary for authorization of appropriations by fiscal years beginning after June 30, 1969, the administrator, in cooperation with state, interstate, and local air pollution control agencies, shall make a detailed estimate of the costs of carrying out the provisions of this act; a comprehensive study of the costs of program implementation by effective units of government; and a comprehensive study of the economic impact of air quality standards on the Nation's industries, communities, and other contributing sources of pollution, including an analysis of the national requirements for and the cost of controlling emissions to attain such standards of air quality as may be established pursuant to this act or applicable state law. The administrator shall submit such detailed estimates and the results of such comprehensive study of cost for the five-year-period beginning July 1, 1969, and the results of such other studies, to the Congress not later than January 10, 1969, and shall submit a re-evaluation of such estimates and studies annually thereafter."

Congress has used the technique of requiring reports from the Executive at a steadily increasing rate since 1947. According to data collected by John R. Johannes, there were approximately 300 statutory reports to be made in that year, 500 in 1957, 750 in 1967, more than 1000 by 1974. The General Accounting Office, using a different data base, which, presumably, includes some nonstatutory requirements, estimated that there were over 2500 report requirements in 1980, resulting in the transmittal to Congress of nearly 4500 reports by 250 agencies.[3] The demand for reports in which executive agencies are asked to make recommendations for legislation has grown at a faster rate than the demand for reports that simply divulge data on past performance, although the latter remain more numerous. Approximately one-fifth of all statutory reports are transmitted to Congress by the President, four-fifths by the departments and agencies.[4]

In 1980 some fifty House and Senate committees received these reports. Fifty-seven percent of the reports were addressed to authorizing committees, 26 percent to the government operations committees, and 17 percent to the appropriations committees. A study of the subcommittee on Health of the House Committee on Interstate and Foreign Commerce (now Energy and Commerce) in the Ninety-second Congress (1971–1972) notes twenty-two required reports on subjects within the subcommittee's jurisdiction; and within the annual HEW departmental report, data were presented in response to reporting requirements for more than fifty programs.[5]

Although one cannot attribute immediate congressional responses to most of these reports, Johannes found that, contrary to the views of many executive officers, the vast majority of reports are read by committee staffs and a significant number of them have a verifiable impact on legislation and administration. By requiring the Executive to give attention to problems that it has identified, the Congress often leads the Executive to initiate legislation. Johannes studied the results of forty-five reporting requirements enacted in the Ninetieth Congress (1967–1968), calling on the Executive to study and recommend. Of these, twenty-five reports recommended legislation—mostly program changes or additions; twelve recommended nonlegislative actions—by the Executive or by state or local governments; three reports recommended no action; and six offered no recommendations. The Executive subsequently initiated legislation in nineteen cases, thirteen of which were enacted, frequently with amendments. In twelve cases members of Congress introduced legislation in response to reports, and four of these were enacted. In eight cases the Executive issued new or revised administrative orders and regulations in response to the reports. Also, by conferring legitimacy on policy ideas, keeping issues alive, and generating information, reporting requirements foster what Johannes calls "issue incubation" and help shape an atmosphere conducive to lawmaking.[6]

Similarly, the influence of required reports on administrative oversight is often the result of an action-forcing process on the Executive. The reports generate within the agencies awareness of problems not previously considered and can lead to new program evaluations and changes in administrative regulations and operating procedures. "Study requirements can furnish administrators with pre-oversight opportunities, enabling or even forcing them to assess, moderate, or stimulate their bureaucracies' activities before having to face congressional committees formally."[7]

The quality of the executive reports depends on a number of factors, none more important than the skill and care with which Congress has drafted the language of the requirement. When Congress does not indicate specifically what it wants, agencies are free to define issues and supply information as they choose, possibly frustrating Congress's purpose in calling for the reports. For this reason, the Budget Control Act of 1974 charged the General Accounting Office (GAO) to "assist committees in developing their information needs, including such needs expressed in legislative requirements . . ." but to date committees have made little use of GAO in drafting executive report instructions.

GAO DATA

The General Accounting Office provides congressional committees with several types of information derived from investigations and audits of the bureaucracy and from evaluations of governmental programs. GAO is part of the legislative branch of government, and statutory provisions relating to tenure of GAO employees and to the agency's operating procedures are designed to guarantee its independence from the executive branch and to give Congress confidence in its audits, investigations, and reports. Thus the Comptroller General of the United States and the Deputy Comptroller General are appointed for terms of fifteen years, longer than any other officers of the United States except judges with life tenure. They are nominated by the President and confirmed by the Senate. When a vacancy occurs in one of these offices, Congress establishes an ad hoc bipartisan commission of ten senior members to submit to the President a list of names for possible appointment. The President is not required to select a name from the list, but in 1981, the first time this recent statutory provision was used, the congressional committee proposed eight names for Comptroller General, and President Ronald Reagan nominated one of them, Charles A. Bowsher, who was subsequently confirmed.

Only Congress can remove the Comptroller General and the Deputy Comptroller General by means either of impeachment or a joint resolution when, in their judgment, these officers have become permanently incapacitated or are guilty of specified categories of misconduct. The President, although he can veto a joint resolution calling for removal, cannot fire them on his own initiative. To avoid any chance that GAO employees may be influenced by the executive branch, they are not subject to rules and regulations issued by the Office of Personnel Management or the Merit Systems Protection Board. A 1980 law, initiated by Congress, requires the GAO to set up its own independent personnel system.

All departments and agencies are required to furnish the GAO with any information that it needs in relation to its audits and investigations, and GAO employees, for the purpose of securing such information, have access to, and the right to examine, all agency records. In 1979 Congress strengthened these provisions by giving GAO the power to issue subpoenas and the authority to sue the Executive in federal courts if information is withheld from them.

About 40 percent of the GAO's staff time is devoted to direct assistance to Congress. The remainder is GAO-initiated, as opposed to congressionally directed, work and includes, in addition to audit reports prepared primarily for the executive agencies and more routine audit activities, a large number of reports addressed to Congress because the Comptroller General believes them to be relevant to Congress's oversight of administration. The direct assistance includes audits, investigations, and program evaluations conducted at the request of congressional committees and, less frequently, of individual members. Also, the GAO, when requested to do so by committees, prepares reports on pending legislation and evaluates the executive's proposals for new programs. The Comptroller General and GAO employees testify before committees on investigations and legislation, and the agency frequently assigns its professional employees on a temporary basis to committees to help them with investigations and program evaluations.

Table 13.1 summarizes these GAO activities for 1977. Data in the table do not include a large volume of informal relations between the GAO and Congress, involving consultations, conferences, oral reports, and correspondence, much of it related to executive agencies and programs that are under investigation by congressional committees or are being considered for possible investigative hearings. Nor do they show the large volume of reporting to Congress by the departments and agencies with regard to GAO audits. Executive agencies must inform the committees on government operations, the committees on appropriations, and the relevant legislative committees of actions that they have taken in response to GAO audit reports.

TABLE 13.1

Direct Assistance of the GAO to Congress, 1977

	Number
Audit reports addressed to Congress as a whole	330
Audit reports addressed to committees and subcommittees	265
Audit reports addressed to members	174
Reports on pending legislation	302
Appearances before committees and subcommittees for testimony	111
Committees and subcommittees served by GAO staff	25
GAO staff assigned to committees and subcommittees	102

SOURCE: GAO reports as compiled by Frederick C. Mosher, *The GAO: The Quest for Accountability in American Government* (Boulder, CO: Westview Press, 1979).

The classification "audit reports" in table 13.1 covers a broad spectrum. These reports may be financial audits, management audits of the efficiency with which agencies use their resources, program evaluations to determine if agencies are achieving the objectives intended in authorizing legislation, and even the Comptroller General's views on broader questions of public policy, frequently in response to inquiries by congressional committees. This last category of audit reports has provoked criticism in recent years from some members of Congress and from executive officials. Questions have been raised about whether the government's auditors should be involved in analysis of politically sensitive and controversial issues of foreign, military, and domestic policy, and, more specifically, whether the GAO has the trained personnel and resources to do this. The Comptroller General need not respond to committee requests for such reports if he finds them to be inappropriate for his agency, but Elmer B. Staats, Comptroller General from 1966 to 1981, was generally eager to do so.

Example. In June 1975 the Subcommittee on Political and Military Affairs of the House Committee on Foreign Affairs, chaired by Dante B. Fascell (D. FL), requested the Comptroller General to report on the Ford Administration's handling of the Mayaguez incident in which a U.S. merchant ship and its crew were captured by Cambodian armed forces in the Gulf of Siam and subsequently retaken by U.S. marines in an assault on the island where the ship was being held. Forty-one American servicemen were killed in the assault.

The Comptroller General's audit report criticized the Administration harshly on both diplomatic and military grounds.[8] It dwelled on "diplomatic options not used," saying that "little weight appears to have been given to indications that the Cambodians might have been working out a political solution" and that "several possibilities for communication with the new Cambodian Government were not attempted." The GAO concluded that the Administration had used force unnecessarily to recover the captured ship and its crew, although the report did not use precisely these words. The Comptroller General examined the military operation itself in great detail and found it wanting in many respects, for example, "the risk of having an aircraft carrying the Marine assault commander fly below a 6,000 foot altitude restriction to obtain first-hand information was deemed unacceptable [by the Comptroller General]." More generally, the military had failed to use important sources of information: ". . . little attempt appears to have been made to use photography or other means to verify reports or obtain additional information." The military had acted precipitously and, therefore, with insufficient planning: "Postponement of the operations would have permitted additional time to plan the assault. Because of lack of time, no detailed operational plan for the Marine assault was prepared." And the military had used excessive force.

The report was completed in April 1976 and given to the House subcommittee, the Senate Foreign Relations Committee, and the House and Senate Armed Services Committees. However, it was not released to the public because the National Security Council said that the report was based on classified information, although the Comptroller General did not agree that it was.

Representative Fascell nonetheless released the report to the press six months later, on October 4, which was approximately one month before the presidential election and immediately prior to a televised foreign policy debate between candidates Gerald R. Ford and Jimmy Carter. In the debate Ford was asked to comment on the report. He responded that it injected partisan politics into the campaign and he questioned its conclusions. "Somebody who sits in D.C. eighteen months after the Mayaguez incident can be a very good grandstand quarterback." Secretary of State Henry A. Kissinger complained that the report was based on "misleading information" and "a misunderstanding of government"; and Deputy Undersecretary of State Lawrence S. Eagleburger said that it "is, by the most generous interpretation I can muster, an exercise in *ex post facto* diplomacy by amateurs. Its conclusions demonstrate a fundamental misunderstanding of the issues involved, and a total disregard of the atmosphere in which the decisions surrounding the Mayaguez incident were made."

Some members, especially those on the House Appropriations Committee, feel strongly that the GAO should not be involved in broad policy evaluations. The committee, in its report on appropriations for GAO for fiscal year 1970 (before the Mayaguez incident), said, for example:

It is a good question as to how far Congress and its committees ought to drag the GAO into preauthorization and preappropriation policy questions and areas. Calling on GAO to make detailed recommendations on pending policy legislation might well in time get them tangled—and mangled—politically, and thus in the long run risk impairing their effectiveness as an impartial, unbiased, independent arm of the Congress in examining and reporting on the adequacy, efficiency, and economy of the management of the countless programs of government. . . . Even conceding that it is not always easy or even possible to draw a fine line of delineation in these respects, nonetheless as a general proposition, it would seem that these latter are the more appropriate and profitable ways to exploit GAO resources for congressional purposes.

The Appropriation Committee's report on GAO funds for fiscal year 1982, designed, no doubt, to give guidance to the new Comptroller General, repeated the same sentiments:

> The committee believes that Congress should review the responsibility and operation of the General Accounting Office to assure that . . . it is concentrating on those areas that are most likely to eliminate waste and fraud and assure the proper use of tax dollars. . . . Additionally, the committee hopes the review would include an analysis of GAO's workload to determine what portion of its work falls into the area of reducing fraud and waste, and how much falls into work of an academic or historical nature.

At the same time Congress, in the Budget Control Act of 1974, strengthened significantly the review and evaluation functions of the Comptroller General. The bill that passed the House had no such provisions; they were added in the Senate, on the recommendation of its Committee on Government Operations, which has been strongly supportive of a broad scope for the GAO. They were agreed to, with amendments, by conferees. The act provides that the GAO shall assist committees in developing "statements of legislative objectives" as well as "methods for assessing program performance." Thus questions concerning the propriety of GAO's broad policy audits remain unanswered, indeed, not even clearly defined by Congress.

When the GAO in the late 1960s began to challenge the judgment and procedures used by the Department of Defense in selecting weapons systems for development and procurement, the department formulated an executive position on the proper role of legislative auditors in this sensitive area. This position and the Comptroller General's response to it were presented at 1969 hearings of the Senate Committee on Government Operations. They represent a serious, if ultimately unsuccessful, effort to define the issues. Dr. John S. Foster, Director of Defense Research and Engineering, testified for the Administration, Comptroller General Staats for the GAO.

The Executive held that the GAO should not initiate studies to independently determine military requirements or recommend weapons systems to Congress. It should be limited to reviewing and evaluating programs that have been approved by the Department of Defense and the President and recommended to Congress; to reviewing the management of major ongoing weapons acquisition programs to determine the adequacy of procedures being used; and to reviewing the procedures of completed programs to identify past deficiencies and make recommendations to be applied to current and future programs.

In reviewing programs that have been recommended to Congress by the Executive, the GAO, according to the Defense Department, should not seek to develop alternatives or to review and make recommendations on questions of national security, threat evaluation, foreign policy, military strategy, or technological issues. It should be limited to evaluating the methodology employed and the validity of the data. According to Foster:

> I see no objection to GAO setting forth in its reports alternatives considered by the [Department of Defense], but I do not believe that the GAO should develop and present alternatives to the Congress on weapons system acquisition programs. I do not believe it to be particularly difficult to come up with alternatives for any program—what is difficult and requires considerable study and staff work is properly assessing the net advantages and disadvantages of each alternative.

The GAO agreed with this position to the extent that "we do not believe that it is the desire of Congress that GAO *initiate* new program proposals to deal with social, economic, national security, or other problems or needs." But the Comptroller General did not agree that the GAO should refrain from proposing alternatives to the Executive's program, although his words were guarded:

> How can GAO be most effective as a staff arm of the Congress and the committee as they consider new legislative proposals? An important need of Congress in its decision-making role is to know specifically what alternatives exist and whether adequate analyses were made of these alternatives. . . . Where the underlying studies of alternatives were made available to the GAO, we believe we were able to make useful summaries, highlight significant points, and develop questions, alternatives, and issues for the committee's use.

The DOD felt strongly that the GAO should conduct audits of proposed weapons systems only in response to requests made by relevant authorizing committees or the appropriations committees and not in response to the requests of individual members of Congress. The Comptroller General did not agree to such a limitation.

In terms of our model of executive–legislative relations, GAO audits, like those of weapons systems, may be desirable in the sense that they assist Congress in focusing on broad rather than narrow policy issues and on general rather than specific features of administrative performance. At the same time, the Executive has raised important questions about the capability of GAO to conduct such audits and about how this activity may compromise the objectivity that is required and expected of the GAO in performing its regular auditing functions. The utility of having the GAO develop alternatives to the programs proposed by the President depends on whether the Executive in proposing a program reports to Congress on the alternatives that it has considered and rejected in arriving at its recommendation. As we shall see, executive agencies, using new techniques of policy and systems analysis, have progressively improved their reports in this respect.

Finally there is the question of the independence of the Comptroller General and the GAO. To the extent that the audit agency is involved in sensitive and controversial policy audits, it becomes important that it be controlled by Congress for whom the studies are made. There is no room in our constitutional system for an independent, fourth branch of government policymakers. Yet the structure of the agency—the fifteen-year term of the Comptroller General, for example—gives the GAO considerable independence. The first Comptroller General, J. Raymond McCarl (1921–1936), used this independence in the mid-1930s to disallow expenditures for a number of New Deal programs which had been established by executive orders of President Franklin D. Roosevelt under the authority of emergency statutes that gave the President very broad discretion to act. As Roosevelt began his second term he was confronted, as he saw it, with a double constitutional crisis: the actions of the Supreme Court in ruling unconstitutional a number of New Deal statutes and the actions of the Comptroller General in doing much the same by disallowing expenditures for a number of New Deal programs. To deal with the first crisis the President proposed legislation to reorganize the Supreme Court, and for the second crisis, legislation to remove from the Comptroller General authority to disallow expenditures (so-called preexpenditure auditing), leaving him the responsibility of auditing expenditures after they had been made. In the end neither legislative proposal was enacted, but the crises had abated: the first one by the Court's reconsidering and reversing its doctrines —the "switch in time that saved nine"; and the second by the termination of McCarl's fifteen-year term in 1936.

As for the contemporary GAO, Comptroller General Staats claimed that he served in a dual capacity—as an independent officer in much of his auditing work and as an officer of Congress in the direct assistance that he provided to committees. This is a difficult script to follow in some circumstances, especially since the Comptroller General deliberately shaded the line separating these two categories of responsibility. For example, he insisted on his independence from Congress in selecting the majority of the agency's projects and in controlling the objectivity of investigations and of the recommendations that grew out of them.[9] Also, he would not agree with the proposal that weapons systems audits for Congress be initiated only by committees, thereby leaving himself great freedom to choose among requests for such audits from any of 635 individual members.

As mentioned previously, there are no systematic studies of the effectiveness of all of these GAO activities in helping Congress to oversee and control the implementation of programs by the bureaucracy, only evidence that the demands on the GAO from committees and individual members for these services have increased markedly in recent years. Whereas an estimated 10 percent of GAO staff time was devoted to direct assistance to Congress in 1969, it was 25 percent in 1973, 33 percent in 1977, and 40 percent in 1981.

In addition to the GAO, other agencies in the legislative branch provide information and analysis to Congress, namely, the Congressional Research Service of the Library of Congress and the Office of Technology Assessment, but they are not nearly as important for this purpose as the GAO and we do not discuss them here.

CASEWORK

A fourth, potential source of information for congressional committees on executive performance is casework done by individual members as constituency service. Constituency service was discussed briefly in chapter 4 where I noted that such service does not translate directly into congressional activity in either the legislative or administrative processes.

Casework, as defined by Johannes, who has done the best research on this subject, includes concrete intervention with agency bureaucracies by congressmen and their staffs on behalf of: (1) individual constituents who seek benefits or register complaints about the treatment or quality of service they have received, in connection with programs as varied as military transfers, veterans' pensions, passport applications, social security payments, immigration papers —80 percent of total cases; (2) business and other groups that seek government contracts, low-interest loans, or relief from federal regulations—12 percent; (3) state and local governments which seek federal grants and loans for local programs and projects as varied as community health centers, sewer systems, housing projects, and airports—8 percent.[10] The Obey Commission report, based on a survey of 131 members of the House, estimated an average 12,000 cases per member annually, or approximately 5 million for the whole House. Johannes, using data obtained from 177 members' offices, estimated a mean weekly caseload of 112, or approximately 2.5 million annually for the whole House. In any case the numbers are very large, and casework would appear to present abundant opportunities for discovering program deficiencies and bureaucratic errors and abuses. Information acquired by casework might be used by congressional committees in hearings for continuous administrative oversight, for investigating charges of executive misconduct, for annual authorizations and appropriations, and for considering remedial amendments to the more permanent basic statutes that govern programs. In fact, this happens only infrequently and sporadically, and the question is why.

Johannes asked a sample of 4 former Senators, 25 former Representatives, and 241 staffers who did casework in members' offices: "How effective and how valuable is constituency service for providing ideas and incentives for legislation or for various oversight activities, formal and informal?" For legislation, approximately 20 percent answered "rarely effective"; 20 percent, "very effective"; and the remainder, "somewhat effective." For administrative oversight, the percentage answering "very effective" was slightly higher. But these data are not entirely relevant to our problem nor are they very reliable. The question asked was not limited, as is our concern, to the impact on *Congress's* activities of information acquired by constituency service, for it comprehended also, especially with regard to "formal and informal oversight activities," the respondents' views of any direct impact of constituency service on the ideas and incentives of administrative agencies. As for reliability, one would expect caseworkers to be partial to the importance of their jobs and, therefore, to overestimate effectiveness, as Johannes readily admits. A more reliable test is evidence that information acquired through casework is in fact used in hearings, and there is little of this. Casework seldom leads to oversight hearings or even to preliminary investigations by committee staffs.

Casework, as a part of constituency service, is related overwhelmingly to members' district activities, rather than to their duties in the legislative and administrative processes. Although many members believe that there are electoral rewards stemming from constituency service, according to Johannes, they do not believe that the primary reason for casework is electoral. It is more nearly humanitarian. "You've got to understand that those are real people out there with real problems. We want to help them—anybody would." Casework, in other words, has a life of its own.

As it has developed, casework is not well designed to support the legislative and administrative processes. It principally involves direct relations between members' offices and the executive branch, both regional administrators in the members' districts and agency liaison officers in Washington. The orientation is toward individual cases, and there is relatively little effort among staffers to generalize from cases to broader propositions for amending programs. Sixty to seventy percent of all casework is done in the members' home district offices where staffers' perceptions of the relation between case data and legislation or general administrative oversight are likely to be more attenuated than they would be in Washington. Each member's office works alone—635 independent enterprises—and there are no systematic efforts to agglomerate data and share experiences. Furthermore, the vast majority of cases—estimates range from 80 to 90 percent—are strictly routine and raise no serious questions that are relevant for new legislation or general administrative oversight. The distribution of cases is markedly uneven over policy areas. A large majority result from a relatively small number of entitlement programs—social security, veterans, military, unemployment compensation —and there are few cases relating to foreign and defense policies, or to energy, environment, and transportation.

Finally, if data acquired through casework are to have an impact on legislative and administrative processes, they would have to be available to congressional committees. Yet there are no institutional means for combining the data of individual offices; and, although members will bring the experiences of their offices to committee deliberations, the overall results of this will be uneven because of committee assignments. Seventy-five percent of a member's casework may relate to social security, veterans, and the unemployed, while he serves on the Armed Services Committee. Members may, of course, tell colleagues on the relevant committees about their casework, or they may speak of it on the House floor. It is in voting on the floor that all members may be able to translate experience acquired from their casework into legislative decisions, but the opportunities for doing this are limited.

Using Data from the Executive

Congressional committees, then, obtain huge quantities of data from the executive agencies. There remains the question of whether the committees have the capacity to put the data to good use, that is, to organize and analyze the data so that they will serve Congress as well as possible for oversight and control of the Executive by means of appropriations, authorizations, and the other techniques discussed in this book.

Normally the most important factor determining the technique of data analysis that Congress uses in any situation is the technique that was used by the Executive in preparing the data for Congress. The Executive sets the legislative agenda in this regard as well. Occasionally Congress will prescribe the form in which executive agencies are to organize and present their data, as in some of the executive report requirements discussed earlier, and less frequently it may prescribe analytical techniques to be used by the Executive. But for the most part these are within the Executive's discretion.

In recent years there have been extraordinary advances in methods of policy analysis, most of them derived from the techniques of systems analysis and dependent on computers for the capacity to use large amounts of basic data. For analyzing public policies, executive agencies have used most of these methods, including benefit-cost analysis *(bca)*, multiple-objective planning, evaluation, planning-programming-budgeting systems *(ppbs)*, management by objective *(mbo)*, technology assessment *(ta)*, environmental impact analysis *(eia)*, and others. To make effective use of these techniques, they have invested heavily in the development of new basic data sets, such as social indicators, to accompany the more traditional economic indicators.

A commonly held view among political scientists is that Congress has resisted these executive developments in data analysis, principally because they reduce opportunities for bargaining among subcommittees, committees, bureaus, and departments. Relating the techniques to the budget, Wildavsky argues as follows: if there were a way to determine the relative merits of alternative expenditures, outside of the political process of partisan mutual adjustment, then such techniques as *ppbs* would have a rationale. But there is no way, so the budget can do no more than "register the constellation of prevailing political forces. There is no need for any special budget review technique. It is sufficient if each actor plays his assigned role. . . ." New policy analysis techniques have the unfortunate effect of denying certain actors in the Executive and Congress their traditional roles, and for this reason they are doomed to failure when the actors rise in opposition to them.[11]

This view is wrong. It is true that certain congressional committees have been wary of the new techniques when they have first confronted them and that others have initially opposed them, but for reasons different from those offered by the critics. Concerned that they may lose information from the Executive on which they previously have relied, congressional committees are circumspect about new techniques with which they are unfamiliar when these are first presented to them. Committees embrace the techniques, however, once they become familiar with them and satisfied that they will gain relevant information, rather than lose it.

Example. In 1946 the Navy Department, in response to a study by its fiscal director, Admiral Wilfred McNeil, altered the method for presenting the budget for the naval shipyards. Previously there had been a direct appropriation to each yard for the cost of overhauling the ships that would be assigned to the yard in the fiscal year. The Navy proposed to have the forces and commands under which the ships steamed pay for their overhaul so as to more nearly represent the cost of operating and maintaining those forces. Thus appropriations would be made to the forces and commands, rather than to the naval shipyards, and the yards would operate on revolving accounts. No sooner had the new budget reached the House Appropriations Committee rooms than it was returned to the department to be put back into the old familiar categories. For one or two years thereafter the Navy submitted its budget in both forms, after which the committee, now familiar with the new form and convinced of its superiority for making rational decisions concerning the maintenance of naval weapons systems, abandoned its demand to see the old categories.

Congressional committees have also been wary of new analytical techniques when they have believed that the Executive was using them for purposes other than policy analysis, for example, to reorganize a department or agency.

Example. In 1961 Robert S. McNamara, Secretary of Defense in the Kennedy and Johnson administrations, introduced new techniques of systems analysis and program budgeting to facilitate a comparative evaluation of alternative weapons systems, which had become hugely expensive in a nuclear era. For this purpose he brought into the Department of Defense (DOD) a number of bright young analysts who had worked previously at the RAND Corporation in Los Angeles and installed them in the Office of the Secretary, with authority to demand of the service departments—the Army, Navy, and Air Force—the data they needed, to analyze the data, and make recommendations to the secretary based on these analyses.

The House and Senate Armed Services Committees initially opposed vigorously McNamara's reliance on systems analysis and program budgeting. The procedures were new and unfamiliar. Also the committees were convinced that McNamara was using the techniques not only to do better analysis of weapons systems, but also and explicitly to reorganize the DOD without the approval of Congress, increasing greatly the power and authority of the secretary's office at the expense of the service departments. They were right about this. While program budgeting of necessity contains a centralizing tendency—for example, one can compare weapons systems proposed by the Navy and Air Force to accomplish the same mission only at a level higher than these two departments—McNamara used the techniques to justify a departmental reorganization. When, in 1968, Melvin R. Laird, who had previously served on the House Armed Services Committee, became Secretary of Defense under President Richard M. Nixon, he dismantled the McNamara superstructure. By this time the use of systems analysis and program budgeting for research, development, testing, and procurement of major weapons systems had become ubiquitous in the defense establishment. Absent the unauthorized use of the techniques for departmental reorganization, the House and Senate Armed Services Committees dropped their opposition and began themselves to use them.

A 1976 study of the Research and Development subcommittee of the Senate Armed Services Committee found that congressional opposition to program budgeting, which characterized congressional oversight in the 1960s, had all but disappeared in the Senate by the early 1970s.[12] Among other reasons, those in Congress who wanted to make selective programmatic cuts in DOD's budget clearly saw the advantages of the open and explicit analysis required by program budgeting.

The reason, perhaps, that the critics have failed to see the real causes of congressional concern about new analytical techniques is that they have used an imperfect lens to observe the phenomenon. The use of partisan mutual adjustment *(pma)* leads an analyst to expect that committees and bureaus will oppose any improvements in rational decision making that reduce opportunities for bargaining and tradeoffs. It is fair to assume that if a scholar of the *pma* persuasion were presented the naval shipyard example as a hypothetical case and without the outcome, he would predict that Congress would reject the new budget because it would reduce opportunities to bargain over appropriations for the naval shipyards in Boston, Philadelphia, Charleston, San Francisco, and Bremerton, Washington. But he would be wrong.

Congress will have more control over the Executive if the programs presented to it by the President are integrated and coherent than if they are fragmented and incoherent. In recent years Congress has enacted statutes that require agencies to conduct elaborate and continuing planning processes involving resources inventories, assessments, and analyses of alternative programs, policies, and categories of benefits and costs. The Forest and Rangeland Renewable Resources Planning Act of 1974 (RPA) and the Soil and Water Resources Conservation Act of 1977 (RCA) are examples. The hearings and reports on this legislation make it clear that the committees intend that the agencies use advanced analytical techniques. The results are to be presented to the Congress so that the legislature, as well as the Executive, can use them for decision making in appropriations, authorizations, and administrative oversight.[13] There is evidence, then, that Congress responds positively to the use of advanced data analysis techniques that are likely to serve its purposes.

14

Congress's Right to Know

DESPITE evidence that congressional committees are normally successful in soliciting information from the Executive and that there is cooperation between the two branches for this purpose, it is the exceptions that earn the headlines: "Nixon Denies White House Tapes to Congress," "Carter Foiled in First Tilt with Executive Privilege," "Watt to Be Cited for Contempt." These exceptions are not rooted necessarily in presidential caprice or executive defiance of the legislature, for Congress's right to know is not absolute. There are, and always have been, certain limits on this right, limits that, as it turns out, have been defined principally by the politics of executive–legislative relations.

Congress's Right to Know: Its Meaning

The right of Congress to information from the Executive is a different issue from the right of the public to such information, although this important distinction is frequently overlooked. To put it another way, the right of the Executive to withhold information from Congress is a different issue from the right of the Executive to withhold information from the public. Congress's right to information rests principally on a special claim, namely Congress's duties in the legislative and administrative processes and its need for information in order to perform these duties. The right of citizens, or the public, to know rests on the broader claim that publicity, sunshine, is necessary for popular control over government. As Jeremy Bentham said in his *Rationale of Judicial Evidence* (1827): "Without publicity all other checks are insufficient; in comparison with publicity all other checks are of small account."

Congress has been much concerned with this broader question of the public's right to know. In this area it has on several occasions exercised its reserve power to initiate legislation for the purpose of improving the public's access to information in the Executive. Thus Congress in 1966 initiated and passed the Freedom of Information Act, to increase the access of citizens to governmental records, over the solid opposition of the executive branch. And Congress, the House Committee on Government Operations in particular, has held periodic hearings to oversee the administration of this act. Congress has been concerned with speeding up the process by which classified documents are declassified and made available to the public and, in this connection, has monitored the work of the Interagency Classification Review Committee in the Executive. But these activities relate to the public's right to know, and our special concern is not this, but Congress's right to know, which, as I have observed, rests on a different claim.

Two types of authority may be available to the Executive for withholding information from Congress: statutes and executive privilege derived directly from the Constitution.

A number of statutes authorize or direct the Executive to withhold data from Congress or to reveal it only under specific conditions. The Internal Revenue Code is an example. The statute states the conditions under which the Secretary of the Treasury is to respond to requests from the House Ways and Means Committee and the Senate Committee on Finance for individual tax returns or any information from them. It prescribes even stricter conditions for such requests from other committees, requiring that their petitions be supported by resolutions passed by the whole House or Senate that specify the purposes for which the returns are to be used and attest that such information cannot reasonably be obtained from any other source. In both cases, any data that can be associated with a particular taxpayer can be furnished only when the committee is sitting in closed executive session.

These statutes, of course, can be repealed or revised. Furthermore, statutes can be written to promote the availability of information to Congress, as well as to restrict it.

Example. The Atomic Energy Act of 1946 provided that the Atomic Energy Commission "shall keep the Joint Committee on Atomic Energy fully and currently informed with respect to the Commission's activities." This requirement was strengthened in 1954, on Congress's initiative, to read "with respect to *all of* the Commission's activities." As a means of enforcing this, the Senate members of the joint committee (now the Senate Committee on Energy and Natural Resources) have systematically questioned those whom the President has nominated to be commissioners and extracted from them at their confirmation hearings promises to abide by this provision. Commissioner Lewis Strauss's failure to keep his promise, as the senators saw it, was in good part responsible for the bitterness of the dispute that developed when he was subsequently nominated by President Dwight D. Eisenhower to be Secretary of Commerce, as described in chapter 10. It will be recalled that the Senate rejected the appointment.

The second source of executive authority for withholding information from Congress is a constitutional power vested in the President, in the absence of specific statutes, and called executive privilege. The Constitution itself does not mention executive privilege, which is said to be an inherent right of the Chief Executive, derived from his broad responsibility to execute the laws and to conduct foreign and military policy. Some of the great conflicts in our history between the President and Congress have been over executive claims of executive privilege. It is informative to examine three of these.

Example. Washington Administration—the St. Clair episode, 1791–1792. On November 3, 1791, Major General Arthur St. Clair and his force of 1400 men were surprised by an Indian attack in the Northwest Territory near what is now Miami, Ohio. Nine hundred men were lost, and the command was driven back in disorder.

In March 1792 the House of Representatives resolved: "That a committee be appointed to inquire into the causes of the failure of the late expedition under Major General St. Clair, and that the said committee be impowered to call for such persons, papers, and records as may be necessary to assist their inquiries." The House committee that was appointed called on the Secretary of War, Henry Knox, to turn over to it all documents relating to the expedition. Knox sought President George Washington's advice on whether to honor the request, and the President then chaired two successive cabinet meetings at which the question was discussed. We know what happened at those meetings because Thomas Jefferson kept careful notes.

The conclusions of the cabinet were the following: "First, that the House was an inquest, and therefore might institute inquiries. Second, that it might call for papers generally. Third, that the Executive ought to communicate such papers as the public good would permit, and ought to refuse those, the disclosure of which would injure the public; consequently the Executive were to exercise a discretion. Fourth, that neither the committee nor the House had a right to call on the head of a department . . . ; but that the committee should instruct their chairman to move the House to address the President." Finally, it was agreed in this case that there was not a paper which might not be properly produced; and that "the Executive should speak separately to the members of the committee and bring them by persuasion into the right channel."

Thus commences the doctrine of executive privilege in the history of executive–legislative relations.

Example. Jackson Administration—the Second Bank of the United States, 1832–1834. Congress chartered the Second Bank of the United States in 1816 for twenty years. The Bank became extraordinarily unpopular in the rural West due to its foreclosures of mortgaged farmlands, and President Andrew Jackson during his first term indicated his opposition to the Bank. Senator Henry Clay (KY), seeking to embarrass the President before the upcoming election, pushed through Congress in 1832 a bill to recharter the Bank, although the existing charter of 1816 still had four years to run. Jackson vetoed this bill, and this action became a major issue in the election.

Jackson swamped Clay in the election of 1832 and took his victory to be a mandate in support of his opposition to the Bank. He, therefore, undertook to kill the Bank, although it still had three years to run under its first charter, by withdrawing U.S. deposits from it. The Bank's charter, however, vested authority to withdraw deposits in the Secretary of the Treasury, not the President. The incumbent Secretary, Louis McLane, was opposed to withdrawing the deposits, so Jackson transferred him to be Secretary of State and appointed William J. Duane as Treasury Secretary. Duane also refused to withdraw the deposits, so Jackson fired him and transferred Roger Brook Taney from Attorney General to Secretary of the Treasury. Taney withdrew the deposits.

As the newly elected Congress was not yet in session, Jackson could make these successive recess appointments to the cabinet without waiting for Senate confirmation. When Congress assembled in December 1833, Clay introduced a resolution, which was approved by the Senate, inquiring of the President whether a certain paper reported to have been read at a cabinet meeting was genuine. This was the paper in which Jackson revealed to his cabinet his determination to have the government deposits withdrawn from the Second Bank of the United States. Jackson refused to comply, citing executive privilege:

"The Executive is a coordinate and independent branch of the government equally with the Senate, and I have yet to learn under what constitutional authority that branch of the legislature has a right to require of me an account of any communication, either verbal or in writing, made to the departments as a cabinet counsel. As well might I be required to detail to the Senate the free and private conversations I have held with those officers on any subject relating to their duties and my own. . . . Knowing the constitutional rights of the Senate, I shall be the last man under any circumstances to interfere with them. Knowing those of the Executive, I shall at all times endeavor to maintain them agreeably to the provisions of the Constitution and the oath I have taken to support and defend it."

Clay responded by putting through the Senate a Resolution Censuring the President. Jackson answered, in turn, in what he called a Protest, that a resolution of censure was unconstitutional. Under the Constitution, he said, Congress could impeach him, but not censure him, and he dared the Senate to impeach him, knowing that the House must first vote a bill of impeachment and that he controlled sufficient votes in the House to prevent this.

Jackson delayed almost as long as he could before submitting Taney's name to the new Senate for confirmation as Treasury secretary. When finally he did so, Taney was rejected (June 24, 1834), and he retired to private life. As the "martyred Secretary," however, he had a claim of sorts to the next vacancy on the Supreme Court, and on January 15, 1835, Jackson nominated Taney for the position of Associate Justice. Clay and the President's other enemies in the Senate defeated the nomination in March by postponing it indefinitely. On December 28 Jackson nominated Taney again, this time for the vacancy created by the death of Chief Justice John Marshall. By 1836 enough changes had taken place in the Senate so that, on March 15, Taney was confirmed as the fifth Chief Justice of the United States.

Finally, in 1837, the Senate expunged Clay's Resolution of Censure from the official records of the Senate.

Example. Nixon Administration—Watergate, 1973–1974. The Senate Select Committee on Presidential Campaign Activities, known popularly as the Watergate committee or Ervin committee, after its chairman, Sam S. Ervin (D. NC), was involved in a lengthy struggle with President Richard M. Nixon over release to the committee of White House documents, including tape recordings. In May 1973 the White House issued guidelines on the use of executive privilege which much resembled those of Andrew Jackson. Executive privilege should be invoked only in connection with conversations with the President, conversations among aides involving communications with the President, and with regard to presidential papers and national security. "The President desires that the invocation of executive privilege be held to a minimum."

Based on these guidelines Nixon subsequently refused to hand over presidential papers. "No President," he said in a July 6 letter to Ervin, "could function if the private papers of his office, prepared by his personal staff, were open to public scrutiny. Formulation of sound public policy requires that the President and his personal staff be able to communicate among themselves in complete candor." The issue assumed new dimensions soon thereafter with revelation that tape recordings had been made of many presidential conversations. The Watergate committee subpoenaed the tapes. The President, based on the guidelines, refused to honor the subpoenas. Senator Ervin then made heroic efforts to get the courts to rule on this great constitutional issue between the legislative and executive branches of government. Indeed, Ervin on several occasions made this the principal concern of the Watergate hearings. Television viewers of the proceedings will recall the dramatic moment, staged by Ervin, when his legislative assistant, Rufus Edmiston, who was also deputy counsel of the committee, slowly and deliberately marched up the long steps of the handsome, Victorian Executive Office Building with a subpoena for the President of the United States. Ervin, being himself a constitutional expert and a court afficionado of the southern tradition, seemed to savor a possible opportunity to himself argue such a case, representing the Congress, before the Supreme Court, although this opportunity never materialized.

The President's argument against relinquishing the tapes to the Senate committee prevailed in the lower courts, so convincingly that in the end no appeal was taken to the Supreme Court. It happened this way. The Senate committee filed a civil suit in the U.S. District Court in Washington asking the court to declare the subpoenas lawful and to order the President to comply with them. On October 17, 1973, the court ruled that it had no jurisdiction to consider the committee's request, since Congress had never enacted legislation giving federal courts jurisdiction in such cases. The committee responded initially by getting the upper chamber to adopt a resolution stating the sense of the Senate that the committee had authority to subpoena the President, and soon thereafter by leading a successful effort to pass legislation specifically granting the federal District Court in Washington jurisdiction over any civil suit brought in the future by the Senate Watergate committee to enforce a subpoena against the President or any other executive branch official. On December 18, 1973, Nixon allowed the bill to become law without his signature. He called the bill bad legislation, applying as it did to a single case, but said that a veto under the circumstances would be misunderstood by the public.

The next day the Senate committee approved new subpoenas, Nixon again refused to comply, and the committee renewed its suit, asking the court to reconsider its earlier opinion in the light of the new legislation. On February 8, 1974, the court refused to require the White House to turn over the tapes, holding that "it has not been demonstrated to the court's satisfaction that the committee has a pressing need for the subpoenaed tapes." The Select Committee appealed this decision to the U.S. Circuit Court of Appeals in Washington, and that court upheld the lower court without dissent, finding that "the subpoenaed material was not critical to the committee's performance of its legislative functions."[1]

Thus ended Senator Ervin's great constitutional debate. As Circuit Judge Malcolm R. Wilkey said, in a concurring opinion: "On my own analysis our logical first conclusion should be that the constitutional principle of separation of powers makes the issue here a political question and therefore not justiciable."

Subsequently, the Supreme Court in *U.S. v. Nixon* (418 U.S. 638, 1974) required Nixon to turn the White House tapes over to the Special Prosecutor. The Court denied the President's claim of executive privilege to withhold evidence from judicial authorities relevant to a criminal trial, where the President had not claimed a need to protect national security interests. But this decision related to the needs of actors in the judicial process, it had nothing to do with Congress's right to executive data for the legislative and administrative processes. Nor had the Senate Select Committee been a party to this suit.

Since Jackson's day many Presidents have used executive privilege to withhold information from Congress—Tyler, Polk, Fillmore, Lincoln, Grant, Hayes, Cleveland, Theodore Roosevelt, Coolidge, and all subsequent Presidents. Jimmy Carter, in his 1976 election campaign, promised that his presidency would be different in this regard, an open presidency in which there would be no need to claim executive privilege. But after taking office he found it expedient to claim the privilege on more than one occasion.

In light of these historical examples, what can be said today about the constitutionality of the doctrine of executive privilege to withhold information from Congress?[2] The need for secrecy in conduct of foreign affairs has been recognized by the Supreme Court as justifying the withholding of information from Congress in the absence of specific statutory authority for doing so (*U.S. v. Curtiss-Wright*, 299 U.S. 304, 1936). But apart from this there are few court determinations of any kind on the right of the Executive to withhold information from Congress, and the Supreme Court has never passed directly on the power of a congressional committee to compel release of White House materials in the face of a claim of privilege by the President. As we saw in the Nixon example, the courts avoid such decisions, leaving the parties to resolve them in the give and take of executive–legislative relations.

In February 1976, the House Intelligence Committee, chaired by Otis G.

Pike (D. NY), went to the precipice with Secretary of State Henry A. Kissinger, voting to recommend that the House cite Kissinger for contempt of Congress for failing to comply with committee subpoenas for certain national security documents. No committee had ever voted previously to cite a cabinet officer for contempt. Kissinger was acting on orders of President Gerald R. Ford, who cited executive privilege. However, before the House debated the contempt resolution, the committee and the President reached an accommodation, as the House leaders in particular, unlike Senator Ervin, wanted to avoid the court case that would follow a contempt citation. This scenario has now become familiar, as for example in a much publicized confrontation in 1982 between Secretary of the Interior James G. Watt and John D. Dingell (D. MI), chairman of the House Committee on Energy and Commerce, over papers relating to attempts by Canadian firms to take over American energy companies. On instructions from President Ronald Reagan, Watt cited executive privilege for failing to comply with committee subpoenas for the papers. The committee voted 23 (22D., 1R.) to 19 (2D., 17R.) to request the House to hold Watt in contempt of Congress. Again, before the House acted, the committee and the Executive reached agreement.*

Since, then, it is unlikely that federal courts will set general guidelines for Congress's right to know or the Executive's privilege to withhold information from Congress, let us examine instead various criteria or standards, most of them proposed in the past by executive officers, to distinguish information that should be withheld from Congress from information that should be released to it. To the extent that any of these standards are convincing, they may come to govern executive–legislative relations in the future.

Congress's Right to Know: Criteria for Disclosure

SUBJECT MATTER

The criterion states that there should be full disclosure for domestic and nonsecurity affairs, but the President should have authority to withhold information from Congress on foreign and national security matters, in recognition of the President's superior constitutional position in the latter areas and the

*On December 16, 1982, the House by a vote of 259 (204D., 55R.) to 105 (4D., 101R.) held Anne M. Gorsuch, administrator of the Environmental Protection Agency, in contempt of Congress for refusing, on President Ronald Reagan's orders, to furnish certain documents to the Subcommittee on Investigations and Oversight of the House Committee on Public Works and Transportation. As of January 1983, it is unclear how this case will be resolved.

need for secrecy. But this is an unsatisfactory criterion principally for two reasons. First is the difficulty of drawing a line between the two categories. Second, for those aspects of foreign and security affairs that require secrecy —presumably from the enemy—should there be no information available to the legislature? Of course there should be. Congress needs secret information to perform its role.

At the same time, there is a problem in connection with making secret data available to Congress, namely, if Congress cannot handle such data responsibly, the Executive will resist providing the data. From World War II until the 1970s there were few disputes here. Members had top-secret information and used it responsibly. The conduct of the Joint Committee on Atomic Energy is a good example. But since 1971 there have been a number of instances in which individual members and committees of Congress have revealed information that the Executive considered to be highly classified and useful to enemies.

Example. On April 25, 1972, Senator Mike Gravel (D. AK) asked unanimous consent to insert in the *Congressional Record* excerpts from a top-secret National Security memorandum. The 500-page document concerning policy options in the Vietnam War had been prepared for President Richard M. Nixon in 1969 by the National Security Council staff under Henry A. Kissinger. The senator's normally routine request was blocked temporarily by minority whip Robert P. Griffin (R. MI). The Senate met on May 2 and 4 in closed executive sessions to consider Gravel's request, but no decision was reached. Then, on May 9, Gravel, without advance notice, read into the *Record*, during debate on the annual State Department authorization bill, excerpts from the memorandum dealing with proposals to mine North Vietnamese ports, an action that had been announced by the President on the previous day. Senator Griffin, who entered the chamber during Gravel's statement, criticized him for acting before the Senate had disposed of the question. The senator responded: "I have an obligation to the American people . . . to let the American people have the information that he [President Nixon] has."
Congressman Ron V. Dellums (D. CA) then obtained from Gravel a copy of the full document which he placed in the *Congressional Record* on May 11, by simply asking unanimous consent to extend his remarks in the *Record*, without giving any hint of their contents.

Such conduct by individual members does more to limit Congress's right to know than to enlarge it. If executive agencies believe that by giving Congress access to classified data they may be giving the public such access, then they will give no special consideration to Congress's right to know and simply release to Congress information that they are required to make public in any case. Congress's right to know and the public's right to know become one and the same.

The Senate appears to have been sensitized to this danger by the Gravel incident, and in August 1972 it passed a resolution, proposed by Jacob K. Javits (R. NY), creating an ad hoc committee of ten senators to study "all questions relating to secrecy, confidentiality, and classification of government documents committed to the Senate or any member thereof." Majority Leader Mike Mansfield (D. MT) was chairman of the committee and minority leader Hugh Scott (R. PA), cochairman. The committee presented its report more than one year later, in October 1973, but it had been unable to deal in any significant way with the questions put to it. The report said that under the speech and debate clause of the Constitution (Article I, Section 6, clause 1) no senator can be prosecuted for any speech or debate on the Senate floor or during a committee hearing in which he reveals the contents of a classified document. But the question before the committee was not prosecution by the Executive; no one questioned the constitutional provision. The question was how the Senate should discipline its members. And on this the committee recommended only that:

> Individual members who have such documents and wish to disclose them should consult with the Senate Ethics Committee prior to such disclosure. The Committee wishes to make it clear that although it recommends consultation with the Ethics Committee, any determination by the Ethics Committee should not be binding on the member. The reason for the recommendation of consultation is to permit a member the opportunity of getting the additional thinking and precedents available to him before making a final decision regarding disclosure.

Nor has the House of Representatives been more successful in dealing with members who break security.

Example. In 1975 Michael J. Harrington (D. MA) was charged by several of his colleagues with disclosing secret testimony presented to the Armed Services Committee by CIA Director William E. Colby in executive session, relating to alleged U.S. efforts to prevent the 1970 election of Salvadore Allende in Chile. Harrington, a member of the Armed Services Committee, admitted to discussing this secret testimony with a number of persons, including a *Washington Post* reporter; and he defended his action as the obligation of a member of Congress to disclose any information he receives that indicates, in his view, illegal governmental activity.

The House Ethics Committee (at that time called the Committee on Standards of Official Conduct), by a 7 to 2 vote on October 21, 1975, ordered a formal investigation and hearing, even though the Democratic leadership, especially Majority Leader Thomas P. O'Neill, Jr. (D. MA), a close friend of Harrington's, tried hard to avoid this. But the Ethics Committee copped out less than two weeks later when it voted 7 to 3 not to conduct the inquiry. The reason given was that the occasion on which Colby testified was not a legal executive session. The Ethics Committee had discovered that the Armed Services Committee had not issued a public notice of its meeting, that a quorum had not been present, and that no vote was taken to meet in executive session, as prescribed in the House rules. "We are required to find," said the chairman, "that the hearing which was believed to have been held was a nullity." None of this, of course, goes to the question of Harrington's admittedly giving secret information to the press because in his view the government had acted immorally or illegally.

The most serious problem for Congress relates to individual members who act on their own. But there have also been problems in recent years with committees that want to reveal secret information without first getting the approval of Congress as a whole, or of the relevant House of Congress. This can be illustrated by two examples, one from the House and one from the Senate.

Example. In January 1976 the House Intelligence Committee, under chairman Otis G. Pike (D. NY), sought to make public a report containing information that the White House considered to be top secret. The House intervened, voting 246 to 124 to block the committee from releasing its report until the President certified that it did not contain information that would adversely affect the nation's intelligence activities. Whereupon Daniel Schorr of CBS *News*, having obtained a copy of the report presumably from a House member or staffer, gave it to the *Village Voice*, which published it, thereby frustrating an overwhelming majority of the House. Schorr was subsequently fired by CBS, and became a cult hero on the college lecture circuit, commanding top fees for one-night stands.

Example. The Senate Intelligence Committee chairman, Frank Church (D. ID), went to the full Senate in November 1975 for approval of release of the committee's report on CIA involvement in assassination attempts on foreign leaders. The report included secret information that the President believed should not be made public. The Senate met in executive, that is, secret, session, and when considerable opposition to release of the report developed, more opposition than Church had anticipated, he and the Democratic majority adjourned the session without a vote, and the committee released the report on its own authority.

Since 1976 there is evidence that both Houses are more willing to face up to these problems than before. They have devised and enacted procedures for handling secret data. Whether or not they have the capacity and will to discipline members or committees that violate the procedures remains to be seen. The 1980 state of the art in both executive–legislative and committee–whole House relations concerning secret data is represented by a statute enacted that year to amend the National Security Act of 1947 with regard to Congress's access to secret intelligence data. It provides that the director of Central Intelligence and the heads of all departments and agencies involved in intelligence activities are to keep the House and Senate Committees on Intelligence "fully and currently informed of all intelligence activities" for which they are responsible, "including any significant anticipated intelligence activity"; and they are to furnish the committees any information that they request in pursuance of their responsibilities. These broad requirements are conditioned by the statement that the Executive's actions under the statute are to be "consistent with all applicable authorities and duties, including those conferred by the Constitution, upon the executive and legislative branches of government, and are to be with due regard for the protection from unauthorized disclosure of classified information." At the same time, the statute states that none of its provisions are to be "construed as authority to withhold information from the intelligence committees on the grounds that providing the information to them would constitute the unauthorized disclosure of classified information"; and the conference committee report on the bill states: "Both branches agree that the intelligence committees continue to have the right to obtain the information they require by subpoena. . . . The statute does not provide a statutory right to withhold information from Congress when subpoenaed by Congress."

As for self-discipline by Congress regarding disclosure of secret information, the law provides that the House and Senate, in consultation with the director of Central Intelligence, shall each establish, by rule or resolution, procedures to protect from unauthorized disclosure all classified information and all information relating to intelligence sources and methods furnished to the intelligence committees or to members of Congress. In response to this requirement, the House of Representatives and its intelligence committee have each adopted rules which, taken together, provide the following:

1. Receipt of classified material. The committee's acceptance of classified material from the Executive constitutes a decision by the committee that the material will not be disclosed except in accordance with procedures summarized in the next paragraph.

2. Committee disclosure of classified material. The committee may disclose publicly any information in its possession under the following conditions: There is to be a roll-call vote by the committee stating that the public interest would be served by such disclosure. If the executive branch requests that the information nonetheless be kept secret, the committee must notify the President of its vote and delay immediate disclosure. If, within five days, the President does not object to disclosure in writing, the committee may proceed to make the information public in accordance with its initial vote. If, on the other hand, the President personally notifies the committee in writing that he objects to the disclosure, provides his reasons, and states that the threat to the national interest is of such gravity that it outweighs any public interest in the disclosure, the committee may not publicly disclose the information without leave of the full House. In that case the committee may by majority vote refer the question to the House with their recommendation. The House then must vote on a motion to go into closed session. If such a motion is adopted, then, after no more than two hours of

debate, the House votes only on whether or not to approve the recommendation of its intelligence committee.

3. Restrictions on intelligence committee members. All members of the committee have access to all documents received from any source. But no member may disclose in whole or in part or by way of summary, to any person not a member of the committee or committee staff for any purpose or in connection with any proceeding, judicial or otherwise, any testimony given before the committee in executive session or the contents of any classified papers, prior to a committee vote to disclose it; and after such vote, he may do so only in accordance with the vote and related provisions in the previous paragraph.

4. Restrictions on noncommittee members. Noncommittee members are to have access to the committee's classified hearings and documents under the following conditions: A request to see information must be in writing. Each such request is to be considered by the committee, a quorum being present, at the earliest practicable opportunity. The committee must determine by record vote whatever action it deems necessary in light of all of the circumstances of the request. The committee is to take into account in its deliberations such considerations as the sensitivity of the information sought to the national defense or the confidential conduct of the foreign relations of the United States, the likelihood of its being directly or indirectly disclosed, and such other concerns—constitutional and otherwise—as affect the public interest of the United States. The committee may approve the request in whole or part, deny the request, or provide information in a different form than requested. If the member making a request objects to the committee's decision, he can notify the committee in writing of the grounds for his disagreement. The committee must then reconsider the matter and decide by record vote what further action or recommendation, if any, it will take. Finally, noncommittee members may not disclose any classified information they have seen except in a closed session of the House.

5. Restrictions on committee staff. Access to classified information is to be limited to those committee staff members with appropriate security clearances and a need-to-know as determined by the committee. Limitations on disclosure of information are the same for staff as for committee members.

6. Enforcement. The Committee on Ethics is to investigate any unauthorized disclosure of intelligence information by a member or employee of the House. If the committee determines that there has been "a significant breach of confidentiality or unauthorized disclosure," it is to report its findings to the House and recommend "appropriate action such as censure, removal from committee membership, or expulsion from the House, in the case of a member, or removal from office or employment or punishment for contempt, in the case of an officer or employee."

The Senate has adopted similar rules.

In conclusion, the proposal that the subject of a document should be the criterion for deciding whether or not the President can withhold it from

Congress is not an acceptable proposal or criterion in terms of the respective roles of Congress and the President, for it would deny Congress information, including secret information, that it needs. But until Congress is able to discipline its members with respect to secret data, the criterion will be propounded and used by officers of the executive branch, thereby denying Congress this information.

FORM AND TIMING OF DOCUMENTS

The criterion states that internal, working, and staff papers need not be revealed to Congress, only formal decisions; also that executive agencies can deny Congress documents relating to pending decisions, releasing only those relating to decisions that have been made. This was for many years supported by the Office of Management and Budget as the standard to be followed by executive agencies, but it has not been acceptable to Congress. In legislative investigations, for example, Congress may need to see internal papers. As for timing, decisions once made become data for new decisions that are pending, so that the rule gives no operable guidance. These concepts may be of use, however, in combination with other criteria, as will be seen below.

LOCATION OF INFORMATION OR INFORMANTS IN THE STRUCTURE OF GOVERNMENT

The criterion states that if the information sought by Congress results from oral or written communications with the President or with his personal staff in the White House, then there is no right of Congress to know, for here executive privilege is at its strongest. If, on the other hand, the information is in the departments and agencies and does not involve the President and his assistants, then it can be withheld from Congress only if a statute authorizes the Executive to suppress it. In this case claims of executive privilege cannot be made since the privilege is derived from the constitutional powers of the President and does not relate to other constitutional or statutory officers of government. Andrew Jackson used this standard in the Second Bank of the United States case. He claimed privilege, it will be recalled, for communications with the departments "acting as a cabinet counsel" not, presumably, for papers in which department secretaries acted as chief executives of their departments rather than as cabinet advisors to the President. Richard M. Nixon used a similar standard in his executive privilege guidelines of March 1973.

President Dwight D. Eisenhower, however, endowed lower level officials, even bureau chiefs, with executive privilege, which brought on a major conflict with Congress. During the McCarthy hearings on alleged Communist infiltration of the Army, the President in a letter directed Secretary of Defense

Charles E. Wilson to instruct employees of his department not to disclose to the McCarthy committee (the Permanent Investigations Subcommittee of the Senate Committee on Government Operations) conversations, communications, or documents relating to any advice given by government employees .on matters under investigation by the committee. The letter said:

> Because it is essential to efficient and effective administration that employees of the executive branch be in a position to be completely candid in advising with each other on official matters, and because it is not in the public interest that any of their conversations or communications, or any documents or reproductions, concerning such advice be disclosed, you will instruct employees of your department that in all of their appearances before the Subcommittee of the Senate Committee on Government Operations regarding the inquiry now before it they are not to testify to any such conversations or communications or to produce any such documents or reproductions. This principle must be maintained regardless of who would be benefited by such disclosures.
>
> I direct this action so as to maintain the proper separation of powers between the executive and legislative branches of the government in accordance with my responsibilities and duties under the Constitution. This separation is vital to preclude the exercise of arbitrary power by any branch of the government.

The Army General Counsel, John Adams, on May 24 cited the President's letter in refusing to answer McCarthy's questions about a January 12 meeting between Attorney General Herbert Brownell, Jr., and himself.

Between 1954 and 1961 this letter was used frequently by officials in the departments, commissions, and even bureaus as their authority for withholding information from Congress, claiming thereby an executive privilege which, as we have said, derives from the inherent constitutional powers of the President. The House Committee on Government Operations reported in 1956 that in the two years since it was written the President's letter had been cited by nineteen departments and agencies as authority to restrict or withhold information from the Congress, and a later report of the committee, covering the five years from June 1955 through June 1960, lists forty-four cases of executive branch officials refusing information on the basis of the principles set forth in Eisenhower's May 1954 letter, although the letter itself may not have been cited in all of these cases. Two examples are given here.

Example. The Dixon-Yates controversy of 1954–1955 concerned the Eisenhower Administration's complex scheme to force the Tennessee Valley Authority (TVA) to increase its electric power rates. The purposes were to blunt the yardstick influence of TVA's low rates on rates charged by private utility companies in the region and to stop the expansion of TVA to serve new customers attracted by the low rates, which was at the expense of the private utilities. All of this was to be accomplished by requiring TVA to meet its expanding load by purchasing electric power from private utility generating plants rather than by building more low-cost plants itself.

Because they feared that Congress would be unreceptive to such a proposal, the Administration undertook to enact it by secret executive action. The Atomic Energy Commission (AEC), which was a large consumer of TVA power at its Oak Ridge, Tennessee, and Huntsville, Alabama, facilities, would contract with a private power combine (Dixon-Yates) to purchase power, which TVA would be required to introduce into its system. Negotiations were conducted secretly by the AEC, Bureau of the Budget, and White House with the private utilities and their bankers. TVA was kept entirely in the dark. When hints of this subreptitious scheme leaked to Congress, several committees sought information about it, which the Administration refused to provide. The general manager of the AEC and the chairman of the Securities and Exchange Commission claimed executive privilege. The director of the Budget and the chairman of the AEC, Admiral Lewis Strauss, did the same by refusing to testify on any matters with respect to which they had had conversations with White House officials. After Congress finally obtained the information from other sources, President Eisenhower canceled the contracts on the advice of Attorney General Herbert Brownell, Jr.

Example. In 1955–1956 the Anti-Trust Subcommittee of the House Committee on the Judiciary, chaired by Emmanuel Cellar (D. NY), conducted an investigation of without-compensation employees, so-called WOCs, who served as advisors and consultants to government while retaining their positions in private industry, and of members of governmental advisory committees, to determine if such employment resulted in giving the persons involved an opportunity to take advantage of inside information that was not available to their competitors. Among other organizations, the committee was interested in the Business Advisory Council (BAC), a privately financed group of senior business executives who met periodically to advise the Commerce Department and the government in general. The general counsel of the Commerce department and then its secretary, Sinclair Weeks, refused the committee's request for the confidential files of the BAC, saying, among other things, that these were private papers since the BAC was not a governmental agency. The committee then called on BAC's executive director to provide the files. He refused, claiming executive privilege, on orders of Secretary Weeks who said the records were in possession of the department.

The practice of the Eisenhower years was reversed with the inauguration of a new President. In February 1962 John E. Moss (D. CA), chairman of the Special Government Information Subcommittee of the House Committee on Government Operations, wrote to President John F. Kennedy asking how the new Administration would handle the problems of executive privilege. Kennedy responded on March 7 that "Executive privilege can be invoked only by the President and will not be used without specific presidential approval." This statement by the President, said an enthused Moss, "is one of the most encouraging developments in the nearly two centuries that executive privilege has been an issue." To consolidate the gain, Moss wrote a similar letter to

President Lyndon B. Johnson, who responded that he would follow the policy laid down by Kennedy—"Thus the claim of executive privilege will continue to be made only by the President"—and to Richard M. Nixon, who responded that he would be the only person to exercise the privilege. Kennedy invoked executive privilege once, Johnson not at all, and Nixon four times.[3]

Eisenhower had, then, delegated to others the authority to claim executive privilege, and in doing so he had explicitly violated the criterion for withholding information that is derived from the structure of government. There are, however, more difficult and subtle problems in applying this criterion, problems that result from the recent multiplication of the number of presidential assistants with whom the departments and agencies communicate, and of the staffs of the several units in the Executive Office of the President (EOP). When executive privilege surrounds this large body of officers, it is a different matter than it was in Andrew Jackson's day. And this raises the broader question: Where should decisions be made in the structure of government? Should decisions on foreign policy be made or proposed to the President by the National Security Council of the White House to which Congress has limited access, or by the Department of State to which it has much greater access? When President Richard M. Nixon transferred Henry A. Kissinger from chairman of the National Security Council to be Secretary of State, many in Congress who were highly critical of Kissinger rejoiced. While they knew that he would continue to be at least as influential as he had been previously, and possibly more so, they also knew that as department head he would be more accessible to Congress than he had been as a White House aide.

Congress's response to the trend toward greater centralization of executive decision making in the White House has been confused and uncertain. But, then, there are no simple solutions. Furthermore, centralization of decision making in the President's office, while it may mean a loss of information to Congress, may be advantageous to it in other ways. As we have seen, Congress can carry out its responsibilities in the legislative and administrative processes more effectively if the agendas before it—the Executive's initiatives—are well-coordinated programs than if they are diffuse, partial, and parochial programs that are likely to come directly from the individual agencies.

In some cases Congress has specified in statutes the duties of officers in the White House and the EOP on the assumption that if their activities are controlled by statute, Congress has a greater claim to know what is done pursuant to the statute than it has where the activities are entirely informal. Congress has, in other cases, required that certain White House assistants and EOP officers be subject to Senate confirmation. It has even gone so far as to propose that a presidential assistant keep certain committees of Congress fully informed of his activities. It is in this light, also, that one should view Congress's aversion to allowing a top executive to wear two hats, if one of these is as a presidential assistant. In the chapter on personnel controls I discussed Congress's concern about President Dwight D. Eisenhower's appointing the same man to serve as chairman of the Civil Service Commission and as presidential assistant for personnel. The following unusual example illustrates the first three of these techniques for gaining access to officials at the top.

Example. The Council on International Economic Policy (CIEP) in the EOP was created by a memorandum of President Richard M. Nixon in January 1971. The council consisted of the President as chairman and the secretaries of State, Treasury, Agriculture, Commerce, Labor, the director of OMB, the assistant to the President for National Security Affairs, the director of the Domestic Council, and the chairman of the Council of Economic Advisors. The executive director of the CIEP was an assistant to the President. Subsequently in 1972 OMB proposed legislation to authorize appropriations for CIEP. The Senate Committee on Foreign Relations reported a bill that established CIEP within EOP by statute; authorized appropriations for one year only; required the executive director of the council, a presidential assistant, to keep the foreign relations committees of both Houses fully and currently informed of the council's activities; and required the President to transmit to Congress an annual report on international economic policies prepared with the council's assistance. On the Senate floor an amendment was adopted to add the Senate Committee on Finance and House Committee on Ways and Means to the list of committees that were to be kept fully informed.

In the House the Banking and Currency Committee reported a bill to establish CIEP within EOP by statute; authorize appropriations for one year; require the President to submit an annual report; require each member of the council other than the President to testify before congressional committees on the annual reports. On the floor the House adopted three amendments proposed by John C. Culver (D. IA) requiring that authority for the council expire within one year unless extended by Congress; the council's executive director keep the appropriate committees of Congress fully and currently informed; and the executive director be appointed by the President with the advice and consent of the Senate.

The Senate and House conferees then agreed to the following provisions which Congress adopted: the council was authorized for one year only; the executive director was required to keep the appropriate committees of Congress fully and currently informed; and the President was directed to submit to Congress an annual report on international economic policy prepared with the council's assistance.

The CIEP had to be reauthorized in 1973. In that year the big issue was Senate confirmation of the executive director. The Senate passed a bill requiring such confirmation of the current director and all future directors; the House bill required confirmation of future directors only. The House bill prevailed.

DUTIES OF THE TWO BRANCHES OF GOVERNMENT

None of these three criteria—subject matter, form and timing of documents, location of information or informants in structure of government—is sufficient, I believe, to determine when Congress should know and when the

Executive should withhold, nor is any combination of them. Let us turn, therefore, to a different type of criterion, which states that access by Congress to information that the Executive wishes to withhold should be decided according to the relationship of the disputed information to the duties of each of the two branches. Consider their duties in the legislative process. Congress needs access to considerable information from the Executive in order to be able to evaluate the President's legislative proposals as well as all reasonable alternatives to them. For this purpose Congress may want to see the various policy proposals that were made to the President by the departments and agencies and by presidential advisors, many of which the President will have rejected. These may constitute the most useful, and in some cases the only, source for alternatives to the proposal that is approved by the President. On the other hand, the President, seeking to achieve a broad view of the public interest in his legislative program, may want to suppress parochial policy proposals made to him by the bureaus. Also, in order to encourage his staff to be imaginative and creative in their advice to him, he may want to assure them that they will not be held accountable to anyone except himself for the advice given in their staff memoranda. Obviously these views are in conflict. To reach a judgment requires, first, a study of comparative effects for each broad class of data. If the impairment of the Executive's function in the legislative process outweighs the benefit to the Congress's function, then the President should have the right to withhold, and vice-versa. This criterion requires, also, an agreement between the two branches on procedures to be followed in cases of conflict.[4]

To illustrate the rule of comparative effects, let us refer again to the benefits and costs of congressional access to legislative recommendations that have been prepared by the departments and agencies. An appropriate resolution might be to release to Congress all such documents, but to do so only after the President has taken a position on them. In this way presidential leadership would be protected significantly. Agencies might continue to support un-cleared drafts authored by themselves, but they would not be able to do so without competing with the President's measure. The balanced presidential program would be well known to Congress, even though this program might face competition from bureau proposals that he had rejected. At the same time the range of congressional choice would be broad, because Congress would have, if it wanted them, the alternative proposals that the President had rejected.

To be sure, this possible resolution of comparative effects for legislative memoranda reintroduces the time criterion which was rejected previously. But here it does not stand alone as the principal criterion for judgment; it has been put into a meaningful context.

The analysis of comparative effects can be further illustrated by the case of internal departmental memoranda in which junior and middle-level officers make policy recommendations to their seniors. Should these memoranda be available to congressional committees? In October 1975 the House Intelligence Committee, chaired by Otis G. Pike (D. NY), demanded to see such a State Department memorandum relating to U.S. policy in the Cyprus dispute. Secretary Henry A. Kissinger responded that, although he was prepared personally to come before the committee to describe in detail the views presented to him in the memorandum and his reasons for accepting or rejecting them, he believed he should not provide the memorandum itself. Instead, Kissinger proposed the following principles and procedures for balancing the needs of the Executive for privacy and those of Congress for information:

1. That individual memoranda of the type requested not be revealed, but that the department instead prepare summaries of the recommendations received from all junior and middle-level officials without indicating which officials were the authors of particular recommendations.

2. That junior and middle-level officials not be allowed to testify about any recommendations that they have made to higher-ups relating to U.S. responses in crisis situations, but that they testify freely about all *facts*, including those in intelligence reports, that they possessed when they made their recommendations.

3. That higher level officials testify on the substance of the policies that were recommended to them by subordinates.

Kissinger's reasons for wanting to limit the availability of memoranda and testimony by junior and middle-level policy men were these. If these officials know that their recommendations will be subject to later scrutiny by Congress, they may become timid—they may pull their punches—and the decision process will suffer. The foreign service has remained very sensitive, understandably, to what happened to the department's China experts in the McCarthy era. Further, to encourage a variety of views, the State Department has a "dissent channel" whereby junior and middle-level officers can offer retrospective criticism of decisions by senior policy-makers. This dissent channel would probably be seriously constricted if the memoranda were to be subject to later scrutiny in Congress.

Congressman Pike did not accept Kissinger's proposals. He insisted that Congress must have every piece of paper that exists in the Executive with regard to any subject that it chooses to investigate. Nonetheless, these proposals seem to strike a reasonable balance between the requirements of the two branches, if one measures comparative effects.

Reaching a judgment on the conflicting claims of the Executive and Congress to executive information requires not only an analysis of comparative effects for each major category of data, but also an accord between Congress and the Executive on a procedure to be followed in those cases where disagreements over comparative effects persist. Such a procedure could be based, I suggest, on three precepts. First, if a committee wants information that an executive agency is not willing to give, the committee should go to the whole House and seek a House or Senate resolution. Second, this resolution should call on the President, not the agency directly, to provide the data. Third, the President should not delegate to subordinates the authority to use executive privilege to withhold information from the Congress. These procedural requirements are based on the assumption that major conflicts between the Executive and Congress should be conducted at the top level. And in the abnormal case where the Executive refuses data, there will be, in all likelihood, a major conflict. Also, these procedures are consistent with those that were stated by Washington's first cabinet in the General St. Clair episode—"the Committee should instruct their chairman to move the House to address the President." Finally, these procedures are likely to reduce the occasions for the exercise of executive privilege. If only the President can employ it, then privilege will be used less frequently than if bureau chiefs can also claim privilege to protect their papers from disclosure to Congress.

In conclusion, it will be observed that this preferred criterion—duties of the two branches of government—for judging what information the Executive may withhold from Congress is derived from the model of executive–legislative relations that has informed the analysis of most subjects treated in this book. This model is related, you will recall, to a formulation of the public interest that emphasizes breadth of view—the general will of the political community.

Notes

A NOTE ON THE NOTES

Most of the examples in the text are parts of legislative and administrative histories. I do not document them because any reader who wants to see the sources can locate them by referring to one or more of the excellent indices to congressional and executive documents that are now available. These include:

1. *Congressional Quarterly Weekly Report; Congressional Quarterly Almanac* (annual); *Congress and the Nation,* vols. I–V 1945–1980. All works available from Washington, D.C.: Congressional Quarterly, Inc.
2. *CIS Annual Abstracts and Indices* (Washington, D.C.: Congressional Information Services, 1970 to date).
3. *Congressional Record, Index to Proceedings and History of Bills and Resolutions* (annual); *Congressional Record, Daily Digest* (annual) (Washington, D.C.: U.S. Government Printing Office).
4. *United States Code : Congressional and Administrative News* (annual) (St. Paul, MN.: West Publishing Co., 1942 to date).
5. *U.S. Code Annotated* (St. Paul, MN.: West Publishing Co., 1927 to date); and *Federal Code Annotated* (Indianapolis: Bobbs-Merrill, 1937–1970), superseded by *United States Code Service, Lawyers Edition* (Rochester, NY: Lawyers Co-operative Publishing Co., 1972 to date).
6. *Monthly Catalogue of U.S. Government Publications* (Washington, D.C.: U.S. Government Printing Office).

CHAPTER 1

1. For a thorough discussion of literature on the *pma* model up to 1970 and a vigorous defense of the model, see David B. Truman, "Introduction to the Second Edition," *The Governmental Process: Political Interests and Public Opinion,* 2nd ed. (New York: Knopf, 1971). (First edition published 1951.)
2. See Richard P. Nathan, *The Plot that Failed: Nixon and the Administrative Presidency* (New York: Wiley, 1975).
3. Commencement address at Syracuse University, June 6, 1965. Reprinted in *Congressional Record* 111, 12762–63.
4. *Schwegmann Bros.* v. *Calvert Distillers Corp.,* 341 U.S. 384, 395–396, 1951.
5. John R. Johannes, *Policy Innovation in Congress* (Morristown, NJ: General Learning Press,

1972); "Congress and the Initiation of Legislation," *Public Policy* 20 (1972): 281–309; and "Where Does the Buck Stop? Congress, President, and the Responsibility for Legislative Initiation," *Western Political Quarterly* 25 (1972): 396–415. The quotation in the Civil Rights Act example which follows is from Johannes, *Policy Innovation*, p. 9. For a good analysis of the President as legislative leader, see Steven J. Wayne, *The Legislative Presidency* (New York: Harper & Row, 1978).

6. This example is derived from Arthur Macmahon, "Specialization and the Public Interest," in O. B. Conway, ed., *Democracy in Federal Administration* (Washington, D.C.: USDA Graduate School, 1955), p. 49.

7. In an important essay on political evaluation Professors Brian Barry and Douglas Rae define public interest in substantive terms. They define it so narrowly that public interest excludes important elements of justice, equality, and freedom. They then reject public interest as the criterion for evaluating political institutions, proposing instead "the amount and distribution of human well-being." Barry and Rae, "Political Evaluation," in Fred I. Greenstein and Nelson W. Polsby, eds. *Handbook of Political Science*, vol. 1 (Reading, MA: Addison-Wesley, 1975), pp. 337–401.

8. Robert A. Dahl, *Modern Political Analysis* (Englewood Cliffs, NJ: Prentice-Hall, 1963), p. 59; Philip Converse, "Public Opinion and Voting Behavior," in Gardner Lindzey and Elliot Aronson, eds., *The Handbook of Social Psychology*, 2nd ed. (Reading, MA: Addison-Wesley, 1969).

9. Morris P. Fiorina, *Retrospective Voting in American National Elections* (New Haven: Yale University Press, 1981), chap. 1; Barbara Hinckley, "The American Voter in Congressional Elections," *American Political Science Review* 74 (1980): 641–650; Thomas E. Mann and Raymond E. Wolfinger, "Candidates and Parties in Congressional Elections," *American Political Science Review* 74 (1980): 617–631.

10. Angus Campbell, Phillip Converse, Warren Miller, and Donald Stokes, *The American Voter* (New York: Wiley, 1960), chap. 8. Fiorina comments on this point, *Retrospective Voting*, pp. 9–10.

11. Fiorina, *Retrospective Voting*, p. 10.

12. V. O. Key, Jr. (with the assistance of Milton C. Cummings, Jr., and a forward by Arthur Maass), *The Responsible Electorate: Rationality in Presidential Voting 1936–1960* (Cambridge, MA: Harvard University Press, 1966).

13. Fiorina, *Retrospective Voting*, p. 200.

14. Norman H. Nie, Sidney Verba, and John R. Petrocik, *The Changing American Voter*, 2nd ed. (Cambridge, MA: Harvard University Press, 1979). Also, Warren E. Miller and Teresa E. Levitin, *Leadership and Change: The New Politics and the American Electorate* (Cambridge, MA: Winthrop, 1976); Gerald Pomper, *Voters' Choice: Varieties of American Behavior* (New York: Dodd, Mead, 1975).

15. Sidney Verba and Norman H. Nie, *Participation in America* (New York: Harper & Row, 1972), chap. 4.

16. Raymond E. Wolfinger and Steven J. Rosentone, *Who Votes?* (New Haven: Yale University Press, 1980). The quotation is taken from their article in the *New York Times*, May 29, 1980, p. A23.

17. Key, *Responsible Electorate*, p. 7.

18. On role differentiation see Anthony Downs, "The Public Interest: Its Meaning in a Democracy," *Social Research* 29 (1962): 18–20.

The birth control experiment is reported by W. W. Charter, Jr., and Theodore M. Newcomb, "Some Attitudinal Effects of Experimentally Increased Salience of Membership Groups," in Eleanor E. Maccoby, Newcomb, and Eugene L. Hartley, *Readings in Social Psychology* (New York: Henry Holt, 1958), pp. 276–281.

For a report on studies in group problem solving see Truman Kelley and Robert Thibault, "Experimental Studies of Group Problem Solving and Process" in Gardner Lindzey and Elliot Aronson, eds., *Handbook of Social Psychology*, 2nd ed. (Reading, MA: Addison-Wesley, 1969).

19. Campbell et al., *The American Voter*, p. 205; James W. Prothro and Charles M. Grigg, "Fundamental Principles of Democracy: Bases of Agreement and Disagreement," *Journal of Politics* 22 (1960): 276–294.

20. Maass letter to Campbell, 25 June 1963; Campbell to Maass, 2 July 1963.

21. Donald K. Kinder and D. Roderick Kiewiet, "Socio-tropic Politics: The American Case," *British Journal of Political Science* 2 (1981): 129–161; "Economic Discontent and Political Behavior: The Role of Personal Grievances and Collective Economic Judgments in Congressional Voting," *American Journal of Political Science* 23 (1979): 519–524. Kiewiet, *Macroeconomics and Micropolitics* (Chicago: University of Chicago Press, 1983). Sears has compared "short-term self-interest" to "long-standing symbolic attitudes" as determinants of policy preferences and voting behavior. The former have very little effect, and the latter, major effects. David O. Sears et al., "Self-Interest vs. Symbolic Politics in Policy Attitudes and Presidential Voting," *American Political Science Review* 74 (1980): 670–684.

22. See for example Gerald H. Kramer, "The Ecological Fallacy Revisited: Aggregate—Versus Individual—Level Findings on Economics and Elections, and Sociotropic Voting," *American Political Science Review* 77 (1983):92–107.

23. For example, M. Stephen Weatherford, "Alternative Sources of Politico-Economic Demands: Carter Policies and the 1978 Congressional Elections" (Paper presented at Annual Meeting, America Political Science Association, Washington, D.C., September 1980); Richard Lau, "Some Political Consequences of Economic Grievances" (Paper presented at Annual Meeting, American Political Science Association, New York, September 1981).

24. Clyde H. Coombs, *A Theory of Data* (New York: Wiley, 1964) and others make this point. The example is from Edwin G. Boring, "The Role of Theory in Experimental Psychology," *American Journal of Psychology* 66 (1953): 169–184.

25. For citations to and comment on these studies see Gary C. Jacobson and Samuel Kernell, *Strategy and Choice in Congressional Elections* (New Haven: Yale University Press, 1981), chaps. 1 and 2.

26. Anthony Downs, "The Public Interest: Its Meaning in a Democracy," *Social Research* 29 (1962): 1–36; Gerhard Colm, "The Public Interest: Essential Key to Public Policy," in Carl J. Friedrich, ed., *The Public Interest* (New York: Atherton, 1962); Jerome Rothenberg, *Measurement of Social Welfare* (Englewood Cliffs, NJ: Prentice-Hall, 1961), pp. 296–297.

27. W. Dean Burnham, "Insulation and Responsiveness in Congressional Elections," *Political Science Quarterly* 90 (1975): 412.

28. Douglas Rivers and Nancy L. Rose, "Passing the President's Program: Public Opinion and Presidential Influence in Congress" (Paper presented at Annual Meeting, Midwestern Political Science Association, Cincinnati, Ohio, April 1981). See also Jacobson and Kernell, *Strategy and Choice*, pp. 10–11; George C. Edwards III, *Presidential Influence in Congress* (San Francisco: W.H. Freeman, 1980).

29. This may be too much of a simplification, for David Truman speaks of a "rich complexity of relations between interest groups and governmental sectors," and says that "initiative, or interest articulation may come from anywhere within the system." Truman, *Governmental Process*, pp. xxv, xxxii.

30. John C. Harsanyi makes this distinction in *Rational Behavior and Bargaining Equilibrium in Games and Social Situations* (Cambridge, England: Cambridge University Press, 1977).

31. A. D. Lindsay, *The Modern Democratic State* (London: Oxford University Press, 1943); Ernest Barker, *Reflections on Government* (London: Oxford University Press, 1942).

32. Lindsay, *The Modern Democratic State*, p. 242

33. J. H. Hexter, "The Birth of Modern Freedom," review article in *Times Literary Supplement*, 21 January 1983.

34. Samuel H. Beer, "The Strengths of Liberal Democracy," in William S. Livingston, ed., *A Prospect of Liberal Democracy* (Austin, TX: University of Texas Press, 1979), p. 222.

35. Truman, *Governmental Process*.

36. Charles E. Lindblom, "The Science of Muddling Through," *Public Administration Review*

19 (1959): 79–88; "Decision-Making in Taxation and Expenditures," in National Bureau of Economic Research, *Public Finances: Needs, Sources and Utilization* (Princeton: Princeton University Press, 1961), pp. 295–336; with David Braybrooke, *A Strategy of Decision* (New York: Free Press, 1963).

37. Arthur F. Bentley, *The Process of Government* (Chicago: University of Chicago Press, 1908).

38. Truman, *Governmental Process*, p. ix.

39. Bentley, *Process of Government*, pp. 208–222. It should be observed that contemporary interpreters of Bentley argue over his meaning, especially the precise meaning of group. See Lewis A. Dexter's introduction to a new edition of Bentley (New York: Transaction Books, forthcoming).

40. *to koinē sympheron*, Book III, 1178b23.

41. The quotation is from *Ethics*, viii, 1160a11.

CHAPTER 2

1. Arthur Maass, *Muddy Waters: The Army Engineers and the Nation's Rivers* (Cambridge, MA: Harvard University Press, 1951), and "Public Investment Planning in the United States," *Public Policy* 18 (1970): 211–243, especially n. 7.

2. As an example of committees as social systems, see Richard F. Fenno, Jr., *The Power of the Purse: Appropriations Politics in Congress* (Boston: Little, Brown, 1966). As an example of the goals and perceptions of committee members, see Fenno's study of six committees, *Congressmen in Committees* (Boston: Little, Brown, 1973). As examples of systems analysis applied to committees, see Joseph Cooper, *The Origins of the Standing Committees and the Development of the Modern House*, vol. 56, no. 3 (Rice University Studies, 1970), pt. 3; also "Organization and Innovation in the U.S. House of Representatives," in Cooper and Gordon Calvin MacKenzie, *Congress at Work* (Austin: University of Texas Press, 1981). For a good collation of these studies and others, see Leroy N. Rieselbach, *Congressional Politics* (New York: McGraw-Hill, 1973), chap. 3.

3. Cooper, *Origins*, pt. 1, 2.

4. See Fenno, *Power of the Purse* and *Congressmen*.

5. Professor Arthur B. Levy of South Florida University did the interviews in 1970. They have not been published.

6. The British have been experimenting with parliamentary committees in recent years. Norman St. John Stevas, Conservative House Leader, said at his 1981 party conference, with some exaggeration: "We [the Conservative government] have already reformed the Commons by setting up a committee system which has done much to redress the balance between Westminster and Whitehall."

7. Frans Bax, "The Committee-Party Nexus: Committee Cues in the House of Representatives" (Ph.D. Diss., Harvard University, 1976). Also John W. Kingdon, in an earlier study, *Congressmen's Voting Decisions* (New York: Harper & Row, 1973), sought to determine the most important cues for members in their voting decisions. Fifteen representative Congressmen were interviewed on fifteen major votes, a total of approximately 225 observations. The alternative cues, with the percentage of observations indicating that the cue was of major importance, are the following: fellow congressmen, 47 percent; constituency, 38 percent; interest groups, 26 percent; Executive, 18 percent; staff, 9 percent; party leadership, 5 percent. See also Matthews, Donald R. and Stimson, James A., *Yeas and Nays: Normal Decision Making in the U.S. House of Representatives* (New York: Wiley, 1975).

8. "Whirlpools" was first used by Ernest Griffith, longtime head of the Legislative Reference Service of the Library of Congress. See his *Impasse of Democracy* (New York: Harrison-Hilton Books, 1939), p. 182, and *Congress: Its Contemporary Role* (New York: New York University Press, 1951).

I am unable to attribute initial use of "iron triangles," but the term has been employed recently by many scholars—for example, Hugh Heclo, *A Government of Strangers* (Washington D.C.,: Brookings Institution, 1977), p. 225. Roger H. Davidson referred to "cozy little triangles" in 1974, "Representation and Congressional Committees," *The Annals of the American Academy* 411 (1974): 48–62. He attributes the term to Dorothy B. James, without further citation.

The concept of subgovernments, consisting of bureaus, committees, and interest groups, which underlies these terms was elaborated by J. Leiper Freeman, *The Political Process: Executive Bureau–Legislative Committee Relations* (Garden City, NY: Doubleday, 1955; rev. ed. New York: Random House, 1965); Douglas Cater, *Power in Washington* (New York: Random House, 1964); and Randall Ripley and Grace A. Franklin, *Congress, the Bureaucracy, and Public Policy* (Homewood, IL: Dorsey Press, 1976), especially pp. 4–7, 74–95, 145–153, 166–170.

9. Robert A. Pastor in a recent study of *Congress and the Politics of Foreign Economic Policy* (Berkeley: University of California Press, 1980) finds that a "lense of interbranch politics," which is similar to our model of executive–legislative relations, is far superior in predicting foreign economic policy from 1929 to 1976 than any of four alternative lenses or models, including one similar to whirlpools.

10. Recently Hugh Heclo has proposed that instead of "iron triangles" we use "issue networks" to study the roles of committees, bureaus, interest groups, and others in public policy. These networks are larger, more amorphous, and more permeable than the triangles, and they involve self-conscious efforts to develop good public policy rather than simply adjustment of narrower interests. See Hugh Heclo, "Issue Networks and the Executive Establishment," in Anthony King, ed., *The New American Political System* (Washington, D.C.: American Enterprise Institute, 1978).

CHAPTER 3

1. Arthur N. Holcombe used these categories in *Our More Perfect Union* (Cambridge, MA: Harvard University Press, 1950), chap. 6. See also Joseph Cooper and David W. Brady, "Institutional Context and Leadership Style: The House from Cannon to Rayburn," *American Political Science Review* 75 (1981): 411–425.

2. Woodrow Wilson, *Congressional Government* (Boston: Houghton-Mifflin, 1885), pp. 332–333.

3. Michael A. Sego, *Who Gets the Cookies? A Realistic Look at American Government* (Brunswick, Ohio: King's Court, 1977); C. Peter Magrath, Elmer E. Cornwell, Jr., and Jay S. Goodman, *The American Democracy* (London: Macmillan, 1969), pp. 317, 393; Clinton Rossiter, "The Presidency—Forces of Leadership," in Peter Woll, *American Government: Readings and Cases*, 3rd ed. (Boston: Little, Brown, 1969), p. 268.

The mode of thought in American politicial science represented by these texts owes much to the early analysis of Harold D. Laswell, *Politics: Who Gets What, When, How?* (New York: McGraw-Hill, 1936).

4. American Political Science Association, Committee on Political Parties, *Toward a More Responsible Two-Party System*, supplement, *American Political Science Review* 44(3) (September 1950).

5. Criticisms of the committee's proposals are found in Julius Turner, "Responsible Parties: A Dissent from the Floor," *American Political Science Review* 45 (1951): 143–152; Austin Ranney, "Toward a More Responsible Two-Party System: A Commentary," *American Political Science Review* 45 (1951): 488–499; M. S. Stedman, Jr., and Herbert Sonthoff, "Party Responsibility—A Critical Inquiry," *Western Political Quarterly* 4 (1951): 454–468; T. W. Goodman, "How Much Political Party Centralization Do We Want?" *Journal of Politics* 13 (1951): 536–569.

6. I do not discuss the Legislative Reorganization Act of 1946 in this chapter because it does not present any major issues that are not covered elsewhere.

7. Conable was testifying before the House Commission on Administrative Review, November 30, 1976.

8. David W. Brady, Joseph Cooper, and Patricia A. Hurley, "The Decline of Party in the U.S. House of Representatives, 1887–1968," *Legislative Studies Quarterly* 4 (1979): 405.

9. *Congresional Quarterly Weekly Report*, 13 September 1980, p. 2696.

10. *Congressional Quarterly Weekly Report*, 21 March 1981, p. 535.

11. Quoted in *Congressional Quarterly Weekly Report*, 8 November 1975, p. 2407.

CHAPTER 4

1. The most important studies of the member's job are those of Lewis A. Dexter, for example, *The Sociology and Politics of Congress* (Chicago: Rand McNally, 1969) and Richard F. Fenno, Jr., *Congressmen in Committees* (Boston: Little, Brown, 1973); *Home Style: House Members in Their Districts* (Boston: Little, Brown, 1978). I have relied on both authors in the pages that follow. The quotation from Fenno is from *Home Style*, p. 168.

2. Fenno uses Goffman's phrase. Erving Goffman, *The Presentation of Self in Everyday Life* (New York: Doubleday, 1959).

3. Raymond A. Bauer, Ithiel de Sola Pool, and Lewis A. Dexter, *American Business and Public Policy* (New York: Atherton, 1963), p. 455.

4. The unnamed congressman is quoted in Thomas E. Cavanagh, "The Two Arenas of Congress," in Joseph Cooper and Gordon Calvin MacKenzie, eds., *Congress at Work* (Austin: University of Texas Press, 1981).

5. The phrase is David Mayhew's, *Congress: The Electoral Connection* (New Haven: Yale University Press, 1974). See also Kenneth A. Shepsle and Barry R. Weingast, "Political Preferences for the Pork Barrel: A Generalization," *American Journal of Political Science* 25 (1981): 96–111.

6. The debate between Fiorina and Johannes and McAdams is in *American Journal of Political Science* 23 (1981): 512–604.

7. *Congressional Quarterly Weekly Report*, 14 February 1981, pp. 316–317.

8. Warren Miller and Donald Stokes, "Constituency Influence in Congress," *American Political Science Review* 57 (1963): 45–56.

CHAPTER 5

1. See Stanley Bach, "The Structure of Choice in the House of Representatives: The Impact of Complex Special Rules," *Harvard Journal of Legislation* 18 (1981): 553–602.

2. Richard F. Fenno, Jr., *Congressmen in Committees* (Boston: Little, Brown, 1973), p. 235.

3. Multiple reference of bills is a recent development, since 1975. See Joseph Cooper and Melissa P. Collie, "Structural Adaptation in the House: Multiple Reference and Interunit Committees in Organizational Perspective" (Paper delivered at 1981 Annual Meeting, American Political Science Association, New York).

4. Fenno, *Congressmen in Committees*, chap. 6.

5. Ibid., p. 234.

6. Fenno holds that the Education Committee's lack of floor success should not be viewed invidiously, for it is the price that members deliberately paid in order to pursue their partisan and individual views of good public policy. This conclusion derives from, and is valid only in relation to, the perspective of his study, namely, the goals of members in committees and how they achieve them.

CHAPTER 6

1. Roger H. Davidson and Walter J. Oleszek have argued in "Adaptation and Integration: Structural Innovation in the House of Representatives," *Legislative Studies Quarterly* 1 (1976): 37–65, that the pursuit of bipartisanship within the Bolling committee made it more difficult to put together an ad hoc majority for the committee's recommendations. It inhibited the Democratic majority members from searching freely among noncommittee Republicans for a majority, since they were expected to work through the minority members of the committee. In decision making for House rules of level one, however, involving, as they do, the fundamental parliamentary procedures of the legislature, it is questionable that the committee would have been more successful if it had abandoned the pattern of strong bipartisanship that had been used in 1946 and 1970.

2. This analysis is derived from an unpublished study by Joseph Cooper.

3. The study is by Kenneth A. Shepsle, *The Giant Jigsaw Puzzle: Democratic Committee Assignments in the Modern House* (Chicago: University of Chicago Press, 1978).

4. Sam M. Gibbons (D. FL) in *Congressional Quarterly Weekly Report*, 10 February 1973, p. 280.

5. On this subject see Roger H. Davidson, "Representation and Congressional Committees," in Norman J. Ornstein, ed., *Changing Congress: The Committee System* (Philadelphia: The Annals of the American Academy of Political and Social Science, 1974).

6. This analysis is derived from an unpublished study by Joseph Cooper.

7. Michael J. Malbin, *Unelected Representatives: Congressional Staff and the Future of Representative Government* (New York: Basic Books, 1980), p. 20.

8. Harold P. Green and Alan Rosenthal, *Government of the Atom* (New York: Atherton, 1963).

9. Robert H. Salisbury and Kenneth A. Shepsle, "Congressional Staff Turnover and the Ties-That-Bind," *American Political Science Review* 75 (1981): 381–396; Malbin, *Unelected Representatives*, p. 239.

10. R. Shep Melnick, *Regulation and the Courts* (Washington, D.C.: Brookings Institution, 1983).

CHAPTER 7

1. Robert W. Shoemaker III, "Creating Legislative Standards and Balancing Administrative Discretion: Considerations in the Formulation of Consumer Protection Legislation" (Senior Honors Thesis, Harvard University, 1973).

2. For fiscal years 1970–1971 and 1982–1983 the foreign aid program had a two-year authorization.

3. There had been tonnage bills for warships.

4. Testimony before House Budget Committee, 1980.

5. Ibid.

6. Morris P. Fiorina in *Congress: Keystone of the Washington Establishment* (New Haven: Yale University Press, 1977) argues that annual and short-term authorizations are importantly a means by which members of Congress influence and even dominate the bureaus for the purpose of advancing programs and projects that are of special interest to their constituencies and, therefore, important for their reelection. Although this may be true in some degree, there is no evidence to support his claim that this is a keystone to government in Washington. Indeed, the evidence points the other way—to broad national standards and criteria—as discussed in chapter 4. The airport program, used as an example there, is subject to periodic reauthorization.

CHAPTER 8

1. Richard F. Fenno, Jr., *The Power of the Purse: Appropriations Politics in Congress* (Boston: Little, Brown, 1966).

2. Ibid., p. 355.

3. Allen Schick, *Congress and Money: Budgeting, Spending, and Taxing* (Washington, D.C.: The Urban Institute, 1980); Lance T. LeLoup, *The Fiscal Congress* (New York: Kings Court Press, 1977).

4. On average the appropriations recommended by the House Committee were 98.2 percent of the President's recommendations for thirty-six bureaus in the five-year period, 1958–1962, according to Fenno, *Power of the Purse.*

5. Schick, *Congress and Money*, p. 432.

6. Ibid., p. 438.

7. Amendments offered in House to twelve regular appropriations bills, 1980:*

Amendments offered	162
Amendments passed	97
Nonrecord votes—no effective demands for roll calls	79
Subcommittee chairman voiced support	62
Subcommittee chairman voiced opposition	3
Subcommittee chairman did not state position	14
Recorded votes	18
Legislative provisions not concerned principally with money	10
Money amendments	8
Opposed by chairman and majority of subcommittee	7
Opposed by chairman but supported by majority of subcommittee	1

*When there are votes on an amendment and on substitutes for the amendment, only the final or controlling vote is counted. Foreign Operations bill not considered on floor.

8. See Michael W. Kirst, *Government Without Passing Laws: Congress' Nonstatutory Techniques for Appropriations Control* (Chapel Hill: University of North Carolina Press, 1969).

9. See Fenno, *Power of the Purse*, chap. 9; also Schick, *Congress and Money*, p. 439.

10. Arthur Smithies, *The Budgetary Process in the United States* (New York: McGraw-Hill, 1955).

11. Aaron Wildavsky, *The Politics of the Budgetary Process*, 2nd ed. (Boston: Little, Brown, 1974).

12. Ibid., pp. 137–138.

13. See Peter B. Natchez and Irvin C. Bupp, "Policy and Priority in the Budgetary Process," *American Political Science Review* 67 (1973): 951–963; also John F. Padgett, "Bounded Rationality in Budgetary Research," *American Political Science Review* 74 (1980): 354–372.

14. Wildavsky, *Politics of the Budgetary Process*, pp. 166–167.

CHAPTER 9

1. A number of points in the analysis that follows are taken from Allen Schick's study, *Congress and Money: Budgeting, Spending and Taxing* (Washington, D.C.: The Urban Institute, 1980).

2. Ibid., pp. 247–249.

3. *Congressional Quarterly Weekly Report*, 31 March 1979.

4. As for Republicans who were selected for the Budget Committee in 1980, four of seven were newly elected to Congress, so that comparable conservative scores cannot be calculated.

5. *Congressional Quarterly Weekly Report*, 13 December 1980, p. 3550.

6. *Congressional Record*, 22 July 1974. Quoted by Schick, *Congress and Money*, p. 85.

7. Schick, *Congress and Money*, p. 442; Lance T. LeLoup, *The Fiscal Congress* (New York: Kings Court Press, 1977), p. 109.

8. Schick, *Congress and Money*, p. 462.

9. Ibid., p. 481.

10. The Budget Control Act states also that Congress can provide in the first resolution that spending bills, both appropriation and entitlement bills, that are reported after enactment of the first resolution, and that exceed the relevant categorical targets in that resolution, not be enrolled and sent to the President for his signature until after the second resolution has been agreed to. This provision was not used until 1980.

11. Allen Schick, "In Congress Reassembled: Reconciliation and the Legislative Process," *PS* 14 (1981): 750.

12. Conable is quoted in *Congressional Quarterly Weekly Report*, 27 July 1981, p. 1127; Proxmire and Jones, ibid., 15 August 1981, pp. 1464–1465.

13. Schick, *Congress and Money*, p. 201.

14. Quoted in *Congressional Quarterly Weekly Report*, 15 August 1981, p. 1464.

15. See, for example, Schick, "Congress Reassembled," pp. 750–751.

16. *New York Times*, 15 September 1981, p. D29.

17. See, for example, testimony of Director, OMB, before House Rules Committee, September 1973.

18. 11 April 1977.

19. Jones, *New York Times*, 5 November 1981; Domenici and Panetta, *Congressional Quarterly Weekly Report*, 7 November 1981, pp. 2164–2165.

CHAPTER 10

1. MacKenzie argues persuasively that Macy's responsibilities, in fact, "became the broadest of any person ever to serve as a personnel advisor to the President, broader even than Philip Young's." Gordon Calvin MacKenzie, "The Paradox of Presidential Personnel Management," in Hugh Heclo and Lester M. Salamon, eds., *The Illusion of Presidential Government* (Boulder, CO: Westview Press, 1981), p. 136.

2. Article II, section 2. The second phrase of this provision reads as follows: "but the Congress may by law vest the appointment of such inferior officers, as they think proper, in the President alone. . . ."

3. In addition the President submits to the Senate for its approval each year between 50,000 and 70,000 nominations for initial appointments and promotions for the armed forces, the Foreign Service, and the Public Health Service, which are considered and passed en bloc. Except for the senior generals and admirals, this is an anachronism in today's government.

4. *Buckley* v. *Valeo*, 242 U.S. 1, 134–143 (1976).

5. This analysis of Senate confirmation relies heavily on Gordon Calvin MacKenzie, *The Politics of Presidential Appointments* (New York: The Free Press, 1981).

6. Ibid., pp. 174–175.

7. Ibid., p. 175.

8. Ibid., p. 105.

9. Ibid., p. 134.

10. Ibid., pp. 145–146.

11. Ibid., p. 124.

12. Ibid., p. 225.

CHAPTER 11

1. Joseph Cooper and Patricia A. Hurley, "The Legislative Veto: A Policy Analysis," *Congress and the Presidency* 10 (Summer 1983). The data in this section are adapted from this article.

2. Cooper and Hurley, "The Legislative Veto"; also William West and Joseph Cooper, "Congressional Adaptation in Modern America: The Legislative Veto and Administrative Rulemaking," *Political Science Quarterly* 97 (Spring 1983).

3. Antonin Scalia, currently a judge on the Circuit Court of Appeals for the District of Columbia, made this argument in testimony before Congress in 1979. See West and Cooper, "Congressional Adaptation."

4. I made this point in a communication to the *Washington Post* (subsequently reprinted in the *Congressional Record*) when the House and Senate conferees were considering the bill. Arthur Maass, "Anti-Impoundment: The House Bill Is Better," *Congressional Record* 119 (1973): 33465.

5. W. P. Schaefer and James A. Thurber, "The Legislative Veto and the Policy Subsystems: Its Impact on Congressional Oversight" (Paper presented at Annual Meeting, Southern Political Science Association, Atlanta, Georgia, 1980). See also Cooper and Hurley, "The Legislative Veto."

6. West and Cooper, "Congressional Adaptation."

7. Quoted in *Congressional Quarterly Weekly Report* 10 April 1982, p. 799.

CHAPTER 12

1. See "Congressional Investigations," in *Congressional Quarterly's Guide to Congress*, 2nd ed. (Washington, D.C.: Congressional Quarterly, 1976) and the references and bibliography therein.

2. Joel D. Aberbach, "Changes in Congressional Oversight," in Carol H. Weiss and Allen H. Barton, *Making Bureaucracies Work* (Beverly Hills, CA: Sage, 1980); and *Final Report of the Select Committee on Committees* (the Patterson committee), 1980.

3. Susan Weber, "Characteristics and Quality of Investigative Oversight by the House Committee on Education and Labor" (Paper written for Seminar on Congressional Supervision of the Executive, Harvard University, 1973).

4. See Frederick C. Mosher, *The GAO: The Quest for Accountability in American Government* (Boulder, CO: Westview Press, 1979); Joseph Pois, *Watchdog on the Potomac: A Study of the Comptroller General of the United States* (Washington, D.C.: University Press of America, 1979); Wallace Earl Walker, "The Bureaucratic Politics of Fault Finding: The Cultures of Auditing in the General Accounting Office" (Ph.D. dissertation, Massachusetts Institute of Technology, 1980).

5. Mosher, *GAO*, p. 281.

6. In 1961 Congress mandated an inspector general for the foreign aid program, with many of the same qualifications. The provision had been opposed by the State Department which then administered foreign aid. It was repealed in 1977 in connection with a reorganization of foreign aid, but legislation to reestablish the position is being considered by Congress (January, 1982).

7. *Congressional Quarterly Weekly Report*, 21 February 1981, p. 342; *New York Times*, 3 February 1981.

8. Report of House Rules Committee on Legislative Reorganization Act of 1970.

9. See John R. Johannes, *Policy Innovation in Congress* (Morristown, NJ: General Learning Press, 1972).

10. Woodrow Wilson, *Congressional Government* (Boston: Houghton-Mifflin, 1884), p. 195.

11. *Eisler* v. *United States,* 338 U.S. 189 (1949).

12. Martin Shapiro, "Judicial Review: Political Reality and Legislative Purpose: The Supreme Court's Supervision of Congressional Investigations," *Vanderbilt Law Review* 15 (1962): 535.

CHAPTER 13

1. For a recent analysis of the information needs of individual members, see part 3 of Joseph Cooper and Gordon Calvin Mackenzie, eds., *The House at Work* (Austin: University of Texas Press, 1981).

2. Committees can also recommend resolutions of inquiry which, if approved by the whole House in the form of a House Resolution, call on executive agencies to furnish data.

Presidential advisory commissions, some of them authorized by law, are also used to solicit information for these purposes. In this connection see Thomas Wolanin, *Presidential Advisory Commissions: Truman to Nixon* (Madison: University of Wisconsin Press, 1975).

3. John R. Johannes, "Study and Recommend: Statutory Reporting Requirements as a Technique of Legislative Initiative in Congress," *Western Political Quarterly* 29 (1976): 589–596; and "Statutory Reporting Requirements: Information and Influence for Congress," in Abdo I. Daaklini and Ames J. Heaphey, eds., *Comparative Legislative Reforms and Innovations* (Albany: State University of New York, 1977). See also General Accounting Office, "Report to the Congress by the Comptroller General of the United States: A Systematic Management Approach Is Needed for Congressional Reporting Requirements," PAD 82–12 (November 1981). The data in these sources include required notifications to Congress of executive decisions, which are not reports in the context of this chapter—approximately 10 percent of Johannes's data, an unknown percent of the GAO's.

4. These are 1974 data from Johannes.

5. Alan Tipermas, "Techniques for Obtaining Information from the Executive Branch: The Case of the House Subcommittee on Public Health and Environment" (Paper written for Seminar on Congressional Supervision of the Executive, Harvard University, 1974).

6. Johannes, "Study and Recommend," p. 595.

7. Ibid., p. 596.

8. U.S. Congress, House Committee on International Relations, *Seizure of the Mayaguez, Part IV: Reports of the Comptroller General of the United States* (Committee Print, 94th Congress, 4 October 1976).

9. Frederick C. Mosher, *The GAO: The Quest for Accountability in American Government* (Boulder, CO: Westview Press, 1979), pp. 240–242.

10. John R. Johannes, "Casework as a Technique of Congressional Oversight of the Executive," *Legislative Studies Quarterly* 4 (1979): 325–351; and "Casework in the House," in Joseph Cooper and Gordon Calvin Mackenzie, eds., *The House at Work* (Austin: University of Texas Press, 1981).

11. Aaron Wildavsky, *The Politics of the Budgetary Process,* 2nd ed. (Boston: Little, Brown, 1974), pp. 223–229.

12. R. Shep Melnick, "Information for Generalists: The Gathering and Use of Information by the Research and Development Subcommittee of the Senate Armed Services Committee" (Paper written for Seminar on Congressional Supervision of the Executive, Harvard University, 1976).

13. Christopher Leman, "Political Dilemmas in Evaluating and Budgeting Soil Conservation Programs: The RCA Process," in Harold Halcrow et al., eds., *Soil Conservation Policy, Institutions and Incentives* (Ankeny, IA: Soil Conservation Society of America, 1982).

CHAPTER 14

1. Senate Select Committee v. Nixon, 498 F. 2nd 725 (1974).

2. I do not deal with Raoul Berger's argument that executive privilege is "a constitutional myth," in *Executive Privilege* (Cambridge, MA: Harvard University Press, 1974).

3. There are other cases in which congressional committees have claimed that the departments have failed to provide requested documents, without authority of the President to withhold them. However, the facts for many of these—that is, whether or not the departments violated the Presidents' policies and even whether or not they provided the information requested—remain in controversy.

4. The rule of comparative effects has been presented by Charles Goodsell, "Congressional Access to Executive Information: A Problem of Executive–Legislative Relations in American National Government" (Ph.D. dissertation, Harvard University 1960).

Index

Aberbach, Joel D., 206
Ad hoc majorities, 48, 49–50; and committee staffs, 112–13; and grants, 70; and public interest, 63
Administrative Review, House Commission on, 54; *see also* Reforms of 1970s
Administrative rulemaking, 201–2
Agriculture, House Committee on, 38–39
Air Quality Act of 1967, 219–20
Allott, Gordon, 189
American Political Science Association (APSA), proposals of 1950, 53–54
American Voter, The, 20–21, 24
Anti-ballistic missile system (ABM), 11
Appropriations, House Committee on, 78, 124, 231; Budget Control Act of 1974, 156–60; control of appropriations, 138–41; and the GAO, 224–25; and the House, 141–43; norms of, 130–32, 132–35; and U.S. budget, 128–30
Appropriations, Senate Committee on: Budget Control Act of 1974, 156–60; control of appropriations, 135–41; role of, 132, 135
Appropriations procedures: congressional control, techniques of, 135–41; discussion model of executive–legislative relations, 141–43; interpretation of Aaron Wildavsky's theory of, 147–49; *see also* Authorization procedure; Budget, U.S.; Budget Control Act of 1974
Aristotle, 31
Armed Services, House Committee on, 232
Armed Services, Senate Committee on, 232
Army Corps of Engineers, 34, 139
Army-McCarthy Hearings, 33, 246–47
Atomic Energy, Joint Committee on, 112, 204, 235–36
Atomic Energy Acts of 1946 and 1954, 235–36
Authorization procedures, 119; annual and short-term authorizations, 121–27; tech-

niques of congressional control, 120–23; *see also* Appropriation procedures; Budget, U.S.; Budget Act of 1974

Bach, Stanley, 260*n*1 (ch. 5)
Badillo, Herman, 101
Bank of the United States (BUS), Second, 236–38
Barker, Ernest F., 30
Barry, Brian, 256*n*7
Bauer, Raymond A., 260*n*3 (ch. 4)
Bax, Frans R., 40
Beer, Samuel H., 257*n*34
Belcher, Page, 38
Bellmon, Henry, 156
Bentham, Jeremy, 234–35
Bentley, Arthur F., 31
Berger, Raoul, 266*n*2
Bills: amendment of, 88–90; discharge from committee, 86–87; multiple referrals, 86–87; scheduling debate on, 77–86; *see also* Rules; Rules Committee
Bolling, Richard, 82, 105, 201
Bolling Committee, *see* Committees, House Select Committee on
Boring, Edwin G., 257*n*24
Brady, David W., 259*n*1, 260*n*8 (ch. 3)
Brownell, Herbert, Jr., 16
Brownlow committee, *see* President's Committee on Administrative Management
Budget, House Committee on, 78, 152–53; characteristics of, 153–54, 155, 156; and House Appropriations Committee, 158–60
Budget, Senate Committee on, 152–53; characteristics of, 156
Budget, U.S., 128–30, 143–45
Budget Control, Joint Study Committee on, 150–51

82173